"fuck, YES!"

A GUIDE TO THE HAPPY ACCEPTANCE OF EVERYTHING

FUCK, YES!

A Guide To the Happy Acceptance of Everything

The Reverend Wing F. Fing

Shepherd Books, Redmond, Washington

LIBRARY OF CONGRESS CATALOGING-IN-PUBLICATION DATA
Wing F. Fing, 1940
    Fuck, Yes! : a guide to the happy acceptance of everything

    1. Conduct of life. I. Title.
BJ1581.2.F55 1988   158 .1   87-4294
ISBN 0-940183-21-8

10 9 8 7

Manufactured in the U.S.A.

Contents

Note to the Reader

Introduction 1 by Bruno Megasavitch
Introduction 2 by Norleen Winkowski
Introduction 3 by Mrs. Astoria Wing

To Astoria

Note To The Reader

As is the case with many of the great leaders in history, Wing F. Fing is, ultimately and finally, a mysterious figure, a man whose deepest heart is likely to remain hidden from us for all time. At present, he is known to the general public primarily through the news media. As might be expected, these news stories focus on the more sensational aspects of his life, on the criminal and sexual adventures which first brought him and his followers to public attention. Forgotten in this storm of vulgar and yet-to-be-proven charges against him is the simple fact that Reverend Wing had the lasting respect of everyone who knew him personally. Regrettably, few of us were privileged to know the true details of his life, or hear the man's teaching from his own lips. Few of us had the opportunity to say to him, "Hi, Wing, how are you?" or to share with him a lambburger sandwich. Therefore, to introduce you, the Reader, to this profound man whose public career was all too brief, we have asked three people who knew him well to share with us their impressions of him. It is our hope that these three short introductions will help you to better understand the great man who gave us the wonderful teachings you are about to read.

The Publishers

Some men are blessed.
Some men are cursed.
Some have brains
Like liverwurst.

Foreword I

by Bruno Megasavitch

It is a great honor and a heavy responsibility for me to introduce you to Master Wing Fu Fing. The task is so important and my powers of expression are so weak that I would almost wish for some other shoulders to carry this burden. Having said this, I can almost hear Master Wing's voice telling me, "Quit worrying, Crunch, just do it." He was a very encouraging man. For him, I shall do my best, poor as that may be.

"Crunch" was one of his pet names for me, as he gave many of his followers nicknames. It was a sign of his lively affection for us. In a world full of shallow relationships, his were deep and true. For our part, we treasured him, and accepted him as our guide and teacher. Fate chose me to be his first, and perhaps most devoted, follower. It was a blessing for me that brought with it joyful duties. He knew he could count on me for anything

11

any time. "Get me out of this, Crunch!" he would say. And I would do it. Or he'd say, "Hey, Gorilla, bust this guy up for me, huh?"

Of course, he would be joking. Blessed Wing was in the prime of his manhood, and perfectly able to take care of himself. His gorgeous body was beautifully muscled. He moved with the hypnotizing grace and power of a fine dancer. I can see him now, standing in the sun: his wonderful tan, the loose curls of his dark-blond hair catching the afternoon rays, his face—as always—serious, calm, confident, showing he was ready for anything, a lion among men. Oh yes, he could take care of himself. He had little need for me as a bodyguard, though I was always ready to take the bullet for him, should that have ever been necessary.

But Blessed Wing hated violence. He was an island of peace in this brutal world. He was totally accepting of people as they were. He wanted you to be yourself, and he loved you for who you were, whoever you were. Take me, for instance. It was of little importance to him that I am seven feet three inches tall, and bald. He treated me as though I were a normal-sized person, and he totally accepted my sexual preference, although he himself preferred females.

For those of you who are wondering, let me say here that the relationship between the Master and myself was purely spiritual. I will admit, though, that once I did desire to have a physical relationship with him. I longed to show him love as only one man can give it to another. Yes, there was a time when my admiration and affection for him grew so intense I longed for us to become sexually intimate. He soon saw the change in me. That's the way he was: sensitive and understanding. He looked up into my face with his beautiful blue eyes gazing into mine. He reached up and put his hand on my shoulder, and said, "You're out of your fucking mind, Bruno."

As you can see, the Master was totally honest. You always

knew where you stood with him. You had the feeling he approved of you and wanted you to be your own person and do your own thing. It was all right with him if I was a giant homosexual who liked to stay up all night writing poetry or perhaps playing my clarinet until dawn. You see, the Master often told us one of the most important things in life was for "people to get the hell off other people's backs." For example, when he and I were roommates—that was before his beautiful wife Astoria joined us—maybe he would be crashed out on the bed, maybe a woman would be there with him, with her breasts hanging out obscenely. It was hard for me to get used to that. Maybe he would be snoring loudly, like he did. He could fall asleep in a second, fall into a deep, peaceful sleep, looking like a baby angel. As he slept, the pain and torment that the world etches into our faces vanished from his. Utter calm would come over him, the years would drop away as he lay there, and you knew you were in the presence of a man touched by God. Yes, he would fall asleep and whatever I, or the rest of the world, did while he was out was all right with him. Sometimes, however, he'd awaken and join in, because he had so much energy. I remember one night in particular. It was about four in the morning, and I had been playing my clarinet for hours. I was playing Bach concertos that really blew great holes of joyful music into the quiet of the night. Looking up, I was surprised to see Master Wing standing there in his shorts in the bedroom doorway. His mouth was half open and his eyes bleary with sleep, as he said to me, "Is that fun, Bruno? Are you enjoying yourself?"

I assured the Master I was.

"Can I try?"

"Of course, Master."

He took the clarinet from me. After looking at it for a moment, he took it with him back into the bedroom, puffing at it a couple of times, making squeaky notes while I followed. Over his shoulder he said to me, "Maybe Alice would like to try." He flopped on the bed, and before I could understand what was happening, he'd flipped back the bedclothes that covered Alice Angsterlobe's nakedness. I could hardly believe my eyes when he propped himself on elbow beside Alice and began rubbing and putting my clarinet into her vagina. Alice half woke up and moaned. "Wing, what are you doing to me, honey?"

"See if you can play this thing through your cunt, will you?"

Alice began squirming and licking her lips and making sounds. It was awful. Master Wing had completely forgotten my feelings about women. I had to leave the room. After a while he opened the door and handed me back my instrument, saying "Play something for me, old buddy."

But by the time I'd sterilized it he'd fallen back to sleep, so I had to wait to play for him at a later time.

But that was the way Wing was: loving and full of fun.

Then suddenly it was all over. Master Wing was gone. Suddenly an enormous void opened in our lives. Wing gone? How could it be? What would happen to us who loved and needed him? His love, guidance, his great supporting strength, his eternal wisdom, and funny little jokes: they were all taken from us so suddenly. There was a great emptiness in our hearts. We ached. It was like being hit in the pit of the stomach; the pain of our loss made it difficult to breathe.

What made it even more terrible was that all we had were our memories of him. For you see, very little of what Blessed Wing had preached to us had been written down. Like most of the great teachers throughout history, our Holy One had relied on the spoken word to carry his Message of Light. For many hours we had gathered around him, listening to his wonderful voice, gazing into his youthful, yet strangely wise face, framed by those radiant golden curls of hair. We had found peace in his deep blue eyes. His eyes seemed to have seen other worlds beyond anything we have even dreamed of. We would sit on the sand in front of him as he told his wonderful little stories that were his way of teaching us how to achieve lives filled with happiness, lives filled with joy and few regrets, lives in which we would happily accept everything that happened to us. Yes, our great teacher relied on the spoken word, relied on "oral tradition" as he called it. He brought this "oral tradition" into our lives in unusual ways. An example of this occurred once while he was interviewing a young woman who wished to become one of the Holy Helpers in our Church. Blessed Wing fell into a trance. He seemed to be almost bored for a moment or two, and then he looked at her with a gleam in his eye and asked her to say the word "oral."

She started to say it, and then stopped and looked suspiciously at him.

"Come on," Wing gently coaxed, "say 'oral'."

She shook her head, but then smiled. Softly she said, "oral."

"Hummmmm, pretty good, but better try it again," Wing said, explaining with twinkling eyes that "we belong to the oral tradition."

She laughed and said, "Oh, go on..." but then as if on a dare she did it, puckering her bright red lips and saying, "Ooooooral."

"Oh, you've got it, you've got it," Wing said.

"Ooooooooooooooooooral," she said.

"You're wonderful," Wing told her, and waved me from the room.

Yes, but now he is gone. Perhaps the Master had weakness in him. He told me he did, but I refused to believe him. Perhaps he meant women were his weakness. Certainly, after Astoria joined us, things changed. Personally, I think it was Norleen Winkowski who did the most damage. I knew she was trouble the minute I saw her sitting cross-legged in front of him hypnotizing him with her eyes. I tried to tell him to be careful, but my warnings—raised eyebrows and little shakes of the head—were ignored by the Master. He was so understanding that perhaps he *did* see into the vast evil depths of her soul. Perhaps he knew that behind her proud, bra-less boobs lay a heart like a cobra's. Perhaps he understood that behind that phony smile lay all the warmth of an iceberg. On the last night he was with us, I tried to stop him when he was leaving to go to her. I cried out, "My God, Master, what do you *see* in her?" He was staring at the door she'd just closed behind her. It was pathetic. His mouth was hanging open. He looked stunned, drained, exhausted. I tried to tell him, "She's just another..." But he held up his hand to silence me. He shook his head and said weakly that he "had to play this out."

"What are you going to do?" I begged him to tell me.

But he had fallen into silence, and after a moment or two he left. Deep in my heart, I knew things had changed forever.

Three years have passed since that night, and now, quite suddenly, Master Wing has come back to us through this wonderful book he has written. The contents of the book, at the present time, are as much a mystery to me as they are to you, because the Publishers—evidently on Master Wing's instructions—have refused to let me read it yet. But I can tell you this much about what's inside these covers: There is joy! Wisdom! There's a message full of hope and cheer that will lift our spirits and fill our hearts with gladness. I've been told he has chosen some of my poems as introductions for some of the chapters. I am deeply honored, but my poems are of hardly any importance compared with his joyful words. Truly, we can all be thankful, because now for the first time his Blessed Teachings are available to everyone. When Wing began to preach, only a small group of us were there to hear his message from his own lips. But today, through this book, everyone in the world can share his knowledge and be guided by him. At last, each of us can fill our lives with happiness and loving acceptance of everything that happens to us.

But you may be asking yourself if it is truly possible that this small book can do so much. Will these few pages really make such a miracle happen in our lives?

I can hear Wing's voice now, answering that question for us all.

"Yes, it will.

"Of course.

"Certainly."

Jumpy? Nervous? At the end of your rope?
Then drink your drink, or toke your smoke.
Spread your legs or grab your dork,
Do something quick, or you'll blow your cork.

Foreword II

By Norleen Winkowski

(The following material is taken from a taped
interview with Ms. Winkowski, and is used
with her permission.)

Look, I hardly knew the guy. I've already told the police all I
could, so maybe you should ask them. I mean, it's okay that you
people need some information on him for the book, but why me?
We spent one night together, so big deal.

Look, I'll tell you this much. The attraction was mainly
physical, if you know what I mean. I have a weakness for blond
guys with good bodies, especially good buns. Also, good hands. I
like good hands on a guy. And this Wing had good hands. I
noticed that the day I caught him stealing Winslow Smagger's
college diploma. In fact, he had all the physical qualities I like.

Well, listen I can tell you this. You know, about the guy's age?
In the newspapers it said he was in his fifties or sixties?

That's bullshit. If he was over thirty-two, I'm Little Orphan Annie. He was built like an athlete. Good muscle definition. Like some soccer players or a gymnast. Really good muscle definition. I'm into bodies. I run myself, see, maybe thirty to forty miles a week, so I pay attention to how bodies look, believe me. His looked good. Fifty years old? That's bull.

So what more can I say? I hardly knew Wing.

Yeah, I can tell you one more thing: he was a vulnerable guy. Know what I mean? You got the feeling that you could hurt him real easy. I could tell that. It looked to me like he had taken some heavy shots recently. I think he was aching inside. Of course, the thing with his wife must have been part of it. But I had a feeling it was more than that. I think he'd been hurt real bad some time, maybe when he was a kid. That's just a guess on my part. But I could see it. See it in his eyes. They looked like he was wondering what was coming next.

I got to say this for him, he had guts. At first I thought he was just another fuck-up. *Men*: what can you do with them anyway? But after a while I got the strong feeling that he might be a very good guy to have around when things got tough. But he would have been tough to have as a lover on a permanent basis. I'm through having lovers on a permanent basis anyway, believe me, I've had enough of that. Besides when he talked sometimes I had the feeling, like, he could read my mind. And that's scary; it makes you feel very, very vulnerable. Very vulnerable. We were too much alike, and at the same time we were too different. I'm a very competitive person, and all his talk about heros ending up like the dinosaurs made me very nervous. He had this big thing about "cooperation".

Maybe I still have to sort out my feelings about him.

He really got me going, I guess. I was really pissed at myself that I could fuck him like that. Excuse me, I got a real foul mouth, you know. It's like everything stood still and we collided, or merged or something. You figure it out.

(pause on the tape)

Say, you really want to know what I think of him? I'll tell you because I've been talking here to you about this and that, and wandering with my words all over the place, but maybe this means something: after he was gone, and after the whole thing died out of the newspapers, I thought to myself, Norleen, you better watch yourself; you better straighten out and fly right. In a way I was glad he was gone because I had a hunch that having to deal with him on a day-to-day basis could really wear a person out. So then my life drifted back into what I call normal, but which is really a constant mess. Anyway, I'm going along living my life, and this newspaper reporter comes by to ask me a few questions. He's doing some sort of follow-up story on Wing and his followers. I say to him that I barely knew Wing, and then me and the reporter talk for a little while and then just after he's starting to leave, he turns back and looks at me and right out of left field he asks, Do I ever miss Wing?

Suddenly, I got this sort of feeling like my life is basically very dull and useless. I mean, what does it all *mean* anyway? I got sort of sad.

Maybe the guy saw it on my face, because he says, "I guess you do."

And I say, "Yeah, I guess I do."

She is turning around, moving her head
first, her body
afterward
in a circle.
Her hair floats like the leaves of a
    California oak in the wind.
You can almost hear it.

Foreword III

By Mrs. Astoria Wing

(The following material is edited from a taped interview with Mrs. Astoria Wing and used with her permission.)

It is certainly my place—rather than anyone else's—to have my thoughts about Wing as the introduction to his book. I certainly knew him better than anyone else. After all, I *was* married to him for fifteen years. You will have to admit that.

Let me first of all say that I considered him a friend. I have nothing against him; I never did. It's just that I fell out of love with him, but that doesn't mean I didn't want to be friends with him.

But you could never rely on him, I'm sure that that was a factor in the difficulties in our marriage.

For one thing we were not sexually compatible. I will admit my sexual needs from time to time caused me to seek affection elsewhere, and I'm not going to apologize for that. I don't feel at all guilty.

He was very smart. I respected him for that. He was perhaps the smartest person I ever met. And he was excellent with words. But he could never earn a living. He was the worst provider in the world. For years I was our sole support; it put a great deal of pressure on me, which is why I left him so many times during our years together. I would keep coming back for the children's sake and because he was so crushed when I left him. It made me very sad to see how much I had hurt him. Those are the only reasons I came back, but finally I was unable to take it anymore.

I have to leave for work now, but I will say this: for years I had allowed him to pursue his various schemes and jobs and what-have-you. I had all that pressure on me, and then he founded his so-called church and got all that money and then—after all those years—he started an extra-marital affair... Well, there is a saying they have in Scandinavia: "The way you shout at the mountains, that's the way the mountains answer back." You know, the echo. Well, if he betrayed me, then I had a right to defend myself. That's why I cooperated with the government investigation. I might have gotten some of the blame you know, so I had to protect myself.

I have always considered him my best friend. I did not mean to hurt him again. It just worked out that way.

FUCK, YES!

The Teachings of Wing F. Fing

Yes is the Key

I am a simple man. That is the secret of my happiness and success. God loves simplicity, and He gives great rewards to those who have it. So my advice to you is Be Simple.

Let me tell you a little story as an example of what I mean. A few years ago I fell in love with a girl who was less than half my age. I was fifty-six and she just twenty-seven. My wife, Astoria, was thirty-three. My wife was very upset by my attention to this young, slender, tender, cheerful, fun-loving, intelligent beauty with a deeply sexual nature.

"Why, Wing? Why?" my wife begged.

"Hard to say," I mumbled honestly, pulling on my coat.

"You're going to her?"

"Yes."

Yes. There it is. The key word. *Yes*, I was going to her. What was it that pulled me to Norleen? Was it her laughter—like crystal goblets thrown against boiler plate? Was it her winning smile that showed her teeth like a million tiny cantaloupe seeds?

The answer was a mystery.

So I asked her.

"Why, Norleen, am I drawn to you like a supertanker is pulled out to the sea by the all-powerful tides?" I said to her on a hot and exciting day at the beach.

"Maybe it's my perfume," she said, stroking my cheek with

her hand so softly that my whole body and soul relaxed in peace.

"Perhaps you're right," I agreed. "There are so many wonderful things about you. But what I really fail to understand is why you're so attracted to me?"

"It's very simple," she said. "It's because you always say Yes."

Yes, And Only *Yes*

In this troubled time in my life, when I am hunted and alone, I realize how fortunate I am. I have *Yes*. It is the *Power of Yes* that keeps me surviving. The *other* word, the word that some people believe is the opposite of *Yes*, has vanished from my life. That word exists for other people, but for me there is only *Yes*. Truly I am lucky.

A person could look at my present situation and say, "Wing, you poor devil, you've lost everything. Norleen, Bruno, and Muggs are all gone. The Harvester Sisters: gone. Your beautiful blonde wife, Astoria: gone. The Feds are on your tail, and you'll probably end up with twenty years in the slammer. You're broke and still...you think you're lucky?"

There is only one answer to that question.

The answer is *Yes*.

For me the answer to *every* question is *Yes*.

And the answer to every request is *Yes*.

Will I live? *Yes*. Will I die? *Yes*. Will you live and die?? *Yes*.

For a long time I was
Bluer than the sky at midnight
Lower than a bug's belly
Less happy than a candidate for
   president who has spent three years
   and thirty million dollars
Failing to get elected.

Discover *Yes*.

I believe in you. I believe in the goodness of you. Your goodness is all that's important. From goodness comes Love. And I do. I love you.

I wish to give all I have to you. I hope you will give something of yourself to me. But now while I am hiding on this fucking sheep ranch, the only thing I can give to you is this small book.

This book is my confession. In it I confess my caring for you, and I offer to you all I have learned in my life. First of all, you would be wrong to think that I was always the happy, content and successful person that I am now. The truth is, most of my life was wasted. Until a few years ago, I was a frustrated, smoker-doper who spent his whole life bouncing back and forth between terrible jobs and the unemployment line.

Why was my life like that?

I know exactly why, and will gladly share the reason with you. It was because I had a serious defect in my character.

But let me ask you (be honest now), do you, too, feel there is room for improvement in your own character?

Of course, you do. We all recognize we could be better people. However, I think it's good to remember our personal weaknesses are very valuable and very important. It's through them that we *learn*. Have you ever noticed how life keeps hitting us right in those very spots where we are weakest? Life hits us right where it hurts the most. Yes, it does. But let's always remember that each hit we endure pushes us a few steps down the road toward becoming a *better human being*.

For example

I remember so clearly when I, personally, took my biggest step toward personal fulfillment and a happy life. I remember so well the night I changed. The night when the whole world was reborn for me.

My teenage son, Quentin, came up to me as I sat exhausted and disgraced in my beat-up old chair at home. I had recently lost another job, and that very evening I'd just returned from an extremely short interview for a position as a zoo keeper. Quentin's face showed many emotions as he stood before me. He had a teenager's awkwardness mixed with a sort of distrust for adults, and a hunger for independence. I knew what he wanted: he wanted to borrow our car, our beat-up heap, the only transportation for our family, the automobile on which my hard working wife, Astoria, depended to carry her back and forth from her job which was our only source of income.

Without respect for me, his father, my son Quentin stood there nodding his head up and down as though he knew all the important answers in life while I was unaware of even the questions. Finally, he asked, "Hey, how about the car?"

What did I respond?

Did I give him a snotty, "Well, say, hey, how about the car? Washed it lately?"

Did I criticize his manners, his clothes, his complexion?

Did I ask him where he was going, or when he'd return? Did I remind him that our financial existence depended on the continued operation of that automobile, which lacked insurance? Or warn him that the tires looked like racing slicks, but were merely bald? Did I discuss with him the three arguments he'd lost last year to various policemen who had questioned his driving performance?

Yes, I did. I *did* say all those things, *but only* to myself. I said them silently in my own mind; for you see, I was so whipped and wiped out that I lacked even the energy to speak.

Quentin continued his nodding as he stood looking down at me who sat defeated in my chair. I wanted to mention all those things a responsible parent is supposed to say. I wanted to give him free advice, like a good parent is supposed to do. I sat quietly trying to gather into myself the energy to do it. I almost had it, I could feel myself getting ready. Soon I would be able to do my duty as a parent; I knew I could do it, just give me one minute more. In a minute I would have the strength. He stood before me, full of youth and strength and inexperience and energy. He was about to speak again. I watched him. I was full of exhaustion and he was full of energy. What did he know of the burdens of life that were crushing me down? What did he know of how hard I had to struggle just to do everything right? Time seemed to slow down. The seconds took minutes to pass. The minutes seemed like hours. I could see his mouth opening to speak but it was a slow motion thing. He was going to speak. Then suddenly the energy began running out of me. My will-power suddenly was draining away. Let other people worry about right and wrong, I was empty, completely empty.

"So, hey, how about the car tonight?"

"Sure." I said.

"What do you mean?" he said.

"Sure."

"What do you mean, 'Sure.'?"

I shrugged, and he realized I was giving him what he asked for.

"Hey, Pa, you all right?"

I shrugged again. I was thinking about how easy "Sure" had been to say. It had been like *letting go*.

"Well, what if I crack it up?" he asked.

"I hope you survive without serious injury."

"Yeah, but how's Ma gonna get to work?"

"Ask *her* about that."

"You okay?"

"I guess so. I feel funny."

"You just gonna let me go?"

"Sure."

He turned to leave the living room, but paused at the door to the kitchen. "I'm just gonna drive over to…"

I held up my hand to stop his explanation. "Where you go is your business."

He came back pointing an accusing finger at me. "You've been taking drugs, right? You're on something? Downers, right?"

"That's my business," I said.

"Otherwise, you'd be giving me a lot of arguments and advice. Do you know what the tires on the car look like? Suppose it rains, what then? I'll be sliding all over the road."

"Yes, that's probably right."

"You *know* what my driving record is like," he said. "Do you know what they'd *do* to me if I had an accident?"

I ignored his question, and also the other things he said immediately afterwards. But I do remember thinking how pleasant it had been to say *Yes* and *Sure*. Those simple words, it seemed, had lifted huge burdens off my back. I felt lighter, almost like I was floating. *Yes*, what a lovely, lovely sounding word. *Yes*, I repeated in my head. Oh, *Yes. Yes*!

Suddenly I found myself looking up at my beautiful wife, Astoria, who was looking down at me. "Why are you sending Quentin out to be killed?" she demanded.

"That's our business."

"You're damn right." Quentin shouted, "and if you think I'm driving that crappy wreck of yours, you're out of your mind." He spun around and left the room, out the front door, nearly colliding with our thirteen-year-old daughter, Dulcinea, who was coming in as he left.

"So what's his story?" Dulcinea asked.

My wife was staring at me, suspicion all over her face. I looked at them as though they were strangers, and, indeed, in a way they were. Previously I had been responsible for my wife, my daughter and my son. Now I was responsible only for myself. And, these people who stood before me were responsible for themselves. I felt that. I felt my freedom. What had freed me? Why did I now feel like this? Why was energy surging back into me? Where had all the burdens gone?

I thought back. It had all started when I said to my son, "Sure" and "*Yes*."

I remember thinking to myself, "Norris... (I had another name in those days. *Norris*, if you can believe that. How strange to have a name that began with the two letters that spell out the word that most people believe is the opposite of *Yes*.) Anyway, I said to myself, "Norris, you may have found the key to the Universe." I was about to advise my wife and daughter of this new way of looking at life. But then I stopped. Offering advice is just another way of taking responsibility for someone else, I realized. Instead, it would be better merely to share with them the lesson I had just learned. I said, "My dear wife, my dear daughter, I have discovered something which may be very helpful. I have discovered for me that the most useful answer to every question is *Yes*."

Dulcinea snorted her peculiarly thirteen-year-old's type snort. Astoria just nodded, as though she was too accustomed to my foolishness to bother trying to correct me anymore. It was Dulcinea who spoke first; her question was full of the sort of special concerns and problems a young girl must face when she is becoming a woman, when her breasts begin to swell and suddenly she becomes the sexual target of boys who are turning into men.

"Well, tell me this," she said. "Is a girl always supposed to say 'Yes' when a boy asks her a question?"

"I think so. Yes," I told her.

"Always? Are you telling me to *always* say *Yes* to a boy?"

"Oh, do you think that I'm telling you what you should do, honey? If you think so, you're wrong. You probably would be best off if you decided for yourself what is good or bad for you. I am only suggesting for you to consider that the best answer you could give to any question is the answer *Yes*."

"You're just trying to get out of it, Pa. Answer me straight. Do you think a girl should answer *Yes* to a boy?" (She thought she had me.) She added "And you know very well what sort of question I'm talking about."

I thought for a moment, considering the possibilities. Finally, I answered her. "Yes, Dulcinea," I said, "you should tell him *Yes*."

My wife slapped her forehead with her open palm and looked up to heaven as though appealing to God for relief from my endless stupidity. Dulcinea stared at me, her mouth hanging slightly open. "Yes, honey," I told her again, "when a boy asks you to have sex with him, then the best answer you can give him is *Yes*."

Say *Yes* To Teenage Sex

Dulcinea, looking puzzled, shook her head. She seemed to be having a hard time believing that I, her own father, would tell her to say *Yes* to any boy who asked her to have sex with him.

I thought about my answer some more, and the more I thought about it, the more sure I was that I was correct. *Yes* was, indeed, the answer to every question.

"Say *Yes*, Dulcinea," I told her again. "It's a good answer. Call him by name. Say, 'Yes, Bill, let's do it if you really want to.'"

While I spoke, Dulcinea's eyes were getting bigger and bigger. She stared at me as though she were thinking, "Is this my dad talking?"

"Yes, Dulcie, this is your dad talking. Look, honey, you could tell him how proud and honored you are that he's asked. You could say, 'Thanks, Bill.' And you could tell him you think he's a very brave guy."

"Huh?"

"Sure, honey. Tell him he's really brave. You could say, 'Bill, there are very few guys who are willing to risk giving up high school for a girl. I appreciate the chance you're taking.' Remind him that the two of you might be lucky enough to have a little baby together. Tell him you'd like to plan the future with him. He can go get some little job—maybe making hamburgers some place—and when he gets home you'll fix him macaroni and cheese."

Dulcinea made a face, "Aughh." She hates macaroni and cheese.

"Well, if you'd like to avoid cooking dinners and skipping high school, you can always kill the kid."

"Dad, that's gross!"

"I know it, honey, so maybe you'd like to have his company when you have to go through it. You could say to him, 'Bill, I think we should get an abortion, but honestly I want to have you there when they do it.' Say to him, 'They stick these metal things up inside a girl and scrape the little baby away, so would you come into the operating room with me? After all, it is our little baby. Ours together, Bill.'"

Dulcinea made a face like someone had just offered her creamed squash. "God, why does anybody do it?"

"Yes, it does get complicated, huh, Dulcie? You know, after you've said all this to Bill, he might be a little less excited about making love than when the idea first hit him, but if he's got any sort of head at all on his shoulders, he'll start thinking about birth control."

Dulcinea smiled a sly little smile and nodded knowingly.

"Well, Dulcie, I think you should tell him that's a good idea, and you'd like to talk it over with him. Say, 'That's a good idea, what do you think we should use?'" (Dulcinea slyly put her hand on her mouth to try to keep from giggling.) "'Wanna use a rubber or that foam stuff? I hear that rubbers break a lot, and that lots of times those little sperm guys go wiggling right through the foam, and there we are with a baby again and you skipping high school so you can become a hamburger engineer to support us, or else you coming to the hospital to watch the doctor go scrape scrape scrape. What do you think, Bill?'"

"He may think that you're talking too much, Dulcie, but women should talk; after all it's your body, right?"

Dulcinea nodded and said, "I guess so."

"After all he loves you, right?"

She shrugged and shook her head. "I guess," she said.

"Well, of course he does. Tell him how happy that makes you. Say, 'I love you, Bill, and I know you love me, and that's going to make my parents very happy. They're going to be thrilled to learn about the intensity of our relationship.' Grab him by the hand and say, 'Let's go tell Mom and Dad right now.' "

Dulcinea put her hand over her mouth again to keep herself from giggling, trying to keep a straight face.

"Say to him, 'It'll be our first night together, Bill. Go rent a room at the Downtown Hilton, and have them send up room service with some champagne so that it'll be really nice for us. It only costs a hundred dollars. Bring me some flowers.' "

"Oh, Pa," Dulcinea said, "lots of guys have a hundred dollars these days." She looked at me, a small smile on her lips, and some affection for me showing in her eyes, as though she was both fond and proud of me for having faith in her, for giving her more freedom and respect than she expected. I had the feeling that she might have come across the room and given me a hug, except that that is an awkward thing to do when you are thirteen and building your independence, your identity.

I would have liked that. A hug.

Rarely able to keep my mouth shut for long, I started talking again, telling her, "See, Dulcie, if you say *Yes* to him this way, you'll avoid having to reject him. He, himself, may reject all the responsibility you're offering him. And maybe you'll both be safer and stronger because you talked about it."

"Yeah, I guess so." she said.

"You see, probably, at first, he would have been thinking that his big problem is to get you to have sex with him, but with this sort of answer you get yourself out of the way, you will stop being the problem, and then he'll notice there are other questions, like: how much do you really care for one another, and what does all of that lead to."

She said, "Hey, yeah, that's right," and then, "Hey, I got to do my homework; we got finals next week."

But she stuck around for a while talking with Astoria about a blouse. A little later she started toward her room, but after a few steps she turned back to face me. There was a tough little gleam in her eye. She very independently said to me, "Well, what if I want to? The pill is very safe, you know. Lots of kids use it, you know."

A wave of tiredness swept over me. I wondered if she'd heard anything I'd tried to tell her. Had anything I'd said made it easier for her to handle her life?

"Well?" she repeated.

She was failing to understand that I was serious, that I was finished with fucking around, that I meant what I said. Was it the same with Astoria, I wondered? Did she fail to understand, too?

"Well, should I say *Yes*," Dulcinea said challengingly.

"I'm your father, honey. I'm happy to share with you everything I know and everything I have. But your life is your own. Live it as best you can."

"Okay," she said, and skipped lightly out of the room.

Self-discipline

Do you sometimes feel the urge to
    fuck off
    when you should be working?

Do you sometimes search for lint in your navel
    when you should be doing
    other things?

When it's time *to get it done,*
    is there a dead elephant
    tied to each of your arms?

Or does it just feel like it?

Say *Yes* To Higher Education

It is true that almost all of us have some schooling. But some fortunate men and women have the foresight and intelligence to get high-powered educations for themselves. For years they study at universities and colleges until they are rewarded with advanced degrees. Afterwards, these educated people are given exciting, challenging, and high-paying jobs. They get to be doctors, lawyers, dentists, engineers, architects, presidents, sex therapists, and the Pope. Look at the great money they make:

> 20 thousand
> 30 thousand
> 50 thousand
> 90 thousand
> 100 thousand
> and even more.

Did you ever get jealous about this? Did you ever say, "Why them instead of me?"

Perhaps you did.

I certainly did.

I used to say, "Why do other people get to be president instead of me? I could do it."

The reason, of course, is that these other people stayed in school and received diplomas, degrees, sheepskins, and Certificates of Achievement, while I, and perhaps you, too, abandoned education early to work on our surfing.

(Ah, the wonderful courage of youth, how beautiful it is!)

But let us ask ourselves this: is it possible for a person to catch up with their lost education?

Yes!

Can a person who has passed beyond school age still obtain advanced degrees, diplomas, and Certificates of Achievement?

Yes!

How?

Steal them.

That's what I do. Schooling, of course, takes time. And yet life is so short. Is it any fun to sit in a stuffy classroom hour after hour, year after year...?

Yes, it *is* fun.

...exam after God-awful exam. Studying, cramming, writing term papers, and answering multiple choice questions by going eeny-meany-miney-mo...?

Yes, it's lots of fun.

...eating strange cafeteria food: carrot and raisin salad lying dead in yellow mayonnaise; eating gray meat from some unknown animal; staring at yellow-green Brussels sprouts left over from last term?

What could be more fun?

Herpes.

Going Bankrupt.

Oral surgery.

So, if there are things you desire more than sitting endlessly in classrooms and libraries, broadening your mind and rear end, then I want to suggest you *do* them. But if you also hunger to take an advanced university degree or two, then I say *take* them. Take them from doctors' offices, lawyers' offices, dentists' offices. Remember that whatever college degree you want, someone has already done the school work for it, and is displaying it on their office wall. They already have the *education*, why should they have the diploma, too?

That's what I say.

Let them have the education, you take the diploma.

That's what I've done.

Many times.

Example

As a matter of fact, that's how I first met Norleen, the young woman I spoke of earlier.

She must have looked plain and ordinary that day. I hardly noticed her. Maybe she had her dark hair pulled back tight in a bun. Glasses. Probably she was wearing make-up, and just a regular dress of some kind.

Besides, I was looking at the university diploma on the wall.

Actually, I was just taking it down.

"May I help you?" she said. She waited, tapping her foot. She had a small smile on her face, like a nurse who has just caught her patient beating off.

"I can handle it, Miss...?"

"Winkowski."

"Thanks anyway, Miss Winkowski. I can manage."

"Manage what?"

"Pardon?"

"What is it you are managing to do with Mr. Smaggers' college diploma in your hand?"

"Do you mean this framed piece of paper belonging to Winslow K. Smaggers, saying that he is a graduate of the University of Chicago?"

"Yes, that is what I was referring to. The thing in your hand."

"Oh, this."

"Yes, that."

44

"I'm stealing it."

"Why?"

"Because I'd like to have one."

She said, "I see," but that may have been an exaggeration. She removed the thing from my hand and replaced it on the wall.

Later on, she stole it for me herself.

Yippee

I can feel myself coming alive.
I feel loved, and jokey, and what's
     more, I've got
a smile stretching across my face
from here to there.

Yes Is Easy

We all struggle.

Why?

Because we try to control our fate. We make decisions and judgements. We worry about success and failure. In short, we attempt to sail our souls through the troubled waters of existence while keeping one eye on the compass of social demands and the other eye on the stars of chance.

It's enough to make you cross-eyed.

Is that any way to live?

Yes, of course it is.

But are there other ways? Better ways?

Yes!

Remember this: if you are struggling and making judgements about things then sometimes you will have to say *Yes* and sometimes you will say the word that some people believe is the opposite of *Yes*. However, if you stop judging, if you make up your mind to answer *Yes* to every question and request, you immediately remove struggle from your life.

Confusion will be gone.

Suddenly you will have the correct answer to everything.

All the energy that you once needed for making judgements and controlling your life can now be used for other things.

Like *love*.

Example

This comes directly from my own experience.

Three years ago, at a crucial time in my life, I *let go*.

Having just discovered *Yes*, I wandered.

Through the streets of L.A.

Through the noise and traffic of struggling people.

To a bus station.

I asked the young ticket girl where I should go. Several sarcastic replies flashed across her face in the form of nasty little smiles and smirks. Here is a true flake, she seemed to be thinking. And then she saw my own face, so simple, plain, calm, gentle, composed, kind, open and forgiving.

Her face softened, too. "Laguna is nice," she said.

"The beach is wonderful," I agreed.

"I love the beach," she said longingly, seated in her cage of glass.

"Come with me?"

"I..." and then she shook her head and said the wrong word.

"It's all right," I said.

She shrugged. She put her hand on the button to punch up a ticket for me.

"One way," I said.

The Homosexual *Yes*

Homosexuality brings a lot of questions to some people's minds.

Is it fun?

Is it here to stay, or just a passing craze?

How do they do it?

Are gay people happy? Are happy people gay?

Should people in general be tolerant of homosexuals?

Or are all people in general sort of, or partly, homosexual? (Only in San Francisco.)

Is it better to be a homosexual or a masturbator? That is, is it better to make contact with another person or with oneself?

Would you rather be a homosexual or a policeman?

Example

The bus brought me to Laguna on a bright afternoon in early June. The sky was the magnificent, pale blue that one finds only above Southern California beach towns. It is a light sky, a thin sky, weightless, stretching from the high heavens down to the earth where it rests gently on the tops of low buildings. The day was calm. It invited a person to wander pleasantly—thoughtlessly—along the pale sidewalks until they felt the urge to relax on a beach-side bench, and perhaps take a nap. Which is what I did.

Awakening.

A disturbance.

A black teenager. A boy, perhaps seventeen.

He stands beside a brand new Cadillac Seville
   with twenty-nine coats of Georgia Peach metal-
      flecked lacquer,
   and on-board computer
   and all the other available options
   including self-cleaning ashtray.

There are two policepersons: a young woman and man in their twenties
   decked out in tan uniforms,
   full of starch.
   He is big shouldered.
   His moustache sits above his lip like a thin, dark wire.
   She has a pony tail, sort of blond.

The parking meter shows a red flag.

In discussion, it is learned the car's registration is missing.

The policeman moves back to his own spiffy vehicle: a pale green Dodge with a rainbow of fright-lights across the roof. Inside are a shotgun, some clubs, an on-board computer, flak jackets, radar, sonar, and medium range missiles.

There is also a communications console which he uses to call Computer Central concerning "Negro suspect" and the possibility that same "Negro suspect" has illegally obtained expensive vehicle with self-cleaning ashtrays.

Black fellow shows his driver's license.

He is asking why police are on his case.

Police refuse to answer.

Watching them, I get the feeling these police-people believe the black youngster has exceeded his civil rights by driving a car with on-board computer and self-cleaning ashtrays.

The young fellow is very calm, seems to have been through this before. He tells police he was in a near-by store to get change for parking meter, and exhibits 4 quarters in pink palm of black hand.

Policewoman strongly suggests that black boy lean with his hands on hood of car and legs spaced widely.

Black says, "Gees" and mutters "Mutherfuck."

Hearing this insult, the policewoman moves her good right hand to the small cannon upholstered on her hip—where she also has handy: one spray can of chemical anti-personnel repellent (mace), one pair of shiny handcuffs encased in black leather, one good-sized club, and two speedy-load revolver cylinders full of .38 caliber bullets tipped with gray lead the color of death.

The policeman ambles slowly back from the spiffy cop car which is additionally equipped with siren, grappling hooks, back-up computer, tactical nuclear device, riot helmets, and a steel-mesh screen separating the back seat from front. However, inside the car the back-door handles are missing—in case some suspect might want to leave a little bit early.

The policeman returns to them, shaking his head to his partner.

Youngster brightens up and straightens up, too, saying, "See, I told you it was my wheels."

Policepersons request that Negro suspect resume his humble posture, hands on hood, wide-spread legs.

Youngster claims his father is a doctor.

"On the hood," the policeman repeats quietly, confidently.

The uniformed young woman stands nearby, watching while her partner frisks the boy, patting the youngster's legs from heel to crotch, searching, searching, searching intently.

What is the policeman's sexual orientation? Is he just doing a job—a dirty job that someone's got to do?

I walk up to pony-tailed policewoman; I pause; she fixes her face into a questioning look, slightly frowning, a little on edge. Tense.

51

Her face is asking me if I am a threat to her.

The answer, of course, is *Yes*. But different from the threat she thinks I am.

"It must be hard for you," I remark, "to tell who is a good person and who's bad." She has a plastic name tag pinned to her chest. Black with white letters. Kimberly Katz.

Kimberly frowns.

She looks irritated.

The summer sun is hot on us. A bright June sun. There is a faint buzzing in the air like bees are loose.

I am suddenly aware of being dressed differently from a stockbroker or politician or insurance salesman, unless they happen to be disguised in cut-off levis and a black T-shirt that looks good with my curly, blond hair. (I bought it after seeing a French gangster movie. They dress good, the French gangsters do.)

"I mean, Kimberly, how do you know..."

She tells me, "Clear the area, please; clear the area."

"Let me introduce myself. My name's Norris, and I've got a suggestion."

"If you'll just stand back now."

"If it's his car, he'll know where the dents are."

She says, "Pardon," but that was just to stall for time while she was smoothly moving her good right hand back to the anti-personnel device in her holster.

What I was trying to suggest to her was that they could stop that humiliating little drama by asking the young man where the little dings and dents were on his new car. Everyone knows that a new car gets one or two immediately after purchase. (That is because it is a Law of Nature that when you buy a new car, someone follows you as you drive away from the new car dealership. They do this so that as soon as possible they can park next to you and bang their door into your twenty-nine coats of metallic lacquer putting a ding in it. Every new car owner sees this dent immediately. However, when you're stealing a car, you are usually in a hurry and often fail to notice such things.)

Of course, there were better ways of dealing with this situation, but the previous two days had tired me, and all I could come up with at the moment was that if the two officers would just talk person-to-person, friendly....

Just about then, the male policeperson forgot his training; he turned to see what was disturbing his partner, Officer Katz. This meant he took his eyes off the alleged doctor's son, who—seeing himself neglected—used the opportunity to sprint.

Yes, he ran. He ran away. That disturbed both officers a great deal. Sensing that their bust was falling apart, they became very defensive, tense and annoyed. They suddenly moved together quickly, back to back, to guard each other's backs, drawing their cannons like two Marshal Dillons, and shouting "Halt" and "Stop" to the boy who was leaving and me who was stiff.

The male policeperson said, "Cover him," which Kim did, while he took off after the boy.

(Let us pause for a moment to think about this interesting fact: The dreaded moray eel which thrives in the blood-warm waters of tropical oceans is far more feared by natives than the great mako shark. That's because sharks sometimes can be scared off by beating the water, and making a disturbance, but the eel, once it has decided you are its next victim, fixes its beady eyes on you and strikes. Quicker than thought, the eel buries its fangs in you, and with enormous power it begins to relentlessly worm downward deeper into the water into its hole in a coral reef. The slimy, snakey creature drags you with it down into the sea. You vainly thrash about as it pulls you toward death. Agony and terror flood through you as you fight to keep your last breath. You kick your legs and beat your arms uselessly, until finally the last bubbles erupt from your mouth and rise toward freedom in the blue sky above—a sky you have seen for the last time. Water floods into your lungs, and you choke and gag soundlessly in the silent, underwater world. And then you are still, motionless. You have entered a coma, you are dying. Still locked in the eel's jaws, you float there, muscles loose, arms outstretched, eyes open and sightless forever.

Except for this...

Except for this...

There is one chance...

Just after the ugly beast grabs you, and just before it begins to drag you down, it loosens its grip, just for a moment, so that it can bite down harder, more securely sinking its fangs into you. In that one second, if you are quick enough, you can pull free. Surprised, the eel watches you lunge away. You have escaped.)

Kimberly, in regulation manner, with her knees slightly bent and her elbows out to the side, holds her gun in both hands pointing at the center of my chest.

And who am I?

She is uncertain.

Am I dangerous?

Perhaps the boy's partner.

A drug contact.

Yes, who am I?

Without money in my pockets, without credit cards.

A wanderer.

Her eyes fix on me. She's got me, her gun at my heart.

She's young. Twenty-something. Nervous as a duck.

Behind her head, her pony tail is hidden from view.

Is she a woman?

Has she the enormous depths of womanhood in her soul?

Is she warm?

Is she caring?

Does she love someone?

Is she tender?

The metal buttons of her uniform jacket glint in the sun.

I think to myself, "Kimberly, oh Kimberly, oh Child of These Troubled Times, is this the life for you? Is it right for you to live such a life as this, a life filled with crimes: murder, robbery, parking tickets?

Yes, of course, it is. It's the life for you.

But there are other lives, Kim.

Perhaps you could go to some place where all the tension and strain will leave your face, where you can smile warm smiles. Oh, do it, Kim. Go somewhere where threats and anxiety will all be things in your past. Go home, Kim. This is such a waste. Leave this policing business to men and women who have strong, peace-filled souls. So what if there are very few of those calm-type people around. We will have a very small police force, that's all. That's the way it should be. Let everybody in the neighborhood take care of their own lives and problems. You could get yourself away from here, Kim. Forget what you've learned about arresting people, and go find out how to set them free.

Kimberly glances briefly in the direction her partner has run. She allows her gun to waver a bit, moving a few inches off the direction of my heart.

For a moment the eel loosens its grip...

Rage and utter abandon fill my chest. I slap the gun away with my palm, and the gun fires with a loud cracking boom that sends a bullet rocketing out to sea. My hands grab her wrists, and suddenly I am behind her and she is cursing.

My arms go around her from back to front. I hold her wrists firmly, and we begin doing a funny little dance in a circle. She mutters, "Shit" as we struggle, and I leap on her back, and wrap my legs around her waist, and yell, "You have turned me into a male chauvinist piggybacker." She does some sort of Kung Fu move on me and we fall to the pavement, and the pistol goes clattering away on the cement. I cling to her with endless affection.

"You son of bitch," she says.

"I love you, Kimmie," I murmur to her breathlessly.

I hop up and run to the gun, grab it and throw it far out onto the sandy beach. Then she and I go sprinting our separate ways: she for her death-dealer, and me for parts unknown. Her partner, Wire-lip, is returning from pursuing the teenager. "Halt or I'll shoot."

Perhaps he will, or perhaps he'll hold his fire for fear of hitting the people coming down the sidewalk. It's impossible for him to catch me on foot. I refuse to be caught. We are running hard. It's the Olympics. It's the first marathon run, and I am Speedy Thermopolee racing to tell the Greeks that Helen of Troy is pregnant.

A shot rings out.

I am A. J. Foyt at Daytona Speedway.

A police whistle.

I am Apollo 7 heading for lunar orbit, around a corner, down an alley. Kim has joined him. They pursue me. I glance back, sweat in my eyes. In theirs, too?

She wears very little make-up. Her pony tail swishes back and forth as she runs.

Their guns are holstered now. They are intent on catching me.

I dash across a busy street and am nearly run over by a new Cadillac Seville with twenty-nine coats of Georgia Peach metal-flecked lacquer. The black kid behind the wheel gives me a friendly wave.

I wonder if he smokes.

I duck into a cocktail lounge called, I notice, The Eight Ball. Although it's still just late afternoon, some couples have already begun the evening's dancing. I quickly move to the back of the room and slide into a dark booth. I am just catching my breath when I notice something odd. I notice that all of the dancers—everyone of them—and also everyone else in the place—is male.

Say *Yes* to Adultery

Later in this book I'll tell you what happened after I ducked into a homosexual bar to hide from the police, but right now I must say a few words about love and marriage, for it's there that you have the most potent opportunities to use the wisdom of *Yes*.

What is love?

If you are a woman, does love mean you must go on receiving the same man time after time in that place where life and love begin, deep in your Furnace of Desire, your Silky Heaven?

If you are a man, does *love* mean nailing, pumping, humping and thumping the same woman time after time, year after endless year?

Is that a true sign of true love?

Yes, of course it is; or can be.

But are there other signs?

Let us remember the words of the marriage ceremony: what does it mean when a man and woman promise to love, honor, and cherish one another, for better or worse, for richer or poorer, in sickness and in health, until death parts them?

Are we to take those words seriously?

Yes, of course, but how seriously?

What kind of deal are any two people making when they take those vows?

Remember they are speaking those words, making that life-long promise, at a particular moment in time *when they are confused.*

If they were thinking clearly how could they possibly make such a deal? Those words of promise are spoken at a *particular moment in time* and then that moment *vanishes*. The world turns, the stars fly through space, trees grow and shed their leaves and die, and nothing is ever again the same as it was when the promise was made. We grow older, we become different. The world is always changing. The day finally comes when, looking at our mate, we suddenly think, "I have seen this person a few times too often. I wish they'd go away." And also, inevitably, some foxy-looking person will come near us and we'll think, "Hey, I'd like to mingle with that one for awhile."

What do these feelings mean?

Do we still care for our spouse?

Of course, we do.

We may still love that person.

Or perhaps hate has replaced love,

Or boredom has arrived.

But since our lives are tied up together with whoever we are married to, we will care about them. We may want them to share our feelings, to give us *understanding*. Or we may want them to go to Egypt and get stepped on by a camel. But we have changed. That is the way the world is.

Suppose we are married to someone who has changed. And suppose our once-adoring spouse is now greatly tempted to dance the rocky tango of sex with another person. Suppose our spouse acts on this temptation and gets together with someone, and they remove all their clothing and begin fondling each other, stroking and twisting and turning, locked together in a warm, delicious erotic sweat, uttering moans of deep sexual satisfaction.

Suppose a person finds out that their wife or husband has done such a thing.

What is that person's usual response?

Usually the person is very *disappointed*!

Yes, that's true. The partner of a cheating spouse usually has a negative reaction on hearing the news. According to a recent survey (conducted by the Southern California Institute for Public Fucking) 97% of the marriage partners interviewed stated that they were *displeased* to learn of their partner's "infidelity." They often stated they felt "betrayed."

But what *is* betrayal? Infidelity?

Remember the world in which you were married, the world where the two of you promised to love, honor, and cherish for better or worse, richer or poorer until death parts you. That world is gone. It died.

But it was born again in a somewhat different shape.

You and your spouse have changed, have grown older, have somewhat different ideas and needs than when you were first married.

The *old* you has died.

A *new* you has been born, a somewhat different you.

This happens over and over again.

Until at last one of you, or both of you, wants to roam.

And does.

Example

I remember the first time Astoria stepped out on me. Things had been rocky for a while. I had just started a new business of my own, and that is a difficult thing to do. We had been snapping at each other, but I just put it down to the usual causes: too little money, too much work, boredom, the pressure of life in general and my new business in particular. But then I began to *suspect* something and finally I confronted her with my suspicions.

She threw it in my face. "Yes," she said. "I have found another man."

I remember we were standing in the bedroom when she told me. She turned away after she said it. She just stood there, with

59

me staring at her back, and then I turned away, too, in the silence of the room and stood there seeing myself in the dresser mirror. At first, it was hard to recognize my face. It looked flat, with my mouth sagging half open, my eyes dull and empty as though I had just learned of a death. Suddenly I was having a hard time breathing; I sat heavily on the bed and she turned to face me.

She looked angry.

Rebellious.

Astoria is so beautiful. Her hair is rich blonde. Her eyes are a lively gray-blue, and when she smiles she gets little crinkle lines of delight around her eyes, and her mouth forms into a curve of delight that makes me happy. She is fairly tall; we are nearly the same height, and the curves of her fit into me as though God meant we should be forever joined together in his great jigsaw puzzle of love.

I begged her to think of what she was doing. I said, "How can you?" and "Why?"

She knew she was inflicting pain on me, and at that moment, that's what she wanted, it seemed.

She also wanted a divorce and started proceedings. She went to live with her new lover, leaving little Quentin and Dulcinea with me. I got a job, bought the kids shoes, and lost weight because it was hard to eat. I pleaded, shouted, threatened, and prayed for her to come back to me.

Finally she did.

It happened this way.

She had started looking increasingly sad. Her lover was sort of a creep, which is often true of the people who build their lives on other people's pain. Astoria's and my jobs were near one another and she began accepting lunch invitations from me. I would carefully pick a small cafe, or make sandwiches for us, and we sat on lawns in parks, and became more and more, gradually more, slowly more, open to one another. Our reconciliation occurred in fits and starts, moving forward with snags and stops, and occasional steps backward. I kept delaying the divorce proceedings. Then one day, when I was mildly sick with a cold, she showed up at our apartment supposedly to visit the kids. But they soon went out to play and she plopped herself on the bed; she sat cross-legged facing me and asked if I wanted to see her new bra.

"Huh?"

She had this bold, foxy little half-smile. It soon became apparent she wanted sex with me. We were both a little frightened.

I was confused. After so many months? Finally?

"Are you kidding?"

"It's a pretty bra," Astoria said, tossing her curly blond hair pertly and smiling with her lovely eyes and sweet lips. Seeing my confused hesitation, thinking I was reluctant, she added, "We're still married. I have my marriage rights, you know."

We started to make love.

But it ended badly.

She was loving, open-hearted and eager, and so was I until after we came, and then suddenly, lying there in the quiet of the room, anger filled my chest. Anger at being hurt, anger at her manipulation of me, anger at her sudden availability to me. I turned on her like a snarling dog as she lay there naked in her softness. I told her, "Now I'm going to fuck you in the ass," Her eyes widened, and she lay there limp and speechless. I just rolled her over on her stomach. I'd show her who was the more powerful of the two of us. In a rage I shoved it into her like a piston. It was the only time we'd ever done that, and she cried out. Soon afterward she went away, practically running from the apartment.

Oddly, our romance, our reconciliation, went on smoothly without interruption. I apologized. Probably she loved me, because the lunches continued; we kept building closeness. We have always loved each other. Finally, she invited *me* somewhere. To a party. I dressed as well as I could, and talked as well as I could, and was impressive enough, I suppose. She seemed proud of us as a couple.

Soon afterwards she said she was leaving her "friend." She said she wanted to get out of there in a hurry, and asked if she could move back into the apartment for a short while until she found a new place for herself.

I said, "Yes, of course."

Silently, we knew we were re-united again.

But there was a heavy feeling inside of me, a weight that sat low in my guts. In my mind there formed the idea that she and I should sleep in separate rooms for awhile; we should do that at least until we had started to figure out what it was that had gone wrong between us. I told her of my feelings and it annoyed her. By the second night she said angrily, *"I am sleeping in our bed,"* and I said, *"Yes."*

Being together was delicious.

She slept in my arms like a beloved kitten.

Say *Yes* To Yourself

Life can teach us things.

But in order to learn we must be willing to accept the lessons life sends us.

What can that story from the last chapter teach us?

Perhaps you've already noticed that all during that whole ugly marriage difficulty I was a total numbskull, idiot, fool, and birdbrain.

When Astoria announced her "infidelity" did I say *Yes* to it?

Only partially. I admitted that, "*Yes*, it is happening," but I avoided accepting it.

Instead, like so many other people who feel they've been hurt by someone, I asked, "How can you?" and "Why?"

These words mean something quite different from *Yes*.

They mean, "I am unhappy with this."

They mean, "You're guilty."

They mean, "Please keep the vows you once made to me." (Even though those vows were made in a world that has died.)

I was trying to change her mind, ignoring her needs, expressing my own. I was refusing to give her a great big, confident *Yes*.

So what happened?

In spite of my attitude, loving me deeply in her soul, she felt the strong urge to taste once more the pleasures of my good-looking body.

And then, finally, I said my first big *Yes*.

But what kind of a *Yes* was it?

A cruddy *Yes*.

Who needs it?

Hardly anybody, that's who.

Naturally, with such a low quality *Yes*, she goes away.

And, naturally, the next move comes only when *she* is good and ready.

For once I do something right. Accepting her invitation to the party, I play it straight, in effect giving her a big, whole-hearted, old-fashioned you-got-it, okay, Amen, *Yes*.

Of course, that warmed her heart, that total acceptance she got from me.

But then my foolishness returned.

I forgot to say *Yes* to *myself*.

I knew it was asking for trouble for us to sleep together right away, acting as though things were all right, before they actually were all right, before we found out what had caused our break up.

I was a coward.

When she said, angrily, "I am sleeping in our bed," I should have said, "Yes, that's fine, that's all right, please *do* sleep in our bed." I should have said that, and then taken my pillow and blanket up to the roof and slept with the pigeons until we had solved our marriage puzzle.

But under the threat of her anger...Oh God, would she leave me again, I had to prevent that from happening...I refused to say *Yes* to my own idea of sleeping apart for a while.

In my own defense, let it be said that she is difficult to resist.

Lying with her in my arms, the world was whole again.

And so...

Can we learn something from all this painful experience?

Yes, I think I learned to accept the inevitable. Astoria and I were happy, quite happy for a while, and then suddenly things went bad between us and she did it again. She found ''another man''.

When she told me the news, all I said was, ''Aw, shit.''

Is *Yes* Safe?

There are only two ways to live.

You can be *safe*.

Or you can be *sane*.

We must ask ourselves, you and I, which way will we live: safely or sanely. We can choose only one, because when we choose one, the other goes out of reach for us. It becomes a passed opportunity.

But before we choose, we should ask ourselves this question: Where do we find *Yes*? Do we find it in safety? Or in sanity? Where does *Yes* live?

Let me share the answer with you.

Yes is dangerous.

Yes lives in sanity.

Sanity is dangerous.

In fact, the idea of being *safe* is an illusion, a dream. Yet think for a moment how much we, as human beings, hope for safety, long for safety, search constantly for safety and security. But it is always out of reach. Always there are dangers, perils, accidents, disease and such things waiting to strike us down, tear us limb from limb, waste us away, leave us crumpled up and crushed like a cigarette butt in the ashtray of life.

Yes, when we realize that safety is only a dream, then suddenly we are sane. When we say *Yes* to the dangers of life, then suddenly we can live peacefully knowing life is going to beat the fuck out of us as it pushes us ever onward toward our final destination, our home in the bosom of the Cosmic Yes.

Example
Here is a letter from a fine young man who belongs to our church.

> Dear Master Wing,
>   I feel I got to write to tell you how much good your Holy Church has done for me. I used to feel awful. Although I am only twenty-two, I was going bald. My boss at the advertising agency where I am an artist was always picking on me and telling me I had zero potential. My darling wife, Darlene, is an alcoholic and often she would leave town unexpectedly for weeks at a time. And I was never breast fed when I was a kid.
>   You can see why I was miserable.
>   But after joining your great Church and accepting *YES* into my life, my whole world was transformed. I lost the rest of my hair and it was OK with me. I told my boss that if he considered my artwork "boring" and my personality somewhat "irritating", then it was obvious to me that he had the brains of a fungus.
>   It felt wonderful to openly and honestly share these feelings with him.
>   After he fired me, I had plenty of time to follow my wife around, and, boy, did we meet some nice people.
>   Now I spend most of my time at the Church

and have told some of our female members about my childhood disappointment, and asked for their help. Well, you know what they said. I have been making up for lost time. We sure have some great boobs around here.

Yours in *YES*,

Toby

Toby Hanratty

Before You Read The Rest

There are two things I should tell you before you read the rest of this book. One is that, yes, I'm a white man, although my name is Chinese. You'll soon find out how that happened.

The other thing is that most of the events in this book occurred in the summer of 1982. That was before AIDS became known as the deadly problem it's turning out to be. So, when the police chased me into the homosexual bar, I had little reason to worry about my health. But I soon had other problems.

The Message of *YES*

Have you noticed how often you feel that you are the victim of the world in which you live? Are you ever tempted to think you are caught in a trap? Do you sometimes feel other people are guilty of raping you either mentally or physically? Are you sometimes afraid of other people?

To achieve the inner peace of *Yes* you must see the world as a place where *everyone is innocent*.

How can we begin to look at the world differently? To begin with, we should try to look at the world through the window of *Yes* rather than the window of fear.

Example

Remember back to the time when the policeman and ponytailed policewoman chased me into The Eight Ball, the homosexual bar.

I ran to the back of the darkened tavern and slid into a dark booth. Glancing around, I saw lots of fellows looking at me. Suddenly the police appeared in the doorway. Whistles and boos rang through the bar. The men showed great courage in the face of this police assault.

"What a gorgeous hunk *he* is," somebody said.

"I want the tall one, boys."

"Oink, oink."

"How'd you like to feel *his* gun?"

One by one the men arose, and started massing in front of the cops, blocking their way into the bar. From out of the darkness in the back of the room, a huge man walked past my booth. The men parted to let him through as he approached the police. He was nine or ten feet tall, it seemed, with massive shoulders. His legs and arms were like tree trunks. His head was shaved completely bald, and his moustache was large and waxed into the shape of the horns of a bull. He had big, wide-spread eyes, and a heavy staring, innocent look on his face. His pants were white like a sailor's and his purple shirt was open to his belt. Heavy gold chains and a gold cross hung down on his chest. He moved slowly, unstoppably, like fate itself, and stood before the cops like a mountain.

He stared down at the police for awhile.

"Fuck off," he said.

And they did.

A crowd of gays cheered loudly, excited by the huge man's victory. Then gradually they dispersed, moving away from the doorway. A lot of them came to my booth, and soon there were all sorts of men staring down at me. They kept on staring, and suddenly I felt like a rabbit. Like a chicken sandwich. Like a plum. Some of them were ordinary looking, and some looked sort of, well, gay and frilly. They kept watching me, and I thought I detected an epidemic of lust in their faces.

A boyish-looking chap with swept-back flaming red hair and beady eyes said boldy, "So what's going on, fella?"

"Hello, men," I said.

This red-haired person, who had spoken, slid down into the booth much too close to me, and I said, "Sorry, I'm married."

"We saved your tutu," somebody said.

Suddenly the booth was filled, and I was surrounded, hemmed in. Somebody was telling me I was cute, and somebody else said I owed them something. "A lot," he said.

"Take it easy, men," I suggested.

"We're just having fun."

"Have a drink, handsome."

The red-haired fellow with beady eyes leaned toward me and said, "I want to fuck you in the mouth."

Somebody said, "Oh, for god's sake, Harold, calm down."

"You're a savage, Harold," said somebody else.

"So what? He's got a mouth, and I want to fuck it. How about it, fella?"

Now there are two ways of looking at this situation. I could have felt like a *victim*. I could have felt *threatened*. Here were these fellows, some of whom were lusting after me quite openly, and perhaps were willing to resort to violence in order to have their way with me.

"The least you could do," someone said to me, "is show a little gratitude and cooperation with Harold...and me."

Or I could look at the situation through the eyes of *Yes*. I could realize that I should accept them as human beings, and understand that even if they forcibly removed me to some discreet place and beat me up and abused me, wounding my body and feelings, subjecting me to shameful sodomies and such —even if they did these things, they were still people—innocent people. They were just doing the best they could, trying—like anyone else—to make the most of their lives pursuing their own satisfactions. This is what we *all* do as we travel on our way along the path toward the warm embrace of the Eternal Yes.

"Well, how about it, cookie?" Harold asked demandingly.

And what's more, I knew I should look at these people as *individuals* rather than as some hostile "they" that were out to get me. Some of the people in the bar were totally ignoring me, and were satisfied to sit on their bar stools, sipping their alcohol, thinking their own private thoughts.

"Cat's got his tongue."

"I want it, too."

Others in the bar thought that the scene was amusing and were just watching the show. Still others objected to the threatening, stressful tactics of Harold and three or four others, and were trying to stop him from bothering me.

"Let him be, Harold. You're giving us a bad rep."

"Fuck off, Nelson. I mean to get me some new butt."

And of course, there was Harold and the others—people who had their own special needs.

"For the last time," Harold said meaningfully and forcefully. "How about it, fella? What do you say?"

There is only one answer.

The answer of acceptance.

Yes.

The answer is *Yes.*

I accepted Harold as a person. I loved Harold as a human being.

I *liked* Harold.

I liked him better than cancer.

I liked him better than dead fish.

But I liked him less than I like a golden sunrise breaking over the mountains.

But I liked him more than I would like to be hanged, or drowned in a tub of cold oatmeal.

But I liked him less than I love the crinkly-eyes Astoria gets when she smiles in the morning.

But more than I like dog droppings.

Less than I like skiing.

Through the kindly eyes of *Yes* I could see their whole situation for what it was. Harold needed my help. He was avoiding my true feelings about the matter. He was refusing to say *Yes* to my proper place in the universe—for I strongly felt I should be somewhere else rather than on the end of Harold's pecker.

Obviously, fate had led me here so I could bring the message of *Yes* to Harold. To all of them.

"Bless you, Harold," I said to him. "Bless you and bless you, too," I said to each of them, one man after another. "Bless you all, beloved instruments of Light." I suddenly stood on the booth seat. They all cleared out of the booth in a hurry in case I might have violent intentions, and there they stood before me, gazing into my face. "My friends," I said, "I have come to endow you with the *Word*. I have come to bring joy and hope and enlightenment to you.

"You are blessed," I told them. "Look at me, oh brothers. What do you see? Just another good looking guy? Just another sperm bank where you'd like to make deposits and withdrawals? Just another gorgeous hunk of male pussy?"

(Several of them nodded.)

"Fie, I say to you. Woe, I say to you. It is an illusion. I am illusion. Everything is an illusion. The road is straight, the road is wide, and we all must journey together down the tunnel of life toward the Eternal Affirmative from which all light comes and illusion dissolves.

"Gather round, brothers and sisters. Hear the Word from which all Light proceeds. It is the Light that gives us form. The Light that gives us substance."

Someone said, "What the hell is he talking about?"

"I am glad you asked that, Brother. Bless you. I am speaking of the Light that brings clarity to our lives. I am speaking..."

"I still want to screw him," Harold said.

"...of the Light that gives shape and meaning to existence. Have you ever been to the movies? Yes, of course you have. At one time or another we've all been to the movies. Nelson, have you been to the movies?"

Nelson said, "Yes."

"Good. Harold, have you been to the movies?"

Harold looked at me suspiciously.

"Yes. We have all been to the movies. And let me ask you this, how did you get there?

74

"Let me answer for you.

"You said to yourself, 'Should I go to the movies?' Or somebody else said to you, 'Hey, let's go to the movies.' Or somebody said, 'Why don't you go to the movies by yourself?' And what did you say?

"You said *Yes*.

"That's how you got to the movies.

"And what did you see there?

"Did you see John Wayne, Clint Eastwood, Rock Hudson? Did you really see them? Think carefully.

"What you saw was the *illusion* of those men. You saw the *illusion*, the images, of men and women, rocks, trees and theatrical sets. You saw light that shined through the celluloid film, streaming forth from the film, projected onto the movie screen. Those images of those men appear to be real. They look real. They move as if they are real. But what are they really? You all know how motion pictures are shown. *Light* flows through the film and travels to the screen where the images appear. *Yes*. What you see in a movie house is only Light playing out a dream for you to watch."

Harold was whispering to the guy next to him, but the rest were watching me.

"And so it is with *life*, my friends. We are only illusions. You and I and all of us. We are only an expression of the powers of Light. All of the rocks and trees and streets are only manifestations of the Divine Light of Creation. This Divine Light comes streaming through all Eternity and with its own magnificent mystical power it creates the thing we call *Life*. What is Life? Life is only a Cosmic Motion Picture."

Quickly stepping up onto the table top, I called out, asking them, "And where does this Eternal Blessed Light of Creation come from? Can you tell me? Do you know? Tell me!! Come on, tell me! Tell me where it comes from, oh, you Blessed Cocksuckers of Laguna! Where can we find it? The Source!!??

The Burning Source of Everything!??!!?!?"

They remained silent, so I told them.

"We find it in the Flaming Heart of the Burning Mind of the Fiery YES!"

Naturally, they wondered what the fuck I was talking about. But I was having fun playing with all these words and seeing their puzzled faces. Daylight streamed through the open doorway and I wondered if it was time to make a break for it. Harold was still plotting with a couple of others.

Still standing on the table I called to them, "Gather around all you seekers of truth. I have come to bring you the powerful Message of *Yes*. The Perfect Positive! The Almighty Allrightee!"

My voice dropped low.

"Yes...

"Each one of us hungers...We all need something...We are always seeking a better life. But the search makes us tired. We get fagged out. But we still go on searching, always searching for something perfect. The gardener searches for the perfect pansy. The ice skater swishes over the ice seeking the perfect figure eight. But always there is disappointment. We try to be gay. We try to put our finger in the dyke of disappointment. We hope that some good fairy will come to help us. But generally it rarely seems to happen."

Harold shouted, "He's putting us on. He's making fun of us."

"Harold," I cried, "Life makes fun of us! The only way we can survive is to say *Yes* to it. *Yes* to all of it."

Harold grabbed at my ankle. I shook him free. Suddenly a couple of others were grasping for me.

"Accept *YES*, Harold!" I cried, aiming a kick at his head.

It was time to leave.

I leaped off the table, heading for the door, but quick as a flit Harold trackled me. Others joined in—soon six, or eight, or ten of us were thrashing around on the floor. Some wanted my butt, some wanted to help me save my butt, and were trying to pull the others off. Determined to defend my honor and my asshole, I fought like a demon. We all fought like demons. It was a real good fight. It was a jumble of bodies, it was pile up at the goal line, it was freight trains colliding, it was a mess.

And the good guys were losing.

Suddenly I was grabbed from above. Someone seized me under the arms and hoisted me high in the air like a baby. From up near the ceiling I looked down and saw the top of a bald head and a purple shirt covering shoulders wide enough to land a jet on. Far below, on the floor, the rest of guys looked respectfully up at the giant who held me in the air, and you could tell from their faces that giving him trouble was last on their list of fun things to do.

"What's your name, big man?" I asked.

In a low voice he growled, "Bruno."

"Get me out of this, Bruno."

Bruno didn't say anything, just stared down at them. Finally, he turned slowly and moved like a Sherman tank toward some stairs at the back of the dark room. On the second stair he turned back to them and said, "You people are full of lust. You don't know how to love. I will show this man that we know how to love." Like fate itself, he turned and continued up the dark stairs and I said to myself, "Aw, shit."

Say *Yes* To Bruno Megasavitch

Everyone has emotions. Everyone has needs.

Reading those words you may have said to yourself, "Yes, of course, we all know that."

But do we truly know it?

Only partially, I think. Only some times.

Often we take people for granted.

Take Adolf Hitler for example.

Do we say to ourselves, "*Yes*, Hitler, he had needs, too; he had emotions?" Do we ever think to ourselves about how bad he must of felt when he was losing World War II which he had started with such hope and confidence?

I am afraid many of us have often ignored Hitler's feelings, his humanity. *Yes*, many people feared Hitler, and reacted negatively to him, which may have brought out the worst in him, and caused him to do so many things people now label as "bad."

There are many examples of such attitudes. We must try to be sensitive to *everyone*.

We must learn to open up to their emotions.

Being open to other people means giving them your full attention, listening to what they're saying, and to what they're afraid to say, too. If you do this you'll *understand* them, and will be able to react to them in a humane and loving way.

Saying *Yes* to people's needs and emotions will open whole new worlds to you.

Example

Big Bruno moved up the dark stairway, carrying me easily, like a big bag of potatoes, over his shoulder. At the top of the stairs he banged open a door and strode to the middle of a huge room. He stood there and turned slowly around as if trying to decide where he should dump me. I could see, as we turned, a small kitchen and dining table; a big desk cluttered with papers, pens and pencils; a long and wide work table covered with artist's materials: paints, glue, exacto knives, a stack of canvases and pieces of clay sculpture. There were many green house plants in pots, hanging from walls and sitting on tall plant stands. The walls were cluttered with paintings—mostly of flowers. There was a gigantic bed, with a canopy over it and pretty pink lace netting hanging all around it, enclosing it.

He began to set me down in the middle of the room. His hands were like steam shovel claws taking hold of each side of my chest and raising me up before lowering me slowly like a doll, down, down from near the ceiling until my face was level with his. And then he stopped. He held me there with my feet off the floor, staring at me with a blank, expressionless face with flat eyes like a mindless animal. I thought of trying to kick him in the balls but was too frightened to look down at the target. Besides, if I did kick him, he'd probably just throw me through a wall or twist my head off like a chicken.

There was total silence.

After a moment or two he began lowering me again like an elevator, past his massive chin and big Adam's apple, past the heavy chains and bright gold cross on his chest, down, down until my feet finally touched the carpet and I was looking straight ahead at his stomach. Then, without pause, he started moving downwards himself; he was slowly bending his knees, sinking, until he knelt in front of me, his flat eyes staring straight ahead at my belt buckle and zipper.

Ah-hah, now's my chance, I thought, I'll knee him in the

face. Very hard. I'll smash my knee into that broad nose and run for it.

But wait.

What will happen, probably, if I do that?

My knee will splinter against that stone head of his. I will probably make him angry, tense. Irritable. He will probably pull me apart like a wishbone.

So I relaxed, sagged.

Resigned, I looked over his shaved head at the eastern window filled with light. Next to it was a picture frame, and inside the frame was a parchment paper with fancy writing. A poem.

> Bless this home
> wherein I dwell
>> Home port in the storm of life.
>
> Where I am safe
> From the ugly hell
>> of the world of pain and strife.
>
> (signed) B.M.

He bowed his head; then slowly he looked up at me.

At last...finally...there was an expression on his face. He was waiting for something. Pleadingly, longingly, he was waiting for me to speak. He was a *person*. I could see that. Suddenly this giant, this brute, this tank car, had changed into a human being who needed something. Something from *me*.

It was my move. I knew that, and I also knew whatever I did was going to be all right. The worst he could do was tear me into little pieces or squash me like a bug.

Gazing down at him kneeling before me, I touched him. I reached out and laid my hand on the shiny dome of his head and said to him, "Bless you, Noble Freak."

He gazed up at me, and slowly his eyes filled with tears.

Moments passed and then he said, all choked up, "It was so beautiful."

"*Yes*, it was," I agreed, wondering what the hell he was talking about.

He shook his head and bit his lip, so full of emotion was he. "So beautiful," he repeated.

"*Yes*," I said. "It *was* beautiful."

"Thank you."

"You're welcome, Bruno."

"Thank you, so much."

"It was the least I could do," I told him.

"They have so little understanding," he said.

"You are right, big man. They fail to understand."

"*Yes*, but I do, sir. I do."

"*Yes*. I believe that, Bruno. I believe you understand."

"I do," he said.

"Tell me."

"What, sir?"

"Tell me what you understand."

"Everything."

"That's a lot of understanding, Bruno."

"Thank you, sir."

"It's unnecessary to call me 'sir'."

"I apologize, Master."

"That's all right, Bruno."

"Tell me again," he asked humbly.

"Okay, I will. That's all right, Bruno."

"I meant about the Light."

"Pardon."

"I meant about the Light that Burns in the Flaming Heart of *Yes*."

"Oh," I said. "You understood *that*."

"*Yes*, I understood."

"It is very difficult. Very few people understand *Yes*."

"I did," he said. "I understood it immediately. It was as though I had been waiting all my life since I was born to hear you say those words. And when they came, your blessed words, my heart was filled with light. I understood. Life is only as real, or as unreal, as a motion picture. We are all only the projected images of Eternal Light. We are acting out the painful drama of existence under the almighty direction to the Divine Creative power. *Yes*, it's true. It's so true!"

"Bruno..."

"Yes?"

"You talk too much."

He bowed his head.

"It's all right, big fellow. We must be careful."

"Yes," he said. "It's only that I want to know more of your holy message. What does *Yes* really mean?"

"*Yes* means *Yes*."

That answer seemed to leave him unsatisfied, so I added, "*Yes* is difficult, Bruno. *Yes* is hard. And yet it's easy. On the other hand, it's complicated, but also it's very simple and basic."

"That's hard to grasp, Master."

"Yes, it is, Bruno. *Yes* is a slippery word."

"What is your name?" he asked reverently.

"My name...?" After all this mystical stuff I could hardly tell him the truth—that my name was Norris. I looked around. There was a half-finished clay sculpture on his big work table. A large bird in flight. One wing was raised high, making a powerful stroke in the air, but the other had broken off and lay useless on the table.

"My name is...Wing," I said. "My name is Wing Fu Fing."

"Are you Chinese?" he asked puzzledly.

"There are very few blond Chinese, Oh Honorable Skin Head."

"What does your name mean?"

"You have a questioning mind, Bruno."

"I am a Seeker of Truth," he said.

"Yes, I see," I said. "You are a Seeker of Truth."

He nodded that I was right.

Suddenly I was bored. The danger, evidently, was gone, and I began getting itchy to leave. I was getting hungry, too. I thought of broiled lambchops, rare, with maybe some zucchini, fresh and lightly steamed.

But he expected more from me.

"You have *always* sought truth," I told him, and he nodded, Yes.

I looked around the room and saw the paintings and statues he must have created.

"You have the hot, feverish soul of a poet, Bruno."

When he smiled his face became all creases and bumps like a globe of the world.

"You have the strong, creative mind of a true artist, my friend. The exact, all-seeing eye of a master painter. The powerful imagination of a superior sculptor."

He grinned happily showing teeth a water buffalo would have been proud of.

He bowed his face to the ground at my feet, crying, "You see right through me, Master."

"Around you, Bruno, I see around you."

"You do?" he asked.

"*Yes*, I see the halo of holiness that surrounds you."

It was embarrassing having him there at my feet. It was strange to receive so much respect.

"Arise, brother."

"I am too miserable a man to be called your brother."

"All right. Arise, son."

But Bruno stayed bowed low. All he did was bend his head upward to look at me. "Tell me why you are here?" he asked.

"I was wondering that myself."

"Have you come to teach us?" he asked, arising again to his kneeling position.

I thought for a moment and then gave him the best answer I could think of. "*Yes*, I have."

"What will you teach us? Will you teach us about motion pictures and *Yes*?" he asked eagerly.

"*Yes*," I said confidently.

"Will you bring *Yes* to the despairing masses that inhabit this town?"

"Yes, I will."

"Will you preach to the people?"

"Of course, I will. Yes, I'll do it."

"I know what you're going to do," he called out joyously.

"Tell me, Bruno. Tell me!"

"You're going to found a church!"

"*Yes*, Bruno," I answered, "I am! I am going to found a church."

He cried louder than me, "A church about *Yes*?"

"*Yes*, certainly! I might as well! I shall found a Church based on the almighty, confusing, contradictory holy message of *Yes*."

"Oh, good!"

"*Yes* is easy, *Yes* is hard. And I shall call our church... Are you ready for this, Bruno...?"

"*Yes*."

"I shall call it the Church of the *Word*."

"*Yes!*"

"The *Holy* Church of the Word."

"*Yes! Yes!*"

"*The Holy Church of the Slippery Word!*"

"Blessed Master!" he cried, falling on his face again at my feet. "I am hungry for your message. We are all hungry for it."

What could I say...?

I had to say it...

"I am hungry, too, Bruno."

"You, Master?" He was amazed.

"For lamb chops."

"Chops?"

"*Lamb* chops. Get me some lamb chops, Bruno."

Without speaking, he went to the door and I called out to him, and he paused and looked back.

"Bruno?"

"Sir?"

"And some zucchini."

Hello.

I miss you.

Everyone Shall Be Free

Yes is a revolutionary idea.

Yes will set you free.

Are you as free as you'd like to be? Or do you want more freedom?

Many of us want more room in our lives, more space to be ourselves. Often we feel we are the prisoners or servants of something or someone. Perhaps that's why there have been so many revolutions in this century we live in. All century long people have been kicking themselves free of their masters, and declaring their independence. In the 1940's alone, almost half the world's population became independent as the result of two huge revolutions: the Chinese Revolution and the Rebellion in India. These revolutions, like most uprisings that are popular and successful, were led by interesting and attractive leaders. The Indians were led by Mahatma Gandhi, the Chinese were led by 隶 .

隶 was tall for a Chinaman.

But Gandhi was the shortest person in India, except for his wife.

隶 had shiny black hair, thick and combed straight back.

Gandhi was bald as an oyster.

隶 had thick powerful shoulders. He wore peasants' clothing of drab cloth: a plain jacket buttoned to the chin, a little workingman's cap perched on his head. His skin was a reddish-yellow, his cheeks full, his eyes were squinty, intelligent and calm. When he walked, he moved slowly and heavily, sort of waddling like a bear standing up.

Gandhi, who was the color of a concert piano, went around half naked most of the time, wearing only a large white cloth, like a big diaper, wrapped between his legs and around his hips. He had a large hooked nose that hung down over his toothless mouth. (He carried his false teeth in his diaper and took them out for meals). Gandhi peered out at the world through round gold-rimmed glasses. So skinny was his body that you could count his ribs easily; his movements were quick and stiff, like a bird catching worms.

You can see how different the two men looked: like a rock and a robin, and ox and a twig.

Yet they had similarities.

Both have been described, by news reporters, as having femininity, suggestions of womanliness, in them.

Farley Ort of the Jacksonville *Times* mentions the weak handshake, the sensual mouth, and high voice of 隶. Likewise, Gandhi had a shrill tone, according to reporter Agnes Smedley of the Daytona *Herald* (who smoked cigars).

Both men were emotional—at times becoming almost hysterical—and they could quite quickly switch, abruptly, from one emotion to another. Both men are said to have had a sixth-sense: a deep understanding that is often found in women, a sensitivity and intuition so fast and sure they seem to know what you are thinking and feeling before you do.

Possessed of immense will-power—backbones of iron, as far as revolutionary matters were concerned—both men had taken on the tremendous job of bringing freedom and dignity to their countries. India and China happen to be neighbors in the Far East, and by the 1940's the whole neighborhood had gone to hell.

There was poverty and misery.

Starvation, humiliation, degradation.

The Businessmen of the West—the Englishmen, French, Germans, Dutch and Americans—had taken over the two countries and were sucking up native gold and shipping it home by the boat-load to their bank accounts in the white countries. The Chinese and Indian "upper classes" joined with these foreign businessmen to prey upon the "lower classes."

Which was most of the people.

There was hunger.

Begging was a national industry.

The stink of disease rose from millions of people who lived in the streets, giving birth and nursing, eating, breeding, and dying in the gutters.

Thank God for religion.

The people had plenty of religion to keep them occupied and justified. In India, religion ranked second only to poverty as the most popular leisure time activity. The Moslems and Hindus continually held church socials, but these affairs were different from Christian church socials where a person gets a pancake breakfast or a spaghetti feed. At a Moslem church social a group of worshipers would gather, praise God, and then go out and kill as many Hindus as they could handle. A Hindu church social was the same, only they killed Moslems.

With rocks, clubs and guns sometimes, but mainly with knives.

That was the situation Gandhi and 隶 faced in trying to improve their countries: powerful foreigners, class victimization, and religious hatred.

Being different men, they had different ways of working. 隶 went to war, and became known as a communist and a murderer. Gandhi opted for peace.

Gandhi believed all life was holy; he was a vegetarian, refusing to allow any animal to be killed just so he could eat.

He was married to the same woman for sixty years; they had four children before he was thirty-seven. However, one day, he told his wife that he was going to become celibate, giving up the pleasure of sexual contact with her.

His wife said, "It's because I'm the shortest woman in India, right?"

He offered her some more vegetables, and explained that he needed all his energies for the revolution. The Indian people gave him the name *Bapu* which means *Father*.

They should have given that name to 隶 because he had four wives, whom he abandoned, one by one, all but the last. He fathered up to ten kids (an accurate count has been lost in history) most of whom he also abandoned here and there in villages as he led the fighting revolutionary armies back and forth across China. As for vegetables, 隶 felt, what difference did they make? His soldiers wore dirty uniforms and little cloth caps that soaked up the blood very well when they got shot in the head. To win China's freedom his soldiers had to kill, and were killed by, their own brothers, those Chinese men who foolishly served the western businessmen and the upper classes who held all China in slavery. What difference did it make, then, if a few cows, pigs, and chickens were added to the corpses lying in the roads and fields getting stiff with their eyes open, with flies buzzing in and out of their mouths? What difference did vegetables make when warplanes built in New Jersey, U.S.A., came screaming through holes in the sky spitting little gray slugs of death at the peasants because the peasants hated working for 8¢ an hour, twelve hours a day, six and a half days a week?

$325 a year bought very few vegetables and very little meat anyway.

So eat anything you could get hold of
so that you could live on
to fight.

That's what 隶 did. He ate what he could, usually spicing it with chili peppers, lots of hot peppers, that he had learned to love back in his boyhood home in southern China. Eating peppers, he said, kept him from getting depressed. The Second World War had just started, and now he had to lead his armies against the Japanese in addition to fighting his Chinese brothers who made up the armies of the western businessmen and Chinese upper classes. One afternoon in the presence of Arley Fort of the Jacksonville *Times*, 隶 was slouched on an army cot with his pants halfway down, hunting for fleas in his pubic hair. He and the army were enduring another endless wait in a campsite in the bush country. Flies buzzed. The heat lay heavily on the men. After a while of dead silence, 隶 spoke softly, almost as if talking to the fleas. "I think it's too difficult sometimes...," he said. His shoulders sagged. Looking up at the reporter, his eyes grew misty, and he said, "Sometimes this fighting for freedom gets so tough you just feel like crawling into bed and beating off." With that he reached for a cigarette and sucked the smoke deep into his lungs.

Gandhi detested smoking and announced he would live to 125 because he treated his body right. He lectured the Indian people to do the same, cutting out alcohol, tobacco, meat and sex if they could stand it.

Gandhi's oldest son, however, was an alcoholic.

Under Gandhi's leadership, the Indian people fought British domination in various peaceful and gentle ways such as serving them creamed Brussels sprouts for dinner. Needled like this, the irritated Englishmen responded by shooting the Indians and clubbing them until their faces looked like bean soup. The Indians, however, kept it up, serving them cauliflower with cheese sauce. The Englishmen finally had all they could take; going nuts, they yelled, "Let 'em ruin India, see if we care." They began throwing their underwear into suitcases. Meanwhile, the Moslems and Hindus pulled their knives, snapped their thumbnails on the razor edges, and gazed at each others' throats.

World War II ended.

The British fled India.

In China, the armies of the West collapsed. 隶 went to Russia, got sick for a few months, came back home and helped to build a country where everyone gets enough to eat now, and children smile a lot.

In India, the religious people went at each other like mad devils, spilling enough blood to paint the moon.

"India," old Gandhi weeped, "is still India." He was then 78 years old. He (and 隶 too) had been fighting for 30 years by then. "The people refuse to join together. To cooperate. To get off each other's backs. To work together. We must cooperate to find the best ways so that each man and woman and child is free to grow in health and peace."

The people refused to listen.

"The fighting must stop," he cried, "or I will starve myself tc death."

He was willing to make the highest sacrifice a man can make.

He was like a child who threatens to hold his breath until he gets his way.

He began losing weight.

117, 115, 113, 109

Bapu was dying.

Panicky, the religious leaders got together, conferred, and agreed to stop socializing.

Gandhi smiled. "I will eat again, and perhaps live to be 125."

He went outside. An assassin pumped him full of bullets.

隶 , although violence swirled around him all his life, lived to a ripe old 82, seeing China become a world power before he died.

Millions of Indians still live in the gutters.

That's the story of the two revolutions.
Did you like it?
I do. I think it's sort of entertaining.
Too bad it's a lie.
Yes, that's what it is. The story is a lie because it focuses on a couple of heroes, and leaves out some important people who should be in there.
You.
It leaves out you.
And me, too.
We're in this together.
It would be better to re-write the story, putting in all the essential participants, including you and me.
Here's what the new story should be like: it's a sunny day at the beach and you and I are standing contentedly, warm and comfortable, at the waterline. Every ocean needs a name, so we'll name this one. We'll call it the East. The East is here lapping at our feet, so, if someone were to ask us where the East was, we could tell them, "Right here, at our feet."
But also the ocean stretches away from us, far out of sight. Our vision, however, is too weak to see the farthest shore. At our feet, close to us, the East is shallow; but out there, where our eyes are too weak to see, we have a strong suspicion that the East is dark and deep.
But here we are on the beach,
standing looking East, with our toes in the water, waiting.
Then we start to feel something.
What is it?
Is it our imagination?
Or are we sensing something real?
What?
Is there something like a gentle swaying? Like the beginning

of an earthquake.

Then it comes to us, as though someone has sent us some sort of dim message that we can barely understand. It's a wave.

Out there in the ocean, a huge wave is building.

Suddenly, although we are still warm—I mean, the sun is shining, so we are still comfortable, but maybe a little nervous now—suddenly we realize, "That wave is coming *toward* us. It's coming toward *us*. A wave."

It must be a very strange wave to be felt before it's seen.

But it's there.

What is it?

This is what it is: it's revolution.

A monstrous wave of revolution is sweeping toward our lives.

Hey, wait a minute, we might say.

Things are okay the way they are.

Why change?

I mean things could be worse.

You could have cancer, you know.

Things could be lots worse.

I mean, we've tolerated things the way they are for such a long time, why change now?

Hey, wait a minute.

Of course we know that even if we would like to wait a minute, the revolution is going to keep coming. We may perhaps turn around and look inland for a place to hide, but the sand stretches away from us as far as the eye can see, like the future, without shelter for us of any kind.

We know the wave is coming, and that it will pick up everything and everyone who's in its path and sweep everything away in its all-powerful flood.

Will we die? Will it kill us? Will we lose ourselves? What is this damn wave anyway?

It is this.

This is what it is.

It is the wave of Freedom.

It is the most powerful force there is.

It crushes everything that stands in its way.

It sweeps out of the past and crashes into the future, carrying people with it.

In fact, the whole wave is made up of *people*. It's made up of the lives of people. All the people. Little people, like you and me. We are the wave. It is our needs, our desires, our work that is always moving forward into the future.

But wait a minute.

There at the top of the wave, look there, look up there.

There's something floating there at the top of the wave, something being carried along by the wave, bobbing like a little cork.... Like two little corks.

What are those two corks bouncing at the top of the wave of history that is rushing forward into the future?

It is Gandhi.

It is 隶.

They were just two little people like us: two corks carried by the enormous power wave of history, the wave of freedom. It is the human drive for freedom that made these men great heros. Like everybody else, they smoked or avoided smoking, ate meat or vegetables or peppers or whatever, fucked or kept their dicks in their pants, killed or loved life, died in bed or in the street. They had only small lives until we made them great because we needed them for a while in our pursuit of the freedom to grow.

隶 understood this, and once told a reporter from the Jacksonville *Times*, "I count for very little. It is the people who matter; they roll into the future like a great wave."

The wave of revolution takes time to build, but gradually it becomes big enough to form a peak, a crest. Then it breaks and comes crashing down on the old way of life. Those who oppose freedom are crushed by it. And even many of those who love freedom, who want to ride with the wave, will suffer losses, too. Many people are hurt. In the end, the old way of living is broken, and many people are lost. They lie in the streets and the alleys, on the beaches, in the mountains, killed in the fear, anger and despair that comes when people are faced with change. Change terrifies the deepest part of the human soul. This terror takes victims. They lie ripped apart and bloody in the path of freedom.

One night, when he was thinking hard, 隶 put it this way:

"A revolution is people acting for themselves.

"Seizing power over their own lives.

"They refuse to let their masters have so much power over them anymore.

"But the masters refuse to let the common people alone, to let them lead their own lives, do what they need to do, become who they want to become.

"And so they fight.

"A revolution is an act of violence."

That's what 隶 said.

"A revolution is different from writing a story or painting a picture," he said.

"A revolution is full of blood.

"It's full of terror.

"A revolution is different from a dinner party."

Example

"It's your fucking dinner party," I screamed at Astoria.

She leaped back like I'd hit her.

"Asshole," I screamed. Grabbing a plate, I frisbeed it into the kitchen wall where it exploded into bits.

Astoria clenched her elbows and arms tight against her chest, biting her knuckles.

"*You* set the fucking table," I ordered as if I'd kill her if she again suggested that I do it.

She bit her lip and shook her head, her blond hair swaying, her lovely blue eyes wetting as she pleaded, "But I just got home from work... I need a break, Norrie, I need a break..."

"I work, too," I snapped at her, but it made me feel like a fool when I remembered I was unemployed. "Do you think it's easy to go out day after day pounding the streets looking for a job?"

It felt so fucking dumb and stupid to say that. And the truth is that I *was* so fucking dumb and stupid at the time. For you see, this particular night on which I was shouting was the very night before *Yes* was revealed to me. It was the night before I told Quentin he could use the car, the night before I told Dulcinea to say *Yes* to any boy who asked to have sex with her. As we stood facing each other, little did Astoria and I realize great changes would soon come into our lives.

"Your unemployment insurance has run out, Norrie, we got to remember that... If I lose this job, how are we going to live?"

She looked neat and respectable and clean in her business clothes. She looked very proper and correct and traditional in her skirt, jacket and blouse, while I felt dirty and awful in my sandals, my ragged cut-off jeans and the black T-shirt I bought after seeing a French gangster movie.

"You're such a stupid, stupid woman; do you call this living?"

When I said that, she looked like she lost all her will to fight, maybe even her will to live. She dropped head into her hands, and choked on her words, "I do the best I can. It's the best I can do, Norrie."

"You invite your fucking boss over, and you think he's going to fire you if the fucking dinner *I cooked* fails to hit the table at the appointed time. Maybe it should hit the wall, how about that, baby, how'd you like it if it hit the *wall*?" I pulled the casserole dish out of the oven and held it in my good right hand, intending to splatter it against the yellow cupboard.

"Please..," she said, "please put it down..."

Such a fool, I felt like such a fool.

I set the food down on top of the stove.

Astoria sagged with relief.

I felt I'd lost something.

She said, "They're going to be here any minute. I'd better go do my hair."

I watched her go toward our bedroom. God, she was lovely.

I turned and looked at the cupboard; then slowly made my way over there and picked up a stack of dishes to set the table. I put glasses on the stack of dishes, and silverware in some of the glasses, and carried them all to the table. I got the table cloth and spread it, and took a dish in my hand, ready to set the table.

Then I paused.

"Fuck it," I told myself.

Gently I set the plate down, and went out the front door.

In the driveway Dulcinea and Quentin were playing basketball, shooting at the backboard I'd set up for them soon after we'd rented this place.

"Hi, Pa," Dulcie shouted, "Wanna play?"

"Yeah, Pa," Quentin chimed in, "Come on, let's play a little two-on-one."

I ran inside to change from sandals to sneakers.

Back in the driveway, we started playing. Quentin was dribbling the ball toward me. At sixteen and a half, he was already a little taller than I, and he has good body control. His body is very lean and hard, like mine, and his hair is the color of straw. He's a good boy.

Dulcinea was moving around under the basket behind me, waving her arms and begging Quentin to throw her the ball. I held my arms up high in front of him to prevent that. Quentin came bouncing the ball within five feet of me, and then stopped dribbling. He held the ball with two hands and, after pausing for a second, he tossed the ball toward Dulcinea.

What a stupid play that was.

The moment he had stopped dribbling, I had taken a step toward him, but I was only faking, and by the time he was tossing the ball toward Dulcie, I was already stepping backwards, and with one hand I reached high in the air; the ball settled gently into my hand. I turned with grace and ease, and flipped the ball into the basket. It swished beautifully through the net. The next time Quentin dribbled toward me, he stopped and again held the ball in his two hands. I stepped backward, and again he paused because he thought I would be too close to Dulcie and would steal the ball again when he passed it. After taking the one backward step toward Dulcie I lunged forward and stripped the ball out of his hands. Turning, I shot and scored again. The third time he dribbled and stopped and held the ball, I began guarding him so closely, waving my arms around pressing him, that he became flustered and when he tried to pass to his sister, he threw the ball past her into the neighbor's yard.

Bringing the ball back into our yard he said nicely to me, "You're pretty tough for an old man."

"Believe me, it's damn easy when I'm playing against somebody as stupid as you," I said.

Dulcie moaned, "It's only a game, Pa."

"Stupid," I yelled at Quentin suddenly. "Stupid, stupid, stupid."

"Maybe we better quit," Quentin said.

"Do you know what *stupid* is," I challenged him. "Do you?"

Quentin was mute, silently staring at me.

"Stupid is doing the same dumb ass thing over and over and over, time after time."

"Pa," Dulcie said, "The neighbors are looking."

She was right.

Yes, there was old Emily Pothers peering out her window curtains across the street, watching me shouting insanely at my son.

"So what?" I snapped at Dulcinea.

"It's humiliating, Pa." She whined.

"Those who refuse to be humble will endure a lifetime of humiliation," I said, trying to sound reasonable like a professor from the unversity. "All right, Pa," Quentin said.

"Forget that *all right* shit; have we talked about this before?"

He knew what I meant and nodded politely to me, "Yes."

"When?"

"Last summer when you coached the park's team."

"When else?"

"The summer before that."

"What are you supposed to do?"

"I'm supposed to keep moving. Keep on dribbling until I pass to a teammate."

"Say it again."

"I'm supposed to keep bouncing the ball as I come toward the basket, and keep dribbling until I pass to a teammate," he recited like a student.

"And how long have I been telling you that?"

"Two years," he said staring at the ground.

"And why do you refuse to do it?"

"Maybe I'm afraid of you," he said defiantly, looking up and staring me right in the eyes.

"Bullshit," I told him.

"Who says?" he challenged me.

"I say. I've seen you playing against other people. When you get a little pressure on you, you stop."

"Maybe I like to stop."

"Maybe you're right when you say you're afraid. Do you want to score?"

"Yes."

"Then go for it. You think the defensive man is going to tear your testicles off?"

"Very funny, Pa." Quentin said.

"You think it's funny...? Well, listen to me, buster, it's time for a change, and we're going to have one right now. We are going to play some more, you gutless little bastard, and if you stop and hold onto the ball like a scared little cunt, I am going to stop letting you use my car. Do you understand that? You are through using the car."

He stared at me with terrible hate in his eyes.

"If you do it just once more..."

He refused to speak or even show that he had heard me. I knew that if he could have beaten me to pulp he would have.

"Listen to me, you fool. You pull up short like that again and I'm going to kick your ass right out of the house. You go live some place else, you hear me?"

He stared at me and shook his head. "You're crazy, man. You're going crazy."

"Now you're catching on, buster. I am going crazy, and I'm through living with cunts."

"Jesus, Pa," Dulcie moaned, "That's a bad word."

"Do you know what a cunt is, Quentin? A cunt is any person, man or woman, who lets people fuck them all the time. They get their heads fucked, their bodies fucked, everybody uses them. Do you know how cunts feel about life. They hate it—and they try to get even with everybody. But they're such chicken-shit people that they try to get revenge in sneaky ways, by humiliation, by

105

by making people feel bad, making them feel guilty, by putting the blame on them. You tried to do that just now when you told me you were playing poorly because you were afraid of me. Quentin, I'm telling you that better be the last time you blame your poor performance on me. Do you understand, boy?''

Quentin stared at me, refusing to say a word. His fists were clenched at his sides.

"Look, Q, you can be as pissed-off at me as you want to. It really makes very little difference. Think of it this way: if you were taking drugs, getting into trouble all the time, then you, and everybody else would sort of understand my getting fed up and booting your ass out of the house. Well, try and understand this: being afraid is *your drug*, pulling up short is *your* drug. If you keep doing it, you're going to be as much a loser as if you were shooting heroin into your blood. So as of now, boy, I am finished watching you doing it. I've seen you do it in sports, in your school work, with your friends, particularly your girl friends. You let other people take advantage of you, push you around and then you blame them for your troubles. Now, if you want to, you can keep doing that, but you are going to be living some place else when you do."

He stared at me very resentfully.

A certain tiredness flooded my body.

Then energy came back.

My voice went low and threatening. "We're going to play a little basketball now, Quentin. You know what you have to do."

He kept quiet, as though trying to decide whether to accept my challenge or just walk away.

I prayed he would accept it. "I'll give you a couple of minutes to figure out whether you want to be a person who takes risks and gives life a full effort, or whether you want to be a jerk."

It was hard to look in his eyes. Turning away, I walked over to Dulcie who was leaning against the garage door, looking grim. I was restless; I paced, thinking how many times I'd told him how to correctly make that basketball play. When he was bringing the ball down court toward the basket, he must keep moving until he found something worthwhile to do with the ball, and then he should do it. Keep moving, dribbling the ball, keeping it in play, and then quickly pass to a teammate, or pull up and take a shot without too much hesitation. For too long he had been wasting his opportunities.

Quentin was facing me, watching me, and then he turned and walked a few steps away. The seconds were ticking off. Finally, he decided, and said, "Let's get it on." There was a certain coldness in his voice that showed his anger and determination.

He knew I'd make it hard for him. If he tried to shoot, I would try to bat the ball back into his face; if he tried to pass to Dulcie I would try to intercept, making him look like a clumsy fool. We started playing. He began dribbling the ball toward me, coming on and on. I went into a defensive crouch, sliding and shuffling across the cement driveway, my arms outstretched to hinder his forward progress toward the basket. Everything was silent except for the bouncing of the ball on the pavement. He eyed me, circling to his left slowly. Dulcie behind me was waving her arms to get Quentin to throw her the ball. I drifted back toward her, then moved quickly closer toward Quentin so he would have a tough time deciding what to do. Then he began dribbling faster, now moving toward the right side of the court, but he was still too far from the basket to get off a good shot. Out of the corner of my eye, I saw Dulcie also moving toward the right. She cried, "Here, here!" Quentin took some steps backwards, putting him even farther from the basket and I drifted toward Dulcie to guard her closer. Quentin began coming straight toward the basket, and I moved toward him to stop him from shooting. While dribbling with his right hand he brought his left up as if to grab the ball with both hands for a pass to his sister. I leaped close to him as he slowed down, swiping my hand at the ball.

But he was only faking.

As soon as I committed myself to moving toward him, he began to dribble around me, so I was heading in one direction and he was going passed me in the opposite direction.

Time seemed to slow down, the world went into slow motion as I realized he fooled me. Instead of passing to Dulcie, or pulling up and taking a long shot, he was speeding around me, going in toward the basket to shoot a nice, easy little lay-up shot.

He was at my side now, and going away from me.

I hated it.

Hated being fooled.

I must be getting old, I thought, to let him do that to me.

I spun toward him and leaped, reaching for the ball, stretching myself out full length in the air, straining with my arm fully extended trying to knock the ball away from him. But it was too late, he was gone; I missed the ball by inches, and swiped his hip instead as he moved in and sank the shot easily while I crashed into the cement, grinding a strip of skin off my thigh.

Cement almost always feels cool when you lie on it.

I could hear the ball bouncing on the pavement.

I rolled over.

The late spring sun was setting.

Quentin stood at the edge of the driveway near the stone walk that leads to the front door. The ball was tucked under his arm. Our eyes met and we stared at each other.

"Fuck you," he said. He heaved the basketball down the street, then spun around and went inside.

Dulcie knelt down beside me. "You all right, Pa?"

"Dulcie, tell me something? Did you see that move Q put on me?"

She was staring at the blood oozing out of my thigh like red sweat.

"Does it hurt?"

"Did you see the way Quentin went around me? It was a very creative solution to his problem."

"Pa, do you know you have rocks in your leg?"

Watching her stare at the goop oozing out of my leg, I could tell Dulcie wanted to operate.

"Go get the basketball and I'll let you fix me up. Get the spray stuff out of the bathroom."

She ran after the ball. With my leg beginning to hurt, I climbed, crab-like, over to the lawn, and lay on my back, thinking about things.

Our guests drove up in an expensive new car.

Out of it, they got.

Marcie and Doyle Tarwater.

We introduced ourselves to each other, and Marcie said, "My God, what happened?"

I said. "Hello. It's okay."

Astoria opened the front door, and stood there smiling, calling "Hello," as the Tarwaters approached her with greetings.

Dulcie pushed passed Astoria in the doorway, her arms carrying pounds of medical supplies. Astoria and the others entered the house with Astoria calling over her shoulder, "Get dressed, Norris, and join us for drinks."

Dulcie washed the wound with a garden hose, patted it dry with gauze, and shook the spray can full of antiseptic.

In the open wound, the medicine burned so good the top of my head became damp with sweat.

"Do you know about Mahatma Gandhi, Dulcie?"

"Who's that?"

She had a large roll of medical tape and dozens of squares of sterile pads, and I knew that it was going to be difficult trying to talk her out of taping all of them to my leg.

"He was a brown fellow, an Indian who was married to a short wife."

"So...?" she said, poised over my leg, with a tweezer in her hand, looking for little rocks to pull out.

"Having fun?" I asked her.

"It's good practice," she said.

"I was really proud of Quentin."

"What about this Gandy guy?"

"Gandhi. He once had his appendix taken out, but he refused to take anything to kill the pain or put him to sleep."

"Really?"

"Yeah, he just laid down and let the doctors cut him open."

"Sounds like a brave guy."

"Yeah, but he was a jerk. He was nasty to his wife in public once, and he just about drove his kids nuts. One of them became an alcoholic. Gandhi was a rotten father."

Astoria is very good at giving dinner parties, a natural-born hostess. That night she was as beautiful as I'd ever seen her. She wore a long dress of shining white material with some red designs on it. "White," I recalled silently to myself, "is the Chinese color for death."

"You poor man. Your leg." Marcie Tarwater cooed. "What are you going to do about your leg?"

I closed the door and bumbled into the room. "I'm going to have an olive, a black olive. Did you know that the Chinese people believe the color black means good luck?"

"Does it really?"

"Yeah," I told her cheerfully, "they have a color for every part of life. For example, the color for death is...."

"Well, what is it?"

"Pea green." Turning to Doyle Tarwater, I stuck out my hand, "Well, it's about time we met." We shook.

"Hey, how's the leg, champ?" he asked pointing down at the yards of bandages and tape my little doctor had wrapped around the thigh. You could tell from his eyes and his manner that he thought I was sort of a jerk for getting hurt.

"Yes...well, let's have a little pain killer," I suggested, heading for the small table where Astoria had put the bottles of liquor we'd bought for this occasion.

Tarwater accepted a Bourbon on the rocks, and I watched him while he sipped it and stared over the rim of the glass at Astoria. Taller than I, he was a husky, successful-looking man with a thick moustache and a small bald spot on the back of his head. He wore an expensive leather jacket and his shoes were shined with great care. He seemed to be a man who had done well enough in the world to have his own successful business, and provide himself and his wife with a comfortable life. You could tell he was a man who liked to *get* things for himself. He eyed Astoria like he'd like to get his dick into her, but his lustful look was an easy going, off-hand sort of thing, like if somebody were to put a plate of barbecued ribs in front of him, well, he might just like to help himself to some, thank you.

As for Astoria, she wanted to get ahead in life. You could tell that just by watching the way she came in and held the appetizer tray in front of him. Sex was far away from her mind. What she wanted most was to be liked; she wanted to be valued, to be valued so much that she could rest easy knowing that her boss needed her, and would keep her forever on the payroll because he recognized what a smart and worthwhile a person she is. That was all that success meant to her. Getting ahead in life was really only a matter of getting safer and safer, making a little more money each year, having a few more people respect you each year, becoming more and more secure. To accomplish that, Astoria seemed to feel that besides working her tail off, she had to be friends with her employer—whoever that might be at the time—smiling too much, smiling too hard. She held out the tray of appetizers for Doyle Tarwater to pick on, as though she was a beautiful and grateful slave and he was the King of England.

"Would you care for a canape?" Astoria asked as cheerfully as if life was a merry-go-around and we all have an endless supply of tickets.

Doyle made some charming reply while she held the tray at tit-level for him to choose, and I wanted to be sick.

I looked at the little table where the liquor was. Jack Daniels, Black Label, Tennessee Whiskey. Bottled in Bond. Aged for Years. Aged for tens of years. Aged for thousands of years. Aged from back when dinosaurs roamed the earth.

Fuck it, I poured myself a great big glassful.

Astoria's mouth dropped open as she watched me. We'd stopped drinking a couple of years before; the habit of boozing had just dropped away from us.

"Honey, are you sure you want to do that?" she asked.

"Oh, I do, I do. How about you, Doyle, that enough for you?"

"Hey, I'm doing great, thanks."

"Marcie?"

"This is perfect," she said about her vodka and seven.

"And you, baby," I said, putting my arm around Storee's shoulders, "What do you want out of life?"

"Maybe some white wine..."

"A small request from such a beautiful woman. Right, Doyle?"

He said, "Hey, a woman like Astoria can have anything she wants."

I thought to myself, "You prick."

"Can you really drink that much?" Marcie chirped to me.

"And after I'm done, Marcie," I told her, "I'm going to run the four minute mile."

Boy, did that sound stupid.

They all looked like it sounded stupid to them, too. They looked at me like I was drunk out of my head already.

"It's the truth," I said earnestly, thinking that actually it *was* the truth, although it would have been hard to explain at the time exactly what sort of truth it was. There was an awkward silence, like what happens when someone says something so far off the wall that everyone else is embarrassed. It was definitely time for me to stop being the center of attention at this party.

"Norris could do anything he set his mind to," Astoria said supportively, and then added, "Did you wash the lettuce, honey."

"Yes," I told her.

Doyle and I walked, drinks in hand, into the backyard, saying little.

He broke the silence with, "I hear you're out in the job market."

I told him, yes, that's true, and suddenly I wondered about my chances of getting a job with him; suddenly I was thinking of him as an "employment opportunity." How desperate I must be, I thought, and shuddered at the idea of working in his plumbing supply house day after endless day.

Astoria slid open the kitchen window and called, "Where's the lettuce you washed, honey?"

"We ate it last night."

She shook her head, closed the window, and began ripping apart a head of lettuce, looking cheerful like we all had plenty of tickets for the loop-de-loop.

The late-spring sun was low on the horizon, and would soon disappear, but the air was still warm as we wandered about the yard with Doyle using a lot of words to tell me what the government had to do to make America healthy again.

Called to dinner, as we gathered around the table, Astoria whispered, "Norrie, get changed, honey?"

"Sure," I said, and pulled off my great black T-shirt, and tossed it under my chair and sat down.

"Norris," Storee cried half-jokingly, "We have guests. Oh, come on, now."

"You're right," I said and got up. "Forgive my party manners; guests should be seated first, right, Doyle?"

"Hey, I suppose so."

I pulled out a chair for him like he was the Queen of England. But instead of sitting, he moved over to pull out Astoria's chair for her. I asked, "Marcie, my turtledove, is it all right with you if I eat dressed this way?" Marcie looked at me with a quick turn of her head. It reminded me of something.

What was it?

Then it came to me.

A bird! I realized that Marcie, instead of being a real person was actually some sort of bird.

"With a body like that you can eat anyway you want," she chirped.

At least she was a bird with good taste. All her movements were short and sharp. Quick. Her hair was cut short, like a fur-feather cap. With her wide eyes, she looked at me and smiled as she sat.

Astoria, wanting to avoid a bad scene, stopped talking and also sat. We all began to eat quietly like this was the White House and we were all dressed in tuxedos. I wondered if their heads were starting to spin, too.

"That Otto Crumbly is really something," Astoria said, opening the conversation. You could tell from the sound of her voice that being "really something" was an awful thing to be.

"What'd he do this time?" Doyle asked with interest.

"Who's Otto Crumbly?" Marcie chirped, but they ignored her, and since Crumbly was a stranger to me, too, it was beyond my power to tell her.

"He gave me a rose at lunch today. A *rose*," Astoria said, "I went to lunch with him today and he brought me a single long-stemmed rose. Can you believe it?"

"What so bad about that?" Marcie cooed. She had small tits like a bird would have if a bird had tits. "Norris, did you really

114

make this wonderful veal scallopini?'' Tweet.

Looking down through the elegant glass-topped table that Astoria had bought for us once when we had money, I could see Marcie's legs, long and thin like a bird's should be, crossed at the ankles.

Still looking down, I nodded, "Yes, like it?" To tell the truth, the "veal" was really chicken thighs cut up, because who the hell could afford to buy real veal at eight dollars a pound? I was angry with myself because I sort of cared whether she liked the food.

"It's delicious," she said. Her nose was very straight. Watching her, I remembered my theory that women who cut their hair very short, like hers, are people who feel deep down that something important is missing from their lives: I looked at Doyle.

"Hey, it's really good," he said staring me right in the face, pretending he was impressed. "Me, I have a tough time boiling water."

"Honey, you just keep making all that money," Marcie twittered, "and I'll boil the water for you."

"Hey, that's all I'm good for," he complained to me. "Making money. I admire you, Norris, for developing all these household skills. Astoria tells me you're a great father to the kids."

I felt like kicking him in the balls.

Instead, I took a long slug of Jack Daniels wonder-working elixer of death.

"So tell us, Astoria, what Otto had to say," Tarwater asked.

"Doyle, what he said was all right. He thinks that he'll win the bids on two big projects, and he promised to order all his plumbing supplies from us. But I kept looking at that awful rose. In the middle of the table, just lying there, with green wax paper around it."

"Really seems to bother you," Marcie said.

Astoria made a gloomy gesture with her hands, opening them in front of her as if to say, "Could anybody please understand how I feel about this?"

"Hey, that's good news for us about the projects," Tarwater said.

"Oh, yes," Astoria said, picking up his idea that her feelings were a lot less important than the money that would be coming in from Crumbly. "Of course, that's the important part; it was a very successful lunch," she said, sounding as though she hoped that someone would tell her what a wonderful person she was to overcome the insult of receiving a single red rose and still have had a successful lunch. She looked at me with a little look of hope in her eyes, and she said, "Do you know what I mean, Norrie?"

"Jesus," I said.

That answer failed to make her happy, and Marcie showed some good heart when she stepped in and said, "Astoria, I know what you mean. One perfect rose, it's sooooooo...romantic. Big deal. I'm waiting for someone to come up with one perfect Cadillac."

"Exactly," Astoria said, "it's such a cheap little thing to do. I hardly know him. We've talked only a few times. You give a rose to someone you love. Someone who means something special to you."

"Doyle," Marcie said, "now you know how we women feel; forget the rose, send the car."

I was beginning to like Marcie, and felt crummy that I had thought she was a feather brain. It's wonderful when people are nice to Astoria.

"Hey, Astoria," Doyle said, "that's what we have to put up with in this business because, although we sell hardware, this is basically a people business. People do the buying, right?"

"Yes, I know," Astoria said too eagerly. She seemed strangely tense. Her jaw was tight, as though she needed to say more and was forcing herself to keep quiet. She stared at me with a pleading look in her eyes, asking for me to understand, pleading with me to agree with her.

I shrugged.

"Oh, it's all right, Astoria," Marcie said, "Men are always attracted to someone who looks like you. You must get a lot of that."

"It's such poor manners, so lacking in politeness," Astoria said as though something important had been stolen from her. She longed for respect, she wanted to be treated gently.

She leaned toward me, her hands on the table on each side of her plate, her eyes fixed on mine. They had a sort of lonely, despairing look in them. "Do you know what I mean? It's just bad manners," she said, almost begging for my agreement.

"So what," I said.

She closed her eyes briefly, then turned toward Doyle and offered him more salad.

I thought of telling her the world is full of bad manners, hers included. It's bad manners to bitch about other people's bad manners. So what if poor Otto Crumbly bought her a rose. She is beautiful. She is the stuff that dreams are made of. Otto Crumbly is to be congratulated for having the guts to bring a present to someone so beautiful as her. Many men would be too timid. So what if he was too dumb to know she'd hate it. He was only asking to be loved a little bit. So what if he was dumb—needing love makes us dumb, makes us do dumb things.

Reaching down, I smoothed some of the tape that had come loose from my leg.

God, I was tired. Collapse was just around the corner. Maybe some more booze would help.

Talking.
Speaking.
Chatting.
They kept on chatting.

Chatting chatting chatting.

Like there was all the time in the world.

So polite. So boringly polite.

Could anyone possibly be interested in what they are talking about?

What the hell are they talking about anyway?

"Marcie."

"Norris?"

"Let's..."

"Let's what...?"

"Go to France."

"France?"

"I mean dance. Let's dance."

They looked at me like I was mad.

"You too, Doyle. Doyle, can you dance?"

"Forget it," Doyle said waving his arm.

Pulling Marcie up by one of her wings, we flew to the stereo, and soon the Rolling Stones were shouting about how tough life is. We danced, the two of us, whirling, bouncing abandonly around the living room.

"All right!" Marcie cried, clapping her hands in rhythm, flicking her head from side to side so that her short hair bounced like she was from Africa. "All right."

We danced into the hall, and into the kitchen, through the dining room, occassionally making sex-eyes at each other. Back into the hall we danced; there I grabbed at her and she came into my arms laughing. I kissed her and she pressed herself against me. Pulling back, she said she suspected me of drinking.

"And you," I babbled at her, "are a sweet bundle of fun. You are chocolate chip ice cream."

Holding my gaze with hers, she scraped her long red fingernail down the center of my chest. "Chocolate chip?" she said, and she flicked her tongue across her upper lip.

"A double scoop."

From the other room, Doyle called, "Hey."

"We've been gone too long," she whispered.

We flapped our wings and danced back into the kitchen, making a pit-stop at the refrigerator for a six-pack of Coors. We danced back into the dining room where I told Doyle, "Doyle, you look basically like a beer guy to me." I cracked us a couple of cans and told him, "I feel like ripping, you feel like ripping, too? How about it?" I shoved a can toward him in a most challenging manner.

He stared at me leaning shirtless toward him, the beers between us like weapons.

"I want to tell you something, Norris." He said the word *Norris* like *Norris* was some sort of disease. It was easy to tell he was annoyed, and I wondered if I had some of his wife's lipstick smeared across my mouth.

"What's that, Doyle?" I asked aggressively.

"Plumbers can out-drink anybody."

"So who's a plumber, Doyle?"

"I am."

"Is he a plumber?" I asked Marcie. "Astoria, have you been laying pipe?"

Marcie said that Doyle used to be a plumber before he got into the plumbing-supply business and made a lot of money. I was pleased to notice that Marcie seemed to have eaten off all her lipstick, so probably there was little danger of evidence being smeared around my face.

Astoria said, "Really, Doyle?" How interesting? She said it in a happy singing voice, as if being a plumber was a strange and wonderful thing, a sort of a gift-job from God.

"You're damn right," Doyle said.

"Well, hell, Doyle, then let's suck up these brews."

We grabbed our beers about the same time and poured them down our throats while keeping an eye on each other. The cans hit back on the table about the same time, and everything was quiet. Doyle looked me straight into my eyes, then taking his can long-ways in his meaty hand, he crumpled it into a ball like it was tissue paper, and I thought to myself, "Jesus, I wish I could do that."

He belched loud enough to put a crack in the wall.

"Doyle!" Marcie said.

I cracked him another can, saying, "I'm beginning to like you, Doyle."

"And I'm beginning to think you're the strangest person I've met all year," he shot back at me. I told him to fuck the flattery and let's go in the backyard and kill the rest of the six-pack while the women did whatever women did while men killed six packs.

"Let them go," Marcie said, "I want to get better acquainted, Astoria. Doyle's told me how valuable you are around the office."

As Doyle and I were leaving the room, a strange thing happened. Astoria caught my eye, and we stared at each other, and something occurred that maybe only happens when you have lived closely with someone for years: the whole world stopped and Astoria and I had a conversation that took place in total silence. In my head I heard her say, "Are you really going to do this?" And without words, I answered her, "Yeah, yeah, I am, baby."

Doyle and I sprawled on lawn chairs in the backyard. Sucking on brews, we talked about this and that and hardly anything in particular, until gradually I realized through the fog in my brain that Doyle was now talking very sincerely about diseases, for God's sake. He told me that he thought most diseases could be cured by electricity. He talked very seriously about that; he was sharing with me a dream of his, a confidence that was very close to his heart. He told me that he was experimenting in his garage, trying to find a cure for diabetes through the use of electricity and some sort of salt bath. It sounded crazy to me, and I almost told him so, but suddenly a wave of exhaustion swept over me again, and I thought what-the-hell maybe he's right. You could tell that he was serious, that he dreamed of medical glory.

"PLUMBER SAVES HUMANITY"

A headline for all time.

He went on talking steadily, intensely, as though he needed to talk to someone, as though he was lonely. "Listen to me, Norris," he said. "You're smart, you could understand this."

Saving humanity, saving humanity....

My mind drifted away.

Once, years before, Storee and I had been on a late evening walk. The street lamps shone on empty streets, the homes were mostly dark, the people sleeping. We had walked a long way talking in a mellow mood. We came upon a dog, a guard dog, a white German shepherd, that saw us as it rounded the corner of a house and growled menacingly. Almost immediately it bared its fangs, and laid its ears back at us. It came at us running low to the ground the way shepherds do when they're attacking. It was understood by the dog and by me that he was going to leap at us and put his teeth into human flesh and rip.

My reaction was instinctive. Without thought, I put my hand on Storee's stomach and pushed her backward and stepped in front of her, standing spread-legged, bending forward a little, ready to take the animal's charge. It was fifteen feet away, getting ready to spring, and I roared. It was a war cry. There was very little fear, rage or hatred in it. My roar was the sound of my total commitment to the fight that was coming, kill or be killed.

The dog stopped so suddenly it was comical. Tucking his tail over his asshole, he turned and looked at me sideways, and you could almost hear him say, "Jesus, if that's the way you feel about it..."

As the dog trotted off into the darkness, Storee and I retreated in the opposite direction, gradually regaining our composure. I waited for her to thank me or say something about my behavior. All she said was, "That was the loudest sound I ever heard a human being make."

Doyle and I went back into the house. Astoria and Marcie were sitting at the dining room table looking at our wedding album.

Storee was slowly flipping the pages, her eyes had a funny look: glazed and staring. Her mouth was going a mile a minute. There was a sort of desperateness in her. "That's my dad," she said. "He was so happy that day. It was a wonderful day, Marcie. Marcie, you should have seen it. The flowers were just lovely. See this veil, I made that, and Norris said that he knew he'd done the right thing to marry me when he saw the veil because I looked so lovely in it." (The photo was of us kissing outside the church.) "It was such a long kiss, indecent." Storee said. "We sort of got lost in each other. It was embarrassing afterward. It really was. But we sort of got lost in each other."

Astoria went on and on, she was talking more to herself than Marcie. Marcie perhaps felt that; she looked up and greeted us as we entered the living room, but Astoria gave only a brief nod and continued talking with her voice rapid and high.

Marcie told me, "Doyle and I got married in one of those Las Vegas marriage mills." She sounded like she wished she'd had a big wedding like Astoria and I, but my wife barely noticed that Marcie had said anything at all. She just talked on and on like she had to make us understand what had happened that day we married.

How can she do that, I wondered? How can she fail to see how ill-at-east Marcie is? Why is she rubbing our nice wedding in Marcie's face? Why is she so blind? So fucking blind?

"We had such nice food. We danced, it was a wonderful

party. Norris looked so handsome, he's always been such a good-looking man. That day was so special, I wish you could have seen it the way everybody looked.'' Smiling almost like a little girl, she said, ''Norrie and I went back to our apartment for a little while, even before we left on our honeymoon.''

Our small apartment with a desk in the living room.
I'd tried to run a business from that desk.
Astoria used to pile things on it.
Shoes.
Magazines.
Coats.
I screamed.
I swept the fucking stuff off the desk.
''But, Norris, it's in the living room. I just naturally put things there.''

The dinner party ground to a halt.
We ended up politely nodding at each other.
They thanked us for asking them over.
We thanked them for coming. Astoria acted like she had a lot of energy left.
''Really wonderful of you to come. So nice.''
A ferris wheel. We have an endless supply of tickets. We can ride around and around this way forever, with music in our ears.
In the kitchen she and I were cleaning up.
She was bringing dishes from the table.
I was at the sink, still in cut-offs.
But with my black tee-shirt on now.
She came up behind me.
I thought she was going to hug me from behind.
The thought gave me a warm feeling.
What she did was put an apron around me. From behind, she slipped the neck loop over my head and tied the strings around

my waist, and went away, saying something pleasant and friendly as she left.

There was a window above the sink, and it was dark.

I trembled.

The tears started coming.

Holding onto the rim of the sink, I began to cry.

In those days we often took a walk before going to bed, getting fresh air into our lungs and talking over the day together. Later we would sleep curled against each other like puppies. On the night of the dinner party, as we began our evening walk, she became intensely happy. Even I got caught up in her giddiness. It was crazy; we skipped down the street, though it was nearly midnight. Hand in hand we went, her blond hair bouncing in the night light as we skipped along.

"It was a good dinner party. I think they liked it; do you think so, Norrie?"

"Yeah, Storee, I think they did like it."

Suddenly she cried out, "I'm so happy, I'm so happy." She let go of my hand, and threw her arm around my neck, hugging me as we skipped higher and harder. She cried out, "I'm so happy. My life is so full."

I was surprised to hear she felt that way.

She still had her arm around my neck, and smiled at me quickly, and looked ahead, skipping with me gaily along.

I felt suddenly annoyed, angry. I realized that she was talking as though she was alone. She was sort of talking to herself. I was waiting for her to say, "Thank you. Thank you, Norris." But now she was only silent.

We stopped skipping along; we began to walk normally.

I was waiting for her to say she loved me. I was waiting for her to admit that I was a part of her happiness.

Living with her was like living alone.

She could have thrown her arm around anyone's neck and said what she'd said.

She had very little idea of where her happiness came from.

My gifts to her: cooking the dinner for her almost every night, organizing the kid's into cleaning brigades because she was too tired on Saturdays from pounding so hard all week at her job, going with her each and every time to the grocery store, helping her figure out how to deal with problems at her work—in every job she had, there was always some crisis that she got into with some co-worker, and it was with my intense help that we would figure out a way to deal with these personality problems, these office politics battles.

Living with her was lonely.

She was ignoring me, ignoring all I had tried to give her.

I wanted her to get closer to me.

I stopped walking; she took another step, then turned to face me.

Stepping up to her, I took her shoulders in my hands, held her an arm's length away and stared into her eyes.

She lowered her eyes, refused to look at me.

It felt lonely. She looked up at me.

I spit in her face.

Hobos wander.
Thinkers ponder.
Cleaners launder.
But I am fonder
Of sitting still.

The Mature *Yes*

Our lives begin with childhood, so perhaps I should say a few words about how *Yes* can help us pass from youthfulness into a more comfortable and effective adulthood.

When we are very young, just little newborn babies, we feel we are as powerful as God. We feel we are in command of everything because whenever we cry, huge human beings take notice of us and come to serve our needs. They change our diapers, offer food, and cuddle us to soothe our discomfort. This naturally gives us—as babies—a feeling that we are mighty. Our cry is law.

But then around two years of age we realize something has gone wrong with the world. Instead of us being the center of the universe, we begin to find out we are off to the side somewhere. We learn we are just another being in a huge crowd of other beings most of whom, in the recent past, used to serve us like slaves.

This is shocking news. Learning we are less powerful than we'd thought is an ugly blow. We begin to fight. We begin to judge things, and strive to get the best things in life for ourselves. Most of us continue this fight until we die. What we fail to realize is that *everything* is good for us. Everything is a gift to us. We should accept everything that happens to us because the purpose of everything that happens is to push us back to where we belong. All the joy, worry, pleasure and pain we experience is meant to force us into submission until at last we accept our ultimate destiny. All the terror, humiliation, and abuse...all the sads, bads, and glads are pushing us in the same direction. We are being pounded, hounded, pushed and driven all our lives, and then when we have been mugged, bugged, drugged and fugged enough, we finally will find peace and bliss as we arrive at the navel of existence, and there at last we finally merge into the magnificent Cosmic Yes.

Example

A handsome man stands before a dresser mirror, gazing at himself and thinking that finally after all these years he's beginning to look a little bit older.

That's all right with him.

His hair which used to be blonde and long is now cut short and dyed very dark. His face is deeply tanned and dried from the wind that sweeps across the vast Wyoming plains. His eyes are deep blue and clear. Above the left one, high on his forehead is a small scar. His nose is straight, his mouth ordinary, his chin is set firm and determined.

Through the open window near the mirror drift the sounds of sheep: baa-ing and bleating aimlessly.

The man looks away from the mirror, and gazes down at a photograph on the dresser in front of him. It is a photo taken with a convenient instant camera. It shows a group of ten people on a bright morning, standing on a beach with their backs to the water. They are looking East; the rising sun is reflected in their faces. At the back of the group stands a monstrous man, immensely tall and heavily muscled. Among the others there are two older women, look-a-likes, sisters. In the middle is a blond-haired man of middle height wearing a toga-like gown. On the left side of his forehead is taped a small white bandage. At his left is a beautiful golden-haired woman, nearly the man's height. He has taken her right hand in his left and their two arms are raised high—like prize fighters—as though someone has won a great victory. At the man's feet a small black puppy dog sits comfortably on the sand gazing thoughtfully at the camera.

Three years?

So long ago.

And still each moment of that time is clearly printed in his memory.

Can it be me? There? So happy looking? On *that* day?

Yes, it is me. But I've changed so much I'm like a stranger to myself, and in the mirror I study myself the way one might watch an interesting foreigner.

The smell of sheep drifts through the open window. A bell clangs. The dark-haired man drops the photo on the dresser, nods to himself in the mirror, and goes to the open doorway of the shack. From somewhere nearby, a voice calls out, "Come on, you farts, let's cut the balls off these little suckers."

The lambs, out of view somewhere, bleat as if they get the message.

Through the doorway, the man gazes across the Wyoming countryside flat, golden, barren, unending.

Only three years ago?

So many friends and lovers gone?

Yes.

It's all right.

He is mature now. Accepting.

"I love you," he says to his distant loves, and goes out the door.

"Come on," the voice calls out again, "before it gets dark."

Yes is Profitable

Many people lead rich, full lives.

However, people are seldom truly satisfied with what they possess. Some of us continually want *more*. We seek more money, more success, more fun, more leisure, and—most of all—more love. Often, we hope other people will satisfy our desires.

Almost always this leads to disappointment. We often feel neglected, rejected, out of luck—like a pile of dirty clothes in the hamper of life.

It is a waste of time trying to find someone who will give to us as much as we think they should. Instead here's what we should do. We should turn the idea around completely, and give to others—love others—as completely as we would like them to respond to us. We should give to them *totally*. And without expecting anything back.

When you give a great big *Yes* to others, you also give *Yes* to yourself. And then you will be fulfilled.

Fulfillment will come through your own giving.

You will stop waiting for other people to give anything to you. But they probably will.

Example:

They were wonderful days—those first days in which Bruno and I founded the Holy Church of the Slippery Word.

I was penniless and homeless, but that hardly mattered. The important thing was that I was serious and dedicated. More dedicated than I had ever been in my life. It was as though some enormous Power was leading me in some direction, toward some goal that my poor eyes were too dim to see, that my poor mind was too weak to understand.

Almost immediately, it seemed, it became harder for me to smile as I became filled with inner peace and happiness. I accepted my new responsibilities as I gazed at the tanned faces that looked passively, like gentle sheep, at me for guidance and instruction.

I say "tanned" faces, because our first services were held at the beach. I would sit, straddling the front of a yellow catamaran. The bow of the boat stuck out under my toga like a huge fiberglass penis and I would share with them the Message of Total Acceptance.

The services would begin with Bruno beating on a huge congo drum, and out of curiosity a crowd would gather. Southern California was the perfect hunting ground for a minister seeking lost souls. So many of those people live in a physically-comfortable, spiritual desert. They dwelt in attractive condos and apartments, ate plenty of many kinds of good food, and they slept well with partner after sexual partner.

Yet they lacked something in their lives.

They lacked a sense of soul-direction.

They lacked a spiritual home in which they could have a deep and resting faith.

Quite naturally, I assumed my leadership position and showed them the Way.

Of course, some people laughed at me and Bruno—though they carefully avoided laughing in Big Bruno's face.

But the laughter and lack of respect of some of them was of little importance, for it happened that others—just a few at first,

131

but later quite a lot of them—began to understand the thrust of *Yes* and began showing up regularly at our noon-time meetings.

Our church was modern. It addressed itself to the concerns of modern people.

One of the greatest of the concerns of these healthy men and women was their bodies, and so our Holy Service began with a ritual aimed at bringing mind and body into harmony.

We did exercises.

Jumping jacks.

Sit ups.

That sort of thing.

Yes, two, three, four.

Yes, two, three, four.

Yes, two, three, four.

I rarely exercised with them, but instead merely sat on the bow of the boat with my fiberglass penis leading the way while the gentle sun shone lovingly on their attractive, bathing-suited bodies glistening with fragrant suntan oils.

Yes, two, three, four.

Yes, two, three, four.

I explained to them that once they, like myself, had perfected their devotion to *Yes*, exercising would cease to be important. Being in Perfect Harmony with *Yes* brings perfect beauty and health without strain or exertion, I told them.

And they believed.

Respect shone in their eyes.

I would invite them to chant with me as they exercised.

Yes, two, three, four.

Yes, two, three, four.

And then I would suggest that they stop exercising and ask them to sit cross-legged on the sand with eyes closed, bodies relaxed, and continue to chant quietly with me.

Yes, two, three, four.

Yes, two, three, four.

After ten minutes of their soft chanting, I would bid them be still. "Listen, now, to your bodies, oh you Tanned Worshipers of Total Tolerance. Be still and let the energy of Love and Peace fill your souls and ease your minds. Feel the gentle calmness heavy in your being, feel it resting inside you and filling you with pure relaxation."

We would sit quietly for ten minutes more.

Then I would awaken them with the soft spoken, mystical words, "We have done well and truly, participating together in this physical communion. We have called into ourselves the strength and power of the Holy Air of Acceptable Meditation. As our reward—a reward that we are giving to ourselves—we shall feel better tomorrow than we do today; and we shall feel still better the next day, and also the next, and so it shall be forever onward, so long as we perform the *Yes*full Meditation."

And then it would be time for the Communion Feast. Money offerings were taken and other preparations made, and soon some of the men and bikini-clad Holy Helpers would approach us across the sand and place before me on the beach blanket the Communion offerings. I would kneel before these gifts and pray, "As we consume these offerings of the Holy Earth, so we know that we too shall live the full time given to us, and then return into the Earth from which we were born." And then I would gaze up and ask, "Okay, who said, 'Hold the onions', and who wants the double cheeseburger...?"

They would munch contentedly in the slow Southern California sunshine, sipping the Holy Tab, Pepsi and Sprite.

But I myself rarely ate with them, as the fast-food stands around there neglected to offer lambburgers.

And then they brought me their problems:

"My twin sister wants to get into porno flicks."

"*Yes*, Mandy, tell me more."

"She wants me to join her. She says we could make a bundle of money."

133

"And so you could, Mandy, do you wish to join her?"

"I'd rather die first."

"Then do so."

"I was only joking."

"That's all right. Go on," I said calmly, peacefully, holding flowers in my lap.

"She wants my help! Can you believe it?"

"*Yes*, I can. And you should help her. You should understand that what you see as a problem is *her* problem. And so participate only as much as you wish to. She must find her own way."

"But I worry about her."

"Perhaps that is what she wants. If she wishes to be in porno films, then perhaps you should buy her a make-up kit so that her cheeks will look attractive under the harsh lights."

"Are you kidding?"

"I'm serious."

Mandy said, "I mean, I'm thinking screwing is great but..."

"We must discuss that later...for now remember that supporting your sister in whatever life she chooses for herself will help to open the Correct Path to her."

I mention this early exchange in my ministry because it worked so well.

I got laid that night.

Mandy did buy her twin sister (Mindy) the make-up kit.

Mindy started fooling with the make-up kit, and was soon creating exotic cosmetic effects, and during the next week she got a job modeling in nearby San Diego, thus putting off porno stardom.

Mindy got Mandy a job, too; and within a week they left for Europe for six months of modeling designer clothes —both of them fucking me blind the night before they departed, and leaving me the keys to their beachfront condo.

Truly, the good works bring their own reward.

It was a wonderful summer. A fine June became a fine July. My hair bleached out blonder than it had ever been, and grew in soft curls that I could see women looking at and wanting to run their hands through. My body had the best suntan of its life, and there was a calmness and peace in my soul that allowed me to move with gracefulness and power, like an athlete in his prime.

Bruno proved to be a great companion, and wrote an excellent poem to our friendship.

(to be spoken in a bold and happy voice)

He's my friend in a robe of white
Who brightens up the darkest night.
A man who's life is full of good.
A sort of holy Robin Hood.

He's my friend, but who am I?
A great big guy, but sort of shy.
But still I'd fight till my last breath
To save my holy friend from death.

If harm should ever threaten him
I'd gladly give my life or limb
To see that he is safe and sound
Because he's great to be around.

I'm his friend and he is mine.
That *puzzles* me, although it's fine.
Oh, what does he see in me?
We're friends!!! What can the reason be?

He says I'm honest, true and strong.
He says he's glad I came along.
He says that I am sensitive.
And that I've got a lot to give.
He says I'm brave, and that I'm happy

Even though I think life's crappy.
I may have ears like an elephant's,
But he likes my intelligence.

So what more is there to say?
I owe him more than I can pay.
The day we met was my best day.

He's a prince. He is royal.
And me? I'm forever loyal.

And fortune smiled on me by bringing other friends, too.

There was Joe Wagonewti, a beer-bellied salesman whom I met during a volleyball tournament.

And Alice Angsterlobe who played on the clarinet for me one night.

And one of the nicest of the newcomers was Chester Grooch & The Orchestra.

We had just finished the communion service one noontime when someone in our small flock of Holy Yessers pointed out an oddly shaped creature approaching us from across the beach. Even at a distance of forty yards he attracted my interest immediately. He and I were wearing the same sort of clothing. Draped over him appeared to be a green sheet with a hole cut for his head. (It turned out to be a thin blanket.) Strangely, his toga garment seemed to conceal some sort of hardware. The sheet stuck out at odd angles and he walked clumsily, so that I soon realized that he must be a severely handicapped person wearing body braces. As he approached my heart went out to him; he had so much difficulty walking, and moved in a stumbling pace. And then I saw that fate had treated him more cruelly than I originally suspected, for there was a large lump between his shoulders; he was a humpback. His thin face was pasty white, as though he'd been in-doors for years. His legs and arms showing outside his toga garment were also painfully thin, and ghostly white, as though he'd been neglecting to feed himself. But as he came near, you could see that in his eyes shone a brilliant inner light such as one sees in the eyes of fanatics, madmen, and geniuses at work. His braces evidently fit badly and made dull clunking sounds as he came up to us. He stuck out his hand to me, and smiling a boyish grin, he said, "Hi, I'm Chester Grooch."

One had to like him immediately, he was so fearless and friendly.

"Hello, I'm Wing. Welcome to our group."

He told me he had heard of our new church, which someone had described to him as "weird." I told him that was right, that we were into a new type of modern devotion. The news pleased him, if one could judge by the increased smile on his face. He said that was great and that he was glad he'd left his basement to check us out. Without further talk, he started to remove his outer clothing, raising the green toga-garment over his head and spreading it on the sand while we Yessers stared at him, astonished. Beneath his toga he wore a hundred pounds of electronic equipment: two piano-like keyboard instruments, a large tan box with tiny dials and buttons, a small portable Apple computer, and the "hump" on his back which turned out to be a portable battery pack. Strapped to his hips were two small (but, as it turned out, quite powerful) stereo speakers.

As he set up The Orchestra, he introduced the pieces to us as though they were people. Working with great efficiency, Chester said, "This is Roland JX-8P. Roland is analogue. Casiotones here is digital." While speaking, he quickly and surely connected his boxes with wires, arranging the equipment in a semi-circle around him. Looking over his gray-white shoulder, I wondered how long it would take him to turn lobster pink in the sun, and what would the music sound like. He flipped open the computer to reveal a monitor screen, on which appeared "Track 1, Track 2". Chester explained to us Yessers in a high voice that he found commercial programming too limiting and had developed a sixteen track capability for himself. Somehow while he was still connecting wires a drum section started sounding, as if by magic, through the speakers. Snare drums, Indian tom-toms, a kettle drum, a deep bass. Then there was the sound of rhythmic clapping of many hands.

"Chester, who's doing that?"

"909." Chester said.

"Oh."

"I like to work to a beat; it's the child in me, I suppose."

We sat around him like an audience around a magician. When all the equipment was wired together he flexed his fingers, then played the keys on one of his piano-like key boards and out came the sound of windchimes. He stopped playing the keyboard, but the windchimes continued. He resumed playing the keyboard, but this time, we heard bubbles... The bubbles floated up through the continuing windchimes. From somewhere, a flute played a riff, then a guitar played the same riff.

Most of the drums had faded away, leaving only a ticking drum rhythmn like the drummer was tapping on glass. A long eerie sound like a whale laughing at a fish story curved out of the speakers. Other whales, a whole pod with deep voices, joined in the merriment. A saxaphone mimicked them. All of this came from the two keyboards played by Chester Grooch's slim, white fingers.

"Let's get this man an umbrella," I said, realizing that genius like this must be protected. I was about to go search for one myself for him when he began to explain himself to me. As he did so he stopped playing the keyboards. But the music continued. The whales, the windchimes, the bubbles, the guitars, flutes, the drums, all of weaving in and out of each other in perfect harmony.

"You, as I understand it," Chester said, "have invented a synthetic religion."

That was the first time I'd heard anyone describe us that way. It seemed like a nice description. "Yes, Chester, that's right."

"Well, I make synthetic music. It is *my* religion."

"Ahhhh."

"And I was wondering if we might join forces. Perhaps we are both on the cutting edge of the future, you with your new philosophy and ethics and I in my musical composition, and recording, and performance. You see, I do all three at once. Does this idea have any appeal to you, Reverend Wing?"

"Do I look like a fool, Mr. Grooch? Of course, it appeals to me." But to be truthful there was some doubt in my mind.

And Chester Grooch sensed it.

"I sense you have some doubts," he said candidly.

"To be truthful, yes, I do. You see, most of our congregation is into rock."

Chester looked pained. He looked insulted.

"What do you think I am, a creep?" he demanded to know.

"Chester, we're all creeps sometimes."

"Maybe so, but I happen to love rock. Say, how do you feel about Rod Stewart?"

"One of my favorites."

Blessed saints in heaven! Almost immediately Rod Stewart began singing *Infatuation* through Chester's speakers. His hit record. But it was different somehow. The man was singing alone. All the background instruments were missing, and it was just Rod singing solo.

What's more, he sounded a little strange, like maybe he'd

been electrocuted so that now his haircut *really* suited him.

But it was Rod, all right. Sort of.

"How do you do that?"

"I build the voice synthetically with the digital. Wave shapes," he said as though we should all know what he was talking about.

"Is that right?"

"You like W.C. Fields?"

"One of my favorites."

W.C. Fields started singing *Infatuation* with Rod Stewart.

We listened in awe.

"Chester," I said to our new friend, "The church needs a choir director."

"I'm aware of that, Reverend Wing."

"Chester, do you think you'd be willing to be our choir director? The choir director of the Holy Church of the Slippery Word?"

But Chester had become lost in his music. Guitars and drums had begun backing up Rod and W.C. Fields. The two voices ceased singing, then started the song again from the beginning, and this time whales were singing in the background. Then church bells began to bong in the bass like it was Easter.

Chester turned to me and smiled. "Church bells," he said. "Just a little joke. I accept your offer."

"Let's get this man a Holy Hamburger and some fries."

Yes, life was good. I had friendship, sex, comfort, all that sort of thing. And yet, there was something lacking in my life. I was content, but I missed, in my weaker moments, my beautiful wife Astoria. Quentin and Dulcinea, too. But mostly Astoria.

My business kept me busy, though. It was nice to have a job again. I continued going to the same beach day after day. Soon, guess who showed up? My first two Laguna friends, the police-person with the thin, little moustache, and his pony-tailed partner, the lovely Kimberly Katz. They stood there at Sunday service in their uniforms—with their black shoes in the hot sand—casting looks of doom on our religious assembly. After the service Kim approached me, arms loose at her sides, to say, "I remember you."

"I'm flattered."

"We'll meet again, buddy."

"Be gentle, Kim."

We began holding evening services in the condo, and I gave sermons off the top of my head. I found that it was a waste of time trying to prepare them beforehand. It was best just to say whatever popped into my mind. The words always came when I needed them. I'd say something positive, and the sermon would just pour out of me. Gradually, in their enthusiasum, my audience fell into the habit of calling out affirmative shouts during these talks, much as Revivalist or Negro congregations will cry "Hallelujah" and "Amen, Brother."

"Aaaalllll Riight!" the Yessers would say.

I remember that one time, out of the blue, the sentence, "God is our Father," popped out of my mouth.

"Ever so true, Wing, ever so true," said one of my agreeable flock.

This happened on the beach, in the shade of a lifeguard tower. I continued: "We are His children. Mankind is. God's children," I said. "It's God's business to run the Universe, Holy Yessers. That's what He does for a living. It's an O.K. job, too. The work is steady, and He's His own Boss."

Some of the Yessers applauded and laughed, but Alice Angsterlobe squirmed on her beach towel, ill-at-ease. Darleen Hanratty took a ladylike sip of sweet, white wine.

"I sometimes wonder about God, Holy Yessers; yes, I do. What kind of a Father is he?"

"The Best!" someone said.

141

"Right on," I agreed. "He's a Father to be proud of. But, on the other hand, in many ways He's just your typical, ordinary Dad. Look how ticked off He got when His first two kids, Uncle Adam and Auntie Eve, got into His private orchard and took a bite of a fruit of the Tree Of Knowledge. You'd think He'd know that kids are always getting into stuff because they're curious and like to explore. But, what-the-fuck? Dad just went crazy and booted them out of the house—just because they messed with the Tree of Knowledge. Say, why did God resent them getting knowledge, how come he wanted them to stay ignorant, anyway? Why, Yessers, why?"

"Ignorance is bliss," yelled some clever Yesser.

"I agree with you completely! But then *everything* is bliss, right?"

"Right," they sang out in chorus like the Mormon Tabernacle Choir.

Except for Alice who made a face.

"Well, what else do we know about God, our famous absentee Father?"

"He's old," somebody said.

"Exactly right, Yessers. He is. But remember this: to a kid, the parents always seem old. Old and powerful. But, in fact, God may be a lot younger than we think. Who knows? But I want to talk to you about something else...something that's just occurring to me now...something that's just coming in over the wires, as it were...A long time ago, our Dad took Uncle Moses aside and gave him Ten Commandments. The first three of these rules said that He was our One and only Father and that we better treat Him right—with a lot of respect—or He'd fuck us."

At this point, Alice Angsterlobe offered the information that I was making her very nervous with this sort of talk; she got up and moved her beach towel away "in case God sent down a lightning bolt."

"Well, Alice, we've all got brains," I responded. "I use mine to think. If God wants to fuck me for that, that's His business. What I'm thinking about—what I'm wondering about—is whether God, back in the old days, was a little concerned about his own self-worth. Maybe He had a lack of self-esteem. It seems to me a little embarrassing that someone would come up and say, 'I'm really important, you gotta respect me.'

"If He's so great, how come he has to say so?" I asked them. "Yessers, my personal feeling is that when He said it, Dad was new on the job, and maybe a little nervous about how people were going to react to Him.

"Later on, His attitude seemed to change, though. After having extensive talks with our sweet Brother Jesus, Dad sent Brother Jesus to tell us simply that we had to love Him, but this time He left out most of the threats and added that we were supposed to love our fellow humans a lot, too.

"Surely this is a softening of the original message.

"Maybe God was a little less tense than He used to be. Maybe He's growing up."

...that was about the end of the sermon, or as much as I remember. But I think I was also feeling how much I hated for anybody to order me around, including God. I'd grown too old to accept that gracefully. But I figured that I was safe from the lightning bolts that Alice feared. It's only when parents get desperate that they hurt their kids. In fact, many parents enjoy it when their children reach maturity and assume their rightful places. If God resented me having a piece of the family business, then I'd start my own Universe, I thought. But most likely God wants us to join the family firm, bringing in some fresh blood and new ideas. Personally, I think He's having a hard time running the Universe, that He's sort of in the dark. Maybe He'd like to take a little time off, or maybe even retire. Whichever or whatever, I'd be happy and honored to cooperate with God, and contribute however I could. It's silly for Him to be afraid of His own kids. Right?

We had about twenty more-or-less regular Holy Yessers. Most of them were lost people who came to us to join in the health exercises and singing, and who sought the meaning and direction which they found in Yes, the Ultimate Answer. We made our living, did our best. Life coasted along peacefully until the Harvester sisters showed up.

Yes At The Office

There is a small fierce animal inside the mind of each of us that tries to protect us from the outside world. It is a tricky beast. It makes us do a wide variety of useless things which are supposed to keep us safe from harm. It makes us shout, joke, resent, hide, cry and laugh at the wrong times; it makes us frown when we should smile, compete when we should cooperate, hit when we should caress.

The name of the animal is Fear.

Example

I had seen them during the evening service and wondered what they were doing there—for most of our Holy Yessers were relatively young. After the closing prayer these three older women approached and stood before me like three time-ripened princesses. Pink prune faces with angelic smiles.

"We're the Harvester Sisters," said the eldest one. "I'm Bertie, and this is Harriet, and Minnie's the youngest."

Minnie seemed to be about fifty, and she still had a reasonable body that looked relatively unused—like a '62 Chevy that had hardly been driven.

"Yes," I said.

"We have a problem," Bertie said.

Harriet—who was over sixty, I guessed—winked at me.

"Tell me about it, Bertie," I said.

"We are being sexually harrassed."

I nodded, wondering who and why?

"You see," Minnie said anxiously. "We have enough money, but we love our jobs and we want to keep them. But it's unnecessary for us to work."

"But we enjoy working," Bertie said.

Harriet smiled winningly at me.

"Yes, I see," I said.

"But things are getting intolerable at the office," Bertie said business-like.

"The manager is just an awful person," Minnie said, shuddering like she'd stepped barefoot on a slug.

"He wants Minnie's bod," Harriet said brightly.

"Please, Harriet!" Minnie cried.

"We work at a stock brokerage firm," Bertie said.

"Minnie's frigid," Harriet volunteered.

"Harriet!" Minnie cried.

"That's beside the point," Bertie said. "We want to continue working together. And Minnie's job is in jeopardy. She is having difficulty defending herself against this awful man's advances. And we're powerless to help her."

"We use our maiden names," Harriet said. "Except for Minnie. Never married, you know. Still intact, if you know what I mean."

Minnie turned her head away, embarrassed.

"That is beside the point," Bertie said matter-of-factly. "What shall we do to protect Minnie's job?"

"It's a case of put-out or get out," Harriet said knowingly.

Minnie slumped into a chair, and began to sniffle. She shook her head despairingly and began to cry. "I'm so confused. Yesterday he pinched my...my...he pinched my..."

"Bottom," I suggested.

"Tit," Harriet said.

Minnie turned halfway in her chair, leaned over the back and sobbed loudly.

We had attracted a crowd of after-service Yespersons who formed a circle around us and felt the natural sympathy that Yespersons achieve for their fellow human beings.

"Let's get Bruno to break the bastard in half," someone suggested.

Bruno, gentle soul, nodded his willingness, but I held up my hand, saying, "There are better ways." They looked at me expectantly, waiting for *Yes*full wisdom. "It is good if we each handle our own problems as best we can," I told them.

Minnie turned back to face me, tears making silver streams along her cheeks. "I'm so confused. He wants to...he said he wants to... He said we could go out for dinner and then go back to his house and get...and get...get..."

"Naked," Harriet offered.

Minnie shuddered again.

"Minnie has avoided dates since she was twelve," Bertie stated calmly, like a reporter for the *Times*. This is the first time she's had to deal with such a situation. If we try to assist her our relationship as sisters might become known. That would cost us our jobs. It's against company policy to have close relatives working together in the firm."

"He said he wants to give me...wants to...wants to give me..."

"Head," Harriet said.

"*Yes*, that's all very well, and okay," I said thoughtfully. "We know what he wants. But what do you want, Minnie?"

Minnie looked at me as if I had asked a very strange question.

"Why have you avoided dating all these years?"

Minnie looked down at her hands. Then looked up at me, and blurted out, "He only wants one thing."

"To get fuc..."

"We know, Harriet, we know," Bertie said.

147

"I suggest you're mistaken, Minnie," I said. "Most likely, he wants many different things from you. Try to put yourself in his place. Here's a man who is attracted to you, so most probably he wants you to think that he, too, is an attractive person, a strong and interesting man. He's asked you to dinner, so probably he hopes you'll want to wine and dine with him, and enjoy the food, and respond to his attentions to you. For example, when he picks you up for your date, he'll want you to be on time and attractively dressed, and of course you would be. During cocktails and dinner, he'll surely want to have ordinary personal conversation with you, share with you some of his life experiences, and learn something of your personal history. True, he may make some sexual references, perhaps tell an obscene joke or two, at which he hopes you'll laugh, or at least be cutely embarrassed. Also, for example, table manners might be important to him. It might turn him off if you burped during dinner or chewed with your mouth open. If, however, all goes well, he'd probably take you somewhere for after-dinner drinking, hoping you'll get a little high and sort of loosey-goosey. And himself, too. Then he can tell you some more dirty jokes, and if you laugh he'll probably get a good hard-on and feel impelled to hurry you to a bed some place where he will *then* want to hurriedly remove your clothes and make love with you time after time after time again, all night long, till morning."

The sisters stared at me, gaping sort of, and everyone else was rather quiet.

"But that's only what he wants. What do you want, Minnie?" She looked confused.

"Do you like nice restaurants?" She nodded.

"Do you like people—people in general—to appreciate you?" She nodded again.

"And yet you are rejecting an invitation to dine out and also rejecting the attention of someone who obviously finds you attractive. Why?''

"But he's...he's so..."

"Horny," Harriet said.

"So is someone else," I guessed out loud.

Harriet beamed a smile at me.

"Minnie, tell me, how do you feel?"

She looked down at her hands, gulped, looked back up at me, and said softly, "I'm scared."

"Yes, Minnie, I think that's the real problem. Sexual aggression, bad manners, and bullying are his problem. Your problem is fear."

She smiled faintly, nodding in shy, self-conscious agreement.

"You have taken the first small step toward freedom," I told her. "Of course, you must say Yes to him, and I'll suggest to you how to do it."

Say *Yes* To The Dogs of War

Often you will say *Yes* to a person, and then realize something is preventing that person from saying *Yes* back to you. In such a case the most you will be able to do is to continue your openness toward that friend. There is a good chance, however, that at first your friend will resent you for your good-heartedness and affection.

Example

Laguna was cooking in the kind of weather that melts driveways and raises the murder rate. Bruno was in L.A. visiting his mother, and I sat naked in the condo thinking that it was definitely a day to avoid working. Leaving my toga where it was, thrown over the back of a chair, I put on my black T-shirt and a pair of cut-off jeans. Through the heat I journeyed to a beach further south than the one where our holy services and friends were located.

Fate had led me there.

I saw her.

She looked familiar. I knew we'd met somewhere, but I was having trouble remembering where or when or what her name was. She had very dark hair, almost black, and a great tan. She was young, with a fine lean body that her pale-colored bikini did very little to hide.

Our eyes met. She stared at me for a moment, but it was hard to tell if she recognized me, too. After a few seconds, she turned away to face across the beach toward the ocean.

Having lost all the shyness that used to bother me before I received the Gift of Agreement, I walked over to her.

She was staring at the sea. I came to her side, and we stood there, shoulder to shoulder, gazing at the eternal water that rose in blue-green curls one after another, endlessly, and crashed heavily on the sand. Though it was a weekday, there were quite a few people on the beach. Kids were playing in the shallow surf, sometimes screaming in a mixture of delight and fear when a wave tumbled them. There were mothers and fathers and brothers and others lounging on beach towels all along the shoreline: an enormous woman with rolls of dimpled fat; a pretty teenage girl riding on the shoulders of a young man as he waded into the water; a black man, short and beefy, built like a refrigerator, with a bullet-shaped head, who walked ankle deep in the surf foam, kicking it. Closer to me was a pale, skinny fellow who arrested my attention for a moment. He was all elbows and knees, as though the mother who'd nourished him had done a poor job of it, as though he was still starved for food and affection. His longish hair hung limp and his skin coloring was so gray that in my mind I named him "Fishbelly." He looked at me and I looked away.

The awful heat was smothering us all, bringing beads of perspiration to everyone's temples, and making us squint, and sending little lines of sweat rolling slowly down our backs.

The two of us, the dark-haired girl and I, stood on the burning sand in an envelope of silence, while all around us was the hum of beach noises. I could tell she knew I was there; I could feel her alertness, feel that her mind was tense although her body was calm. It seemed to be okay with her if I stood alongside her as long as I left her alone for now, keeping out of her way while she concentrated on something else.

Finally, out of the corner of my eye, I saw her shrug, relax a little and glance over at me.

It was time for my opening line.

In order to avoid prying into her private life, asking her name and other personal questions, all I said was, "I read something very interesting in a book last night."

She shot back, "So you spend your nights reading, do you?"

Her response was so quick and sharp, I laughed. Evidently she was suspicious, but that was certainly okay with me, if that's the way she wanted to be. I merely continued, "Yes, this fellow who wrote the book was saying something about revolution."

"Who's revolution is that?"

"His. Mine. Anybody's, I guess."

"So you're revolting, huh?"

"Everybody's revolting sometimes."

She laughed a small and wicked laugh from deep inside her.

In the heat, a strand of her lovely dark hair clung to her face in a damp curl. She had small silver hoop earrings pierced through her ears, and I felt a sudden urge to bite gently on her ear lobes. Her eyes were dark and bright. I noticed she wore a wedding ring, but it was on her right hand.

"Well," she said in a challenging manner.

"Well, what?" I asked, looking closely at her, at all of her, her body and soul, trying to figure out if she were gentle, if she had tenderness in her. It had been a long time since I'd met a woman who was both intelligent and gentle.

"Well, what did you read in the book?" she asked as though she were annoyed because I was being slow and slightly dumb.

I told her, "This fellow in the book said, '*A revolution marches a crooked path. It must wander where it can. It retreats before superior forces, advances when it has room to advance, and is possessed of enormous patience.*' ".

"So what does that mean to you? It means very little to me," she said as though she were being honest with me, just telling me the truth as though it was her duty.

"It means that when we try to change our lives, we're in for a tough time. It means that sooner or later we'll find ourselves in strange places. We'll be in a whole new world that's different from what we'd dreamed of, and planned for."

She looked at me closer now, as though trying to figure me out. Her eyes squinted in thought, her head was tilted to one side, as she seemed to be wondering whether I was smart or nuts.

Since I chose to remain silent while she was thinking, she was the one who finally spoke after a few moments.

"So...who is this guy you're talking about?"

"He was sort of a Chinese Robin Hood."

"What did he do, poach the King's egg foo yong?"

I laughed and felt very happy toward her. Sparks came from her eyes when she talked.

"Here's something else he said," I told her enthusiastically, wanting to share with her something that I thought was exceptionally wonderful. "You see, this Chinese Robin Hood was very successful in his revolution. He managed to bring lots of fried rice to the starving peasants. And yet here's what he had to say about all his victories and work. He said, *'Above all, we must conquer our feelings of being satisfied with what we have accomplished, we must conquer all our feelings of pride, everything that makes us believe we are heroes.'*"

I paused, waiting to hear how she felt about the wonderful thing this man had said.

"That's bullshit," she said, almost without pausing to think. Her words hit me like a knife, but my face stayed pretty much the same, as she continued energetically. "I mean, come on now. That's against human nature. It's just plain wrong, that's what I think anyway. I mean it's very *obvious* to me that the world needs heroes. That's one of the big things we lack. Where would we be without heroes in the past? Without women and men who strained themselves to the limit, who challenged themselves, who brought out the very best they had—mentally and physically—and accomplished all the great achievements that have enriched mankind?'' She talked quickly and forcefully, gesturing with her hands. ''Think what's been done in science. In art. Einstein. Georgia O'Keefe. Margaret Mead. Margaret Sanger. What about the great athletes who show us what the human body is capable of? Oh, forget it, we need heroes. An individual's accomplishments are absolutely of the *utmost* importance. They form the basis of a person's whole life. As far as I'm concerned, that quote of yours is way off base. It's bullshit. Sorry.''

She talked as though my idea was a pedestrian, and it was her duty to drive trucks over him until he was definitely dead and flat as a nickel.

I liked her a lot, and was attracted to her. She had brains and more spirit than anyone who'd come my way in a long time. However, I knew that some people would consider her just a pain in the ass as she went on to say ''We need heroes. People we can look up to.'' I wondered why she needed so much to be right, to be correct. I wondered why she failed to see that what she was saying was sort of silly because my quote had had very little to do with how we should look at other people. It had only been about how we should look at ourselves. About how we should conquer *our own* feelings of foolish pride.

''Yes,'' I told her, ''you may be right.''

She nodded at me as though she'd won her point, and then, suddenly, she tensed up as she glanced toward the ocean. Then she looked back at me and there was a small questioning look in her eyes. That look seemed familiar, and once again I had the feeling that we'd met someplace once before.

''Perhaps you're right,'' I repeated, ''but you know, I keep having this feeling that we've met somewhere, but where?''

''Winslow K. Smaggers' office,'' she said with a small smile like a night nurse who has caught her patient beating off again.

"Winslow K. Smaggers?"

"You were stealing his college diploma."

"Yes, yes, I was," I said, suddenly remembering. "You look different. How nice to see you."

"Nice to see you, too," she said, but again she glanced away as she spoke, her attention captured by something else. A feeling of jealousy swept through me. For some reason, I felt sure that there was another man on the beach that she was interested in. A previous lover, perhaps. Although we'd just met, I felt afraid I'd lose her.

I knew that she was of great importance to me. She was a very tough person—dark and mysterious. She was a fighter, she would fight about anything. Already she had interfered with my theft of Winslow Smagger's diploma and had driven her trucks over my Chinese Robin Hood. She had a quick tongue and was smart as hell and deep as the ocean. Facing her, I felt weak, as though I lacked the energy and spirit to deal with her. There is much peace and gentleness in me, and she was a warrior, a soldier, one of life's commandos. As she stood there before me with her dark, brilliant eyes and energy-charged body, I stared at her and wondered, How could a person cope with her? Also, I worried, What if I should lose her? It was a though I'd discovered someone I'd been searching for for years without my ever having suspected that she existed. I wanted her.

I'd fallen for her.

It was a crisis.

A time of opportunity and danger.

But I was at a loss as to what to do next.

So I did the only thing that occurred to me to do. I started talking.

Calming down, the gift of ordinary conversation came back to me.

I smiled, and began to charm the shit out of her.

She obviously took good care of herself physically, so I began talking about sports. She was a runner, she said, and I told her that I ran, too, sometimes. She said it looked as though I took care of myself, and she offered the opinion that it was okay to drink booze and consume other recreational chemicals as long as you kept them within reasonable limits. She told me she took a few golf lessons every year but always gave up after awhile because when she hit the ball it went every direction but backwards. She thought she may have even accomplished that a few times, too, she said. It was easy to imagine her swinging at the golf ball like she wanted to beat it up, like maybe it had insulted her or something. I offered the opinion that golf was more of a man's game anyway...

"Fuck you," she said.

Going right on from there... we began talking about other interests and hobbies. Skiing was her winter sport, and in the summer she backpacked. We agreed backpacking was a wonderful sport, and I said I'd like to try it sometime. She said I impressed her as the type of person who went out into the deep woods and got himself lost. She laughed when I agreed with her, and I said it would be nice to have a beautiful guide.

"Listen to him," She said, smiling broadly, pleased I found her attractive. "The most—the absolute most—you can say is that I'm *interesting* looking."

It was clear she actually thought that: she was blind to her own beauty.

Immense as it was.

We fell silent.

"How about a soft drink?" I offered.

"Sure, that'd be nice."

From her nearby beach chair and towel she picked up her sun glasses and a little white sun visor that looked good against her dark hair when she slipped it on with a quick, easy movement. The sun flashed on the gold wedding band on her right hand.

I pointed at the ring, "Married?"

"Divorced."

"I noticed the ring."

"I just like it as a ring," she said, shrugging as though it was of little importance. "You married?"

"Half and half."

"Things have yet to be finalized, right?" she said as though she'd heard my story a hundred times.

I said, "It's true, we're still waiting to see what happens next."

She shook her head, "Boy, you married guys."

"All I did was offer you a soft drink," I said.

She smiled like the night nurse again, and nodded, "Sure."

As we began walking toward the concession stand, she said, "Well, at least you were honest about it."

"And I got two kids," I volunteered. "How about you? Any kids?"

"Zero," she said like it was final.

Already I was having the fantasy that she and I might have some children together. They would be little brown-haired sons and daughters, champion athletes, jumpy energetic kids that we would marvel at.

"Do you want kids?" I asked her. "Someday?"

"I had my tubes tied."

"What?"

"I had my tubes tied. Tubal ligation."

I stopped walking. She had made herself barren. The news made a hole in my belly and my energy began draining out.

She turned to face me.

"You look like a woman..." I said softly, "who would want kids."

"I love children," she said.

Her voice was bright, but I thought I heard sadness buried in it somewhere.

As I look back on that moment and see her standing there before me, lean, supple and firm, she seemed to be watching me, waiting for something.

She shrugged, then smoothed her hands down over her thighs.

She seemed so right for me that I was surprised then that God had decided that we should be without children of our own. Well, if that was the way it was going to be, then okay, I would accept that, would take whatever the future would bring us.

She looked at me, and her face took on a hard look, her eyes narrowing and she said, "Men are so fucking weak."

"What?"

"Oh, forget it. Let's go," she said and started walking in the direction of the concession stand far off in the distance.

It was hard to move, knowing she was barren.

"Coming?" she said. Then I saw her look past me, over my shoulder, some concern showing in her eyes.

I turned around, wondering what the hell it was that kept capturing her attention. The only person I saw was the short beefy black guy that I'd noticed earlier wading in the shallow surf. He stood now, absolutely still, looking into the sun. He was massive like a rhino.

"That man's so high he's going to explode," she said. "Believe me, I know drugs."

I believed her, but so what? Fuck him, I thought. It was hard to believe that she, so young, would do that to herself, that her nursery would be empty forever. I thought of killing the doctor who had performed the operation. Would that be a positive act?

Walking across the beach, the mood was heavy until we began to share with each other our personal histories, and things began to lighten up. She told me she had a job in the computer industry—training people to use certain types of software. When she asked what I did, I told her I was an arc welder. She was surprised, and wondered if that was an intellectual enough job for me. "It's challenging work," I told her, and said she seemed to be too energetic a person to sit in front of a machine all day. She said her job took her all over the country; the software she worked with was used by amusement centers and theme parks like Disneyland and Six Flags. Already that year she'd been to Tampa Bay, Detroit, and St. Paul, Minnesota.

Immediately I felt a loss: her going out of town, and me waiting for her to come back.

"Maybe we could do something together," I asked. "I'd like to see you. Maybe we could go running."

She shrugged, "That might be nice."

As we crossed the sand toward a concession stand, I was about to ask her name when accidentally we discovered we had something important in common. We passed a family (mom, dad, and a couple of small ones) gathered under a beach umbrella watching a small portable T.V. set. A game show.

"Can you believe that!" she asked.

"Yes."

"They've got all this beautiful nature, this beach, this sand, the sun, and they pollute themselves with that shit."

"You're wonderful," I told her. "I hate it, too."

"I detest television," she practically hissed—narrowing her eyes like a snake would, if a snake could narrow its eyes.

"I hate it even more than you."

"That would be very, very difficult. Very difficult," she said. She told me that several years previously she had found herself watching a soap opera on a sunny afternoon, and had been so disgusted with her passivity ("Sitting there like a turnip," she called it) that she had arisen, turned off the small set, carried it to her car, driven ten miles to the city trash collection facility, and paid $5.50 to hurl it into a giant compacter that had crushed it like a grape.

"That's pretty violent," I said.

"Pure hatred," she said.

I told her how Mindy and Mandy had had an enormous wide-screen T.V. that was too much to even have in the same condo with me, even though it was always turned off. So I had given it away, donated it to an old people's home.

"Oh, yeah?" she said sort of pleased.

"Yes, I figured anybody who watches T.V. deserves to be old."

She and I walked on talking in perfect harmony, listing for each other the things we hated most about television. Television religion headed the list for us both. (Television preachers tell you to send your money to the Lord, but they give you their address.) Television interviewers were next on our list, and their guests, too. We wondered how many blow dryers they wore out a week. The whole thing was a pack of lies, we agreed: Sesame Street was evil, and each time you watch T.V. a little bit of you dies.

"We could make enemies talking like this," I said.

"So who gives a fuck?"

"That's right," I agreed, "it's hard to live your life, your own life, without offending somebody."

"That's right," she said, and we stopped and looked at each other. There was silence between us—like a bond—like we had both found someone we felt comfortable with, someone with whom we could be ourselves, with whom we could have fun. When we turned to continue walking, I put my arm around her shoulder. It was a natural thing to do. We were friends. It was exciting, too, because it was the first time we'd touched.

But then, after walking a little ways in silence, she said, "Of course, there *are* a *few* good things on the tube. But just a couple."

It was hard to believe she could say that.

Why did she do it? Break the mood? End the harmony?

"The only good thing on T.V. is the Off button," I said.

"I watch the news."

"I thought you crushed your T.V."

"Like a grape," she said smiling.

"So...?"

"I usually have dinner at my cousin's. We watch the news. Just a habit, I guess. Or I watch in hotels when I'm on the road."

I sighed.

"I consider *Sixty Minutes* a very good show," she said evenly like someone giving a weather report.

"You're right. It's a show. A performance. A piece of entertainment pretending that it's journalism. It's a pack of lies and half-lies, and anybody who likes it likes being lied to."

She snarled at me, "Sick people need T.V. to keep them from dying of boredom."

"May I use a favorite word of yours? Bullshit!"

"How can you be so fucking narrow minded?"

"It's easy once you know how."

I suspected now that she had deliberately broken the mood of agreement that had existed between us. I understood that she *wanted* to disagree with me. Something was going on here, but exactly what it was was a mystery to me. Someday maybe I'd know what the mystery was, but right now I realized I'd have to wage war with this woman, this beautiful woman, or she would walk all over me for the rest of our lives together.

Yes, I'd have to fight.

Even though I might lose her.

I might offend her permanently, and she'd be gone, but that was a chance I'd have to take.

"What about sports?" she said angrily, daring me to object, like she held a golf club above her head, and would beat me with it if I disagreed. "Think of the magnificent sports performances that are televised. "What about the Winter Olympics? Christ!"

"Christ rarely skied."

"Very funny," she said.

"Thanks. You can have any opinion you want..."

"How kind of you...

"...but if you spend your time watching other athletes, you're just masturbating."

"What???" she squealed.

"You're getting off an other people performances; you're living in fantasy land. It's a form of pornography. Only instead of women getting fucked there on the screen, it's athletes getting fucked. They get used. They get used by their teams, their agents, their sponsors. They do what they do for money, for glory, for lack of anything else better to do.''

''So what's so wrong with that. They can always quit, and get other jobs. Are you so stupid as to think that they're being forced to compete.''

''The women in porno films could get other jobs too, but instead they're up there fucking for money or drugs, or for the glory of seeing themselves on the screen, or for lack of anything else better to do. In a way, they're sexual athletes.''

''Excuse me, but *you* are *out* of your mind. Those women are *exploited*...''

''So are athletes exploited by the people who make money off them, and by the viewing public who treats them like heroes instead of like ordinary human beings.''

''There you go about *heroes* again,'' she said shaking her head as though I was a hopeless case.

''Athletes, movie stars, rock stars, porno stars and politicians are all involved in the same game. They're competing. They compete with each other, and they compete for your attention.''

''Competition is absolutely basic to the human condition,'' she said. ''That's why people enjoy watching it so much, that's why billions upon billions of dollars are spent on watching it, and participating in it, and everything like that. So there.''

''Competition is dead. Or to be more correct, it's dying. Athletes, rock stars, politicians, all those people in the headlines, are like dinosaurs—the whole breed is dying out, becoming extinct.''

''Says who?''

(If she was asking questions like that, she was weakening, I realized.)

''Lot's of people know it,'' I told her. ''Teenagers know it most of all. A lot of them have lost interest in competition.

163

Organized sport has gone too far; it's become too intense; the money has gotten too important. It's going to consume itself and burn out like a flame. It's gone about as far as it can go, and now it's going to be replaced.''

"By what?''

She said it testily, as if daring me to tell her.

I kept quiet.

"Is it a secret?'' she asked.

"Yes.''

"Well, go on, you've made your big speech now finish it.

What surprised me was how easily she had given in. She had almost, like, wanted to give in, halt the argument.

"Can you keep a secret?'' I asked her.

"Yes.''

"Good word.''

"*Do* tell me what is going to give us the thrills of a downhill ski race, the drama of a heavyweight title fight...? What will replace the competitive instincts that have kept man alive and interested in life for five million years.''

I said it softly.

"Pardon?'' she asked.

"Lean closer.''

She did, leaning forward so I could whisper the secret in her ear.

"Cooperation,'' I whispered, and, while she was so close, I bent further forward and kissed her gently on the temple. Her skin smelled of the earth and sky.

She said, "Cooperation?''

I nodded.

Smiling, she shook her head like I was wacko, and we resumed walking toward the concession stands. Our shoulders bumped and our arms went around each other's waist in a relaxed, natural manner. "Do you really believe,'' she asked softly, "all that shit you were feeding me?''

I told her, "Sort of," and at the concession stand I offered her the whole menu, but she only had a double cheeseburger, a large side of fries, a medium Coke, and a Snickers Bar. Since they were out of lambburger as usual, I went hungry. As we walked away a kid on roller skates came rocketing down the sidewalk. I stepped in front of her, and intercepted him, hanging on to his arm to keep him from crashing into anyone or anything; although it was close, we all got out of that one okay.

My beautiful dark-haired woman and I crossed the sidewalk, wandering out onto the sand, and we sat with her sitting between my legs, her back to my chest and my arms loosely around her waist. She munched her burger and we both looked out to sea and talked just for the sake of being together and hearing each other. The sun was kind to us, keeping us nicely warm, and after a while we got up and walked, strolled, down the beach hardly talking at all. We wandered around like that for a couple of hours, loafing and relaxing, getting comfortable, splashing in the water when it got too hot, like we'd known each other a long time. Maybe the sun broiled our brains. At times I felt dizzy; the day was so bright it hurt. One of us suggested a swim. We went back to her towel where she dropped her shades, and I impulsively borrowed a large inner tube from some kids near by. We slipped into the water, which was warm, and lazily we paddled away from the crowd. Her eyes had a soft look, and we took our time going out to sea, holding onto the inner tube, floating away from the beach. The sun was hot on our heads. The water was all glint and sparkle. About seventy-five yards out, we kissed, our tongues meeting and our bodies tight together as we clung to each other and the inner tube. The scent of her filled me; she was soft as twilight. My dick got hard. I reached for her breasts, and she laid her head in the crook of my shoulder and kissed me there. Her arm was around my neck. We held onto the inner tube, and I moved my head to look in her eyes. She smiled.

I asked her, "Let's fuck?"

She kept quiet for the longest time, just holding me with one arm and the tube with the other. And then she surprised me.

"Yes," she said. "All right."

I hesitated. She was so open and vulnerable. It was then I remembered we were strangers. Maybe she realized it too, because a small look of doubt came into her eyes. We liked each other a lot, but we were strangers. I knew I could wait, that there would be other times, that rushing it might be harmful. Her bikini bra was loose above her breasts now, and my free hand was at her firm, strong tits. I paused, feeling sort of honored, you know, to be there, to have heard her say, "*Yes.*" The thought crossed my mind that maybe I should wait—wait until a better time—wait until some time when the doubt had left her eyes. My hand dropped to her cunt, it was slick and warm inside.

Fuck waiting.

It was like a slow-starting avalanche, our getting started, me pulling off her bottoms and stuffing them safely into the pocket of my cut-offs, moving faster, down with my zipper, out with my dick, working quickly as I could to get it in, pump pump pump for a while and then it was all over.

All over but the shouting.

We clung to the inner tube and to each other for a little while. We gave each other timid smiles, maybe a kiss or two, wet, salty, us bobbing in the ocean. I zipped my pants and dove under the water to help her on with her bottoms, slipping them up her legs and kissing her in the pubic hair before raising them over her hips. But her only reaction was to reach down to adjust the bottoms evenly. When I popped to the surface we floated in to shore, both of us holding the tube.

Trying to find out what was on her mind, I said, "That was sort of crazy of us."

Quietly she said, "I've done crazier."

Coming out of the surf, I reached for her hand, but right away she slipped it out of mine, and adjusted her hair and kept her hand to herself. We passed the beefy, black man who she'd said was full of drugs. Still pacing in the water, he looked like he'd been cooking his head in the sun all day. I returned the inner tube to the kids I'd borrowed it from, and went to lie next to her on her beach towel.

She was leafing through a magazine.

She was quiet.

"First times are often less... less successful than they might be." I reminded her.

"It was fine," she said.

"What do you want?" I asked her, feeling that she was slipping away from me.

She focused hard on my face. Her eyes narrowed and she practically hissed, "I want it *all*, I want it *all*."

My heart sank. I could hardly give Astoria anything. How could I give this woman—what ever her name was—everything?

What *was* her name anyway?

"You know," she said casually, her voice becoming strangely conversational, like suddenly we were sitting around having coffee after dinner. "All the women I know are more powerful than their men."

The expression on my face stayed the same, but I understood she was baiting me, she wanted to argue and fight; she wanted war again. Since we'd argued earlier, about T.V., and since I felt in some vague way that I'd done something wrong (but what was wrong I'd have had a hard time saying), I decided arguing with her would be a poor choice of responses. Instead, I decided to agree with everything she said. Maybe that would take the fight out of her.

"Perhaps you're right."

"My friends are all stronger then their men."

"What's your name?"

"That about says it all, eh?"

"What do you mean?"

"Norleen," she said.

"I used to have a name like that," I told her.

It failed to amuse her. She squinted at me and her mouth got very tight. "You know something," she said to me with anger buried in her words "you come off like Mr. Nice Guy, but I have a sneaking suspicion that you have a real mean streak in you. I bet you can shove the knife into people real good. I bet you can be a real nasty son of a bitch."

Why was she so angry?

What had I done to her?

Did she think I was a threat to her?

Her words stirred so many feelings in me that all I could do was nod in agreement.

There was silence between us.

Finally, I said, "But still I'd like to see you."

"I have someone."

What? Earlier she had told me that, yes, sometime we could get together. Now all of a sudden she "had someone". After we had fucked, too. This was going to be a very rocky romance.

"A boy friend?" I asked surprised, hesitating to believe it.

"A lover," she said, slamming her five-iron into my ear and making me dizzy.

What was going on? Where the hell did I stand with this lady?

She continued, "I was real lucky; I met him even before the divorce was final, and we've been together a year."

I listened with my head tilted to one side like a miniature poodle.

"I love him a lot. It's real."

"Oh."

"He lives in L.A., so we only get to see each other on weekends mostly."

I had a sudden vision of the two of them locked in wild love making sessions Friday through Sunday. "Uh huh," I responded to her.

"But I'm a very independent person. I need my time alone. We both keep our freedom. So, I can go running with you."

She seemed to be angry with me and interested at the same time.

She really had me confused. "Great let's do it," I said.

"You're a very agreeable guy, right? Always ready with a smile and a joke."

"Yeah, that's why you like me so much."

She laughed, "Who said I like you at all?" she said, punching me on the shoulder.

It was nice for us to be smiling at one another again.

"Well, I know why I like you. You're..."

And then words failed me; I thought about her and my mind went speechless. I wanted to say something about how womanly she was, about how... But as I looked at her, I became dizzy. It was as though I were looking into some huge, dark space. I felt fear as I realized that I could fall into her and be swallowed up forever.

She shrugged. That movement of hers brought me back to reality. "Maybe it's my perfume," she said lightly.

It was then that the black guy who was high on drugs started to go crazy. His craziness interfered with the progress I was trying to make with the dark-haired girl (who I now knew was named Norleen, but who—in my mind—would always remain *the dark-haired girl*.) As the disturbance took shape, our day together came to a screeching halt, and I lost her. There was a loud noise, someone shouting, or a yell or curse or something. The black man was standing over the pale skinny fellow, the one whose skin was fish-belly white. The pale guy sat on a pink towel at the big man's feet. The black towered over him on enormous thighs that would have supported big Bruno's weight. On his

169

chest, curly black hair covered great pectoral muscles that stood out on his body like armor. His upper arms were the thickness of my thighs, and he raised his right one straight in the air with his fist clenched, and he cried out in a voice like a steel mill, "I AM A SOLDIER." He moved his head from side to side, looking down on us little people, and he cried out again, loud enough for God Himself to hear, "I AM A DOG OF WAR."

The people nearby, being a lot closer to him than God, began to get nervous. A woman started gathering her blankets and kids. The Fishbelly fellow, perhaps hoping the big man was looking away, turned onto his hands and knees and started creeping away. The Dog of War reached down and grabbed the Fishbelly's ankle. Straightening up, he half-turned and looked at Norleen and me sitting about thirty feet away; this stretched his prisoner out behind him on the sand, scared, and stiff as a plucked chicken. Dragging the white guy behind him, the soldier, like a caveman heading home for dinner, began trudging toward Norleen and me. We arose to meet him at the door. Fishbelly's head and shoulders made furrows in the sand. As they got close I noticed he had acne. Panicking, he began kicking furiously to free himself. The Dog of War stopped. Turning, he peered down at his prisoner who quickly froze in place, up-ended, like a human letter "L".

"Hey, I say, hey," the black man said.

A silence followed. The pale fellow began to tremble. We watched as a wet spot appeared on his dry, blue bathing suit; it spread downward as the urine seeped beneath the waist band of his trunks and trickled across his pale belly and hairless chest toward his neck, dripping off him into the sand.

"Hey, you tell me, man? What I need medicine for?"

Fishbelly shook his head passionately, as though agreeing that medicine was the last thing his captor needed.

"Man, I need a job, you hear? I am a soldier. I live in blood. I *deal* in blood. You hear me talking?" He straightened up, and looked at Norleen and me, only ten feet away from us now. It was obvious that something had to be done. I had to keep Norleen from harm. Me, too.

Turning his attention to us, the Dog of War continued his conversation, "I want my weapon back. Get back to my outfit with my buddies. Kill us some gooks, you hear what I'm saying?"

What could I do? I had doubts that this fellow was ready for the message of *Yes*. Nudging Norleen with my shoulder, I said softly, "Buy you a soda pop, cutie."

She turned to face me directly. "Cut it out," she said. "Just cut out the bullshit for once."

When she said it, I thought, "Wow." She had a lot of surprises in her. Man, this woman is great, I thought. I asked her quickly, "After this is all over will you see me?"

"Do you ever think of anybody but yourself?"

"Yes."

We were both trying to keep an eye on the soldier who'd turned his attention back to his prisoner.

I asked her again, "Will you?"

She waited a few seconds before answering. "All right, maybe."

"Do you promise?"

"I said, 'Maybe'," she snapped.

The Dog of War had begun talking to the other guy like they were buddies sharing burgers and beer at a tavern somewhere. The soldier was explaining, "I want my buddies back. My old buddies. Where's Andrew? I want to see Andrew."

He turned his attention toward us and stared.

Norleen talked to him plainly. "Are you all right" she asked, walking toward him, and standing just a few feet away.

He was angry. "I'm through taking lithium. I'm through with that shit."

"Are you all right?" she asked again with her voice firm but warm.

171

"What do I have to take that shit for?"

Again she asked in a calm voice wanting to know how he was, "Are you okay?"

He paused; her words had finally reached him, "Hey," he said, shrugging.

Norleen said, "It's hard, huh? It's really hard?"

"Oh, yeah. Oh, yeah." He laughed saying, "And it stays that way, too."

She moved very close to him, taking off her sun visor as she went. He looked at her suspiciously, and I got nervous. She stopped in front of him—they were about the same height—and with a nice easy motion she slipped her sun visor onto his head.

He smiled a big grin—easy and loose.

She laid her hand on his forehead.

"You're real hot."

"Hot day, lady."

"Let's you and me sit down." She put her hand on his massive biceps.

Behind them, Fishbelly had crawled away, gathered his towel and was fleeing across the beach.

The dark-haired girl turned to me and asked, "Would you go wet my towel and bring it to me?"

I nodded.

They sat.

Full of respect for her, I walked back to her beach towel.

As I picked it up I heard someone speaking nearby.

The person said, "Here they come. Finally."

Looking up I saw that, yes, indeed *they* were coming.

Someone had called the cops.

It was Kimberly and Wire-Moustache themselves trotting across the beach toward us, all decked out in their spiffy tan uniforms and black shoes.

What would the cops do, I asked myself quickly.

They would probably be hostile to the soldier, sort of climbing all over his back like they did with the kid in the Cadillac Seville with twenty-nine coats of Georgia Peach lacquer. They would probably hassle the soldier into a rage.

Maybe they'd show him the inside of the Laguna jail. Or maybe kill him if he got out of control.

Right when he was getting a little peace in his angry mind.

I looked back just as the dark-haired girl glanced up and saw the on-coming cops. She winced slightly.

I hated to leave her.

But it was my duty.

"Call me," I shouted to her, and she nodded back that she would.

Yes, I had to leave.

Yes, once again I would have to act in the service of truth and justice.

Once again I would have to employ my clever mind in the service of peace and harmony.

What the hell would I do, I wondered?

I began moving.

Moving toward the cops.

They were sort of trotting across the burning sand, getting their feet hot, looking for the disturbance they had been called out to calm down, but were having difficulty finding.

They kept coming on and on, their night sticks banging against their sides.

I was walking toward them rapidly.

Suddenly, passing a fellow on a beach blanket, I reached down and grabbed his cigarettes, took one, and tossed the pack back to him. He looked angry, and I told him, "You ought to thank me, these things are terrible for your body."

This only seemed to make him more annoyed, and I began running, running in a slow jogging sort of pace toward the cops while rolling the cigarette between my palms and spilling some of the tobacco from the ends and dirtying the paper. Kim and her partner recognized me approaching, and I thought I saw suspicion come into their eyes. I twisted the ends of the cigarette paper and began jogging faster, smiling at them broadly, looking as cheerful as a happy spring flower. "Hi, guys," I sang out pleasantly, "What do you say we split a joint?"

I tossed the fake marijuana cigarette to Wire-lip and he suddenly looked like he was going to be happy in the next few minutes doing his duty as he saw it. Then I was seized with a sudden inspiration. I was filled with an overwhelming affection and sexual desire for Kim. I cried, "Kiss me, Kimberly. It's been so long, baby." I leaped at her trying to jump her bones, but she was too quick and dodged away and I flew by her, managing only to catch with my fingers the cloth of her shirt on top of her left shoulder. I hung on as she began falling on top of me, crying out, "Fucking asshole."

I fell on my back on the sand and she crashed down on me. She lay on my chest for half a second and we gazed into each other's eyes. It was a quiet moment, a lovely moment, that we two shared in this continual hassle of the modern world. For a moment the noise in the world stopped.

There was only one thing to do.

I clamped my arms around her, and gave her a great big kiss.

And, damn, if it might just be possible that she kissed me back for a tiny fraction of a second before she remembered she was a cop.

(Humbly, I say that it is the Power of *Yes* that makes me so attractive.)

(On the other hand, it might just be my imagination.)

In any case it was an exceedingly small fraction of a second because Kim started wiggling and slid off me, and I jumped up like Peter Rabbit, and was off and running like dogs were after me.

But after a few steps I stopped.

I turned and asked them an important question.

"Tell me the truth, you guys: Do you want to know where the cocaine is?

Yes, they did.

You bet they did.

Clubs in hand they chased me.

Now that I think of it, much of my association with these two people, Kim and her partner, Gilford Worthingglass, was spent playing tag.

This time they caught me.

I was careful to stop near a crowded food concession stand, and I made sure I was laughing good and hard so everyone around could see that I was a harmless fellow.

I held my hands straight out in front of me, and to their credit Kim and Gilford, were gentle, and clamped the handcuffs on me without beating my brains out first.

"She's a wonderful woman, Gilford, your partner is. I was unable to stop myself." And Gilford, himself, I suddenly realized, thought the whole thing was pretty funny and was having a hard time trying to keep a straight face.

They gave me a ride in their spiffy green Dodge without handles on the inside of the back doors in case I wanted to leave early.

As we drove away, I looked back trying to catch one last look at the dark haired girl, but she and soldierman were out of sight.

Kimberly turned to me, and shouted out in exasperation and confusion, "What is your story?"

"Have I told you guys about *Yes*?"

The Gift That Goes On Giving

Life is like disarmament talks.

Sure it is.

Often we would like to be friends, or lovers, with someone, but often each of us is waiting for the other one to make the first move.

We have our defenses up.

It's sometimes hard to know whether you should open your arms and touch someone. Or wait for them to open up to you.

The best way to reach most people—the best way to begin the difficult emotional task of getting close to them—is to whisper *Yes* to them.

Give them the Gift of Your Complete Compliance.

This will leave you defenseless—which is the best protection there is. They will begin to trust you.

Make a gift of yourself to others, and continue to make the gift of yourself. Usually they will respond in the same manner. You will begin giving and getting, getting and giving from one another. Every day will be like Christmas.

Example

Women were on my mind.

Astoria.

And the dark haired girl at the beach.

I was in bed.

But leaving my whanger alone.

I have stopped beating off—even when dreaming of women I love.

Or like.

Or just want to roll around with.

I heard the door of the condo open.

We rarely bothered to lock it.

The late morning August sun streamed through curtains.

Bruno stooped to enter the doorway, and stood there so big that the door disappeared behind him.

"Master, there is a little old lady here to see you."

"Bruno, when are you going to cut out that 'master' shit?"

"Your eternal humility is a magnificent example to us all, Blessed Wing."

"It's dumb," I said.

"You fail to realize how good you are."

"Wanna bet?"

"She says she has something for you."

"How big is it?"

"It's in an envelope."

"Maybe it's a birthday card."

Bruno looked startled. "Is today your birthday?"

"What day is it?"

"August Eight."

"Yesterday was my birthday. The Golden Shining Month of August: when else would the Messenger of Light and Truth be born?"

Without a word Bruno left quickly—showing great agility slipping through the doorway without breaking the walls down.

And then she stood before me.

Horny Harriet Harvester.

She smiled coyly and sat on the bed.

"I have just a little thank-you present for you. From us sisters."

Accepting the envelope she handed me, I opened it and out tumbled a cashier's check for $10,000.

"Hummmm," I said.

She smiled at me waiting for more reaction.

"Things must have worked out well for Minnie."

"Oh, yes. Things turned out quite nicely."

I handed her the check back. "It's too much."

She looked distressed, "Oh, keep it, Wing," she said. "We can afford it. You opened up a whole new world for Minnie."

"What happened?"

"She's pregnant."

I laughed. God, I laughed. It's so great when the only thing you can do is laugh, when something grabs you in the stomach and forces out of you great bursts of rolling laughter that keep coming and coming, making you throw your head back and laugh because that's the only thing you can do; when tears of laughter fill your eyes and you clutch your stomach, or pound a pillow, or roll around spilling out laughter that keeps coming on and on and on...

"I knew you'd see how wonderful it is," she said.

"*Yes*, it is wonderful."

"*Yes*, it is. So please keep the check."

"Is she happy about it?"

"So happy!"

"What happened?"

"She wrote you a letter." Harriet took another envelope out of her purse and handed it to me. "She would have come herself," Harriet said, "but she's on her honeymoon. On a cruise ship."

"Pardon?"

"The letter will explain everything."

I stared at the two pieces of paper: the envelope and check. $10,000.

Useless.

So late.

I was remembering back to my marriage. I remembered how Astoria and I had always been broke... especially those years in the mid-west when she had had to take the lousy municipal bus to work, rain and shine, summer and winter... when sometimes it had been snowing and I would worry that she would slip on black ice, hurting herself... when she had worked her so hard to keep us afloat... when she would return home, cold and tired on dark December evenings, to a husband who was useless at making a living and supporting her... when $10,000 would have made us feel like millionaires.

I could see her.

Astoria.

Her beautiful face smiling lovingly at me, looking for a compliment or thanks or approval because she had hunted-out and bought for the kids a couple of sweaters which she had found for only a dollar or two in the crummy bargain basement of some department store... where up the escalator in the same store other women, luckier women, were spending hundreds of dollars on fine silk blouses for themselves.

"Thanks, Harriet. I have someone I love who can make very good use of this money."

"It's for you."

"I have enough."

"We want you to be happy."

"I am happy, good looking."

She smiled mischievously at that.

"But can you really afford this." I asked.

"My dear man, surely you realize who we are?"

"Who are you?"

"The Harvester sisters."

"Yes?"

"Cyrus Harvester was our great grandfather."

"Do I know him?"

"International Harvester, dear man. On the New York Stock

Exchange. Old Cyrus invented the automatic green bean picker. Then the automatic corn plucker. One thing led to another and he founded International Harvester. We're heiresses, you know. We're filthy rich, you lovely man," she said leaning over and laying her hand on top of mine. "So please take it." Her gentle eyes begged me to accept her gift.

I held the envelope up, reading the return address: it was from the Carribean, from the Virgin Islands.

Well, it certainly would be interesting to find out how Minnie had traveled so far so fast, and I would have found out too, except that I noticed that Harriet's hand had moved and was now resting on my thigh, sort of squeezing it through the bedclothes. Her eyes were appealing to me to accept another gift she had in mind.

"How old are you Harriet?"

She slipped her hand under the covers.

"You're going to love it," she said.

She was right. I did. She was wonderful and her heavenly hot spot was just right; she had the moves of a belly dancer and could have squeezed lemons with that thing. If it had lasted all day it still would have been over too soon. As it was, we were just finishing up, real pleased with each other, when we heard a familiar tune being played on a clarinet outside the bedroom door. Beneath the covers, Harriet curled herself contentedly under my arm. The door banged open and Bruno burst in holding his instrument in one hand and a set of golf clubs in the other. He was followed by four or five Holy Yessers all singing in joyful harmony:

"Happy birthday to you, Happy birthday to you. Happy birthday, dear Wi-i-i-ing. Happy birthday to you."

"Bruno. I'm screwing."

"...Oh."

Minnie Harvester's Letter

I have lost Minnie Harvester's letter.

Maybe one of the sheep on this fucking ranch has eaten it.

But more likely, it was left behind in Laguna.

The last time I saw the letter was when Horny Harriet made a grab for my dong, and I dropped it. It slid off the bed and lay on the floor, still sealed in its envelope near the $10,000 check Harriet had given me.

Now somebody else has the letter, and only that person knows for sure what happened to Minnie. The rest of us are still in the dark. All we can do is make some guesses based on the sketchy information Harriet gave out that day. That is, it seems Minnie used the magnificent power of *Yes* to deal with her office manager, and this somehow led to further adventures for her which seem to have included marriage and honeymooning on a cruise ship. Perhaps, as Harriet said, she is also pregnant, although considering the short time span it's hard to see how she would know so quickly. I have the feeling, and perhaps you do, too, that Minnie went fucking wild, and frankly I'm interested in that sort of thing.

Perhaps you are, too.

So it would be very good if the person who has Minnie's letter would send it to me. In turn, I'd find some way to get the information to all of you readers. Free of charge, of course. You already bought the book, so it would hardly be fair to ask you to spend more money to fill this hole we've got in our story now.

I'd be willing to pay to get the letter back. I'd be willing to give a cash reward if the person who has it would return it.

Oh, I know what you're thinking, some of you people who are suspicious types. You're thinking to yourselves, "If he's giving a reward he'll get a lot of phony letters from people who want the money. After all, how will he know which is the real letter because Horny Harriet grabbed his dong before he got to read it?"

Maybe that's true, maybe dozens of letters, or more, might come in.

Well, that's okay.

I could handle that.

Send all the letters you want. I'm one of those people who enjoys getting mail. Besides, who am I to say what's right or wrong—what's true or false? Here's what we could do. We could have a little cooperative story telling here. Anyone who wants to send a letter, please do so, and I'll read them all and pick the one that most honestly seems to tell what happened to Minnie. We'll accept that that's as close to the truth as we're going to get right now. The writer of that letter will get the cash reward; let's say something in five figures; let's say $10,000.

All letters are welcome. Whoever thinks they know what happened to Minnie is welcome to share his or her ideas with the rest of us.

It occurs to me that this might lead to a problem. What if more than one letter is very, very appealing? Perhaps we should have more than one reward. Let's have additional prizes for the top three or four or five most interesting letters. Those writers, too, will get $10,000 each.

(The reason that the prize money is the same for everybody is that we want to get rid of the idea competition. Everybody does the best they can.)

So there you have it. Done.

Maybe this way we'll get to know what happened when Minnie said *Yes* to her boss and got herself married and maybe even pregnant. And what was she doing on a cruise ship anyway?

Okay?

You can reach me at:

Shepherd Books
Box 2290
Redmond, Wa. 98073

Why ARE you so silent?
Do you know How lonely
    it is AwAy from you.

Say *Yes* To Vegetables

Keeping our bodies healthy is a challenge to us as human beings, especially when the strains and pressures of ordinary daily life become intense.

Sad to say, often when the going gets rough we just make things rougher by abusing ourselves. We light cigarettes, we reach for alcoholic drinks, or perhaps even try to lose ourselves in sex or drugs. In other words, we molest our bodies. What's more, our destructiveness often extends to other people and we begin abusing our loved ones, and our friends, and, finally, strangers.

It's a lucky day for some of us when we realize the human body must be treated with love and respect. It's the Temple of the Soul. It's where our personal power is stored.

Doctors and religious ministers, like myself, understand these things, and that's why we play golf on Wednesdays.

Example

Horny Harriet stayed nestled under my arm as I laid there looking at the golf clubs the Holy Yessers had given to me. Tears of joy filled my eyes. "This is almost too much," I said gratefully.

Everyone stood around smiling affectionately at Horny Harriet and me, in perfect acceptance of the fact that she and I had just mingled the juices of love. The feeling came to me, then, that I must mean something special to them. I realized everything I did seemed to be all right with them. They had accepted me as a part of themselves. Maybe I was the part that was brave, that dared to do things they were afraid to do, or said things that were locked inside of them. Or maybe they thought I represented the insane part of themselves. I felt a danger that we might become a cult, and I might become arrogant and evil.

"It's been a long time since I played golf," I told them.

"Hey, we got some great courses around here," Daryl Spagnoff said.

"Bruno?" I asked.

"Yes, Master."

"Do you play golf? Do you have clubs?"

"It may surprise you to know that, yes, I do. A set of Macgregor Muirfields, with persimmon woods. I got them from my good friend Wilt Chamberlain as a thank-you for a bronze statue I did of him dunking a basketball. That was in 1974, he's a very nice person, maybe it was 1975..."

"Bruno..."

"Yes, Master...?"

"I only wanted to know if you had some golf clubs."

"...Oh."

Soon afterward those new clubs were used for the first time. On a humid but pleasant August afternoon, Joe Wagonewti, Daryl Spanoff, Bruno and I were participating in a friendly round of golf, whacking the little white balls around with some success. We had arrived at the eleventh hole. Joe, in addition to being a fine salesman, was an exceptional athelete (we'd met playing volleyball). He was forty or so, and had a world-class beer gut, but you could tell by the way he moved, and by the day's golf score, that he was a ruthless competitor and used to winning. At this hole he had the honor of going first. Dropping his cigar on the grass beside him, be began to line up his tee shot. Ignoring the smoke that curled up around his face, he stiffened his body, relaxed it, waggled his butt, waggled his club, and then finally began taking his club in a backswing, long and very very slowly, until, at the peak of his swing, without pausing, he began bringing the club down in a great wide, flashing arc, smacking the little white ball, driving it far away into the broad green fairway that stretched before us.

"Gees," I muttered to myself, "I wish I could do that."

"It'll play," Joe said, bending over to pick up his tee and his cigar which he stuck in his pocket and mouth. "Lemme ask you this, Wing," he said, coming toward me and staring into my face in a challenging manner. "Would you rather hit the perfect golf shot... I mean the *perfect* golf shot? Or would you rather have sex with a great looking woman?"

It was a surprising question. A good one.

I thought about it for a moment.

First off, a woman's looks had very little to do with anything. I understood that. Then vague memories began floating through my head, memories of all the beds I'd been in, all the sexual grabbing and groping I'd been part of. Some of it was very fine, and some of it was less than fine. But very little of it was what you'd call perfect.

"You know, Joe, I think I might just go for the golf shot."

"See, you guys, I knew there was something wrong with his head." He and Daryl burst out laughing, and so did I, at this lack of sexual aggressiveness on my part, but big Bruno just stood there wearing menacing storm lines above his eye brows.

"What's wrong with the Master's head?" he said like somebody had insulted his mother.

"For God's sake, Bruno," Joe said, "It was a joke. A joke. You remember what a joke is? God, Wing, does he ever laugh?"

"Yes." I said.

"You people better pay attention," Bruno told us. "The world is in very terrible shape. Who hits next? There is very little to laugh about."

189

"Lighten up, Bruno, you're making me old," Daryl said. He is a young surfer, tall and rangy, a boy actually, whose only two strong urges in life are to ride waves and ride women.

Daryl put his ball on a tee and got ready to hit, but he was still chuckling and so he had to wait until his chuckling would go away. Finally he relaxed his grip on the club and said, "That reminds me of this girl I had in the wagon."

He'd just met her, Daryl said, but right away he's getting it on with her in the back of his station wagon, and although the screwing was adequate, it was also only sort of average, so he asked her to give him head.

"Forget it, fella," she said.

"Come on."

"That's a dirty idea," she said.

"For me, baby."

"I stayed away from that dirty stuff all my life and if you think you're going to be the first, you're crazy."

"This is the last night you're ever gonna be able to say that, sweetheart."

"There's something ladies refuse to do."

"Oh, baby..."

"It's ugly, I would only do it with someone I truly loved, and even then I'd have to learn how, and which would be something I'd have to force myself to do, and due to my total lack of experience the whole thing would fall far short of your expectations, so forget it, your chances are zero and zip."

"But, honey, I do love you," Daryl said, and he gets her down there ready to start and she looks up and says, "Well, tell me when you're gonna shoot, I hate the taste."

We laughed and chuckled, and finally Daryl hit his tee shot, a decent shot, a respectable shot for a man to hit.

Then it was my turn.

My nerves started going. Shakiness spread into my arms and hands. My ego was slipping out of control. Here I was in a competitive situation, for the first time in a long time, and my ego wanted me to be a hero. Or at least avoid looking like a fool. You'd think that after receiving all my recent gifts of good luck from *Yes*, I would have learned to stop worrying. But, sadly, I'm a very slow learner, a dense person who sometimes forgets what he trys so hard to learn. That's why I was a little shaky.

Fortunately, Joe Wagonewti interrupted my anxieties by telling us Daryl's story reminded him of this girl he'd known for years who was a very straight and proper type of person. One night he found himself, almost by accident, on a date with her. When they got back to her place she invited him in, which sort of surprised him because she was so well-brought up, well-mannered, and sort of up-tight, if we knew what he meant. She talked very refined and cultured like she was from finishing school, he told us. He said he poured him some la-dee-dah *liqueur* in one of those itty-bitty glasses.

"Gees, I can hardly believe it, guys, when I find myself in bed with her, and what's more she's giving me head. I think to myself, gees, with a girl like this I want to act like a gentleman. So when I start to come, I pull out real quick. Well, she starts grabbing for my dick, and it's dancing around, shooting all over the place and she finally gets hold of it, but it's too late. Real mad, she points her finger in my face, and says, 'You owe me one, sucker.'"

When the laughs faded, it was time to prove that I was a worthy human being by hitting a manly tee shot, by over-coming my fear and shooting the ball in a spurt of whiteness toward the dark hole on the close-cropped green.

To do that sort of thing, one needs a firm ego. A real man's ego is a lean thing. Hard and small. It does it's work quietly, and needs very little to keep it going.

I wish I had one.

I hit a medium poor shot: short and crooked.

As the ball rolled to a stop on the side of the fairway, I nodded toward it. I accepted my bad shot. It was a part of me, something I had done, something that was mine. I looked at the ball and felt my failure, accepting it. For a short moment I was thankful for having had the opportunity of hitting a bad shot and seeing it so clearly.

Then it was Bruno's turn. He cranked up, coiling his body slowly, taking the clubhead away from the ball in a long slow arc that took a long time to complete and that—upon reaching a point high above his head—immediately changed into a flashing downward arc of increasing speed as though some enormous spring inside him had let loose. The clubhead smacked into the ball with a gunshot sound and the ball rocketed away, flying low to the ground for a long ways until it began rising slowly, straight as a frozen rope, driven by the power of Bruno's great personality, up and up into the sky.

We searched around for it for a while, but in my opinion that ball is still in the air somewhere, high above the earth.

Waiting for me back at the condo after the golf game was the lovely and talented Alice Angsterlobe, a woman in her thirties who wanted to send me on a trip to Paris. She owns a travel agency and once had said I was just the sort of person who would love France. I said I bet she told that to all the boys, and she told me I was being silly.

Alice has hair of red and gold that glows like the setting sun. She has a world class body and heavenly breasts. "Hello," I said, "You look good enough to eat."

"You're hungry?" she said.

"Only for you."

"Peel me."

But we were both joking and we both knew it.

"I bet you came here for some other reason." I said, kissing her lightly on the cheek. She and I had slept together twice, but I had a vague feeling twice was all there was ever going to be. For one thing, I was saving myself for the dark-haired girl now.

"As a matter of fact..." she said.

Alice was stalling, getting her sales pitch ready.

She was dressed in travel agency clothes.

A normal blouse. A normal skirt. Normal shoes.

She stood in the doorway of the bedroom while I set birthday golf clubs in a corner. Lowering my zipper, I dropped my cut-offs and shorts to the floor and pulled off my gangster tee-shirt. That left me standing before her naked as a California buzzard with it's pud hanging loose while it looked around for its toga.

"You're a very shy person, I see," she said.

"I was brought up quite strictly by nuns."

"I bet."

The toga was behind a chair. Picking it up, I held it in my hand, standing and looking at her. She returned my gaze.

"Well, my dear, do you want to get out of those clothes or should I get into mine?"

"Wing, it's still only daylight."

"We can pull the curtains."

"Wing, be serious."

How could she fail to understand I'm always serious?

"Fine then," I said, pulling on my toga, standing in front of her like Julius Caesar if Julius Caesar had come to the beach for the summer.

Her mind was at work. You could almost hear it going like a small motor boat puttering across a lake.

"Alice, you want me to go away. I can feel it."

"I would miss you terribly if you left. Whatever gave you that idea?"

Alice is nice, but she has about as much sense of humor as a horse.

"You want me to go away and come back."

"Oh, you mean the Paris trip," she said as if I'd reminded her of the farthest thing from her mind on that summer afternoon in Laguna. She smoothed her hair. "I *would* like to talk about that." We sat on the sofa and she began to speak of the joys of seeing the wonderful sights of France.

"Have you had lunch?" I asked her because a sea-sick feeling was taking over my stomach.

"In a bit," she answered and went right on with her speech about the ecstasy of European travel. "...as a religious leader, Wing, you really ought to see the great churches of Europe."

Could she possibly mean that?

"What I have in mind," she said, "is for you to lead a group of our church members on a tour of the great French houses of worship."

I felt like I was being used.

For the first time in months I wanted a cigarette. How wonderful it would be to suck the poisonous smoke deep into my lungs.

Alice had started blinking a lot under the pressure of getting her sales pitch right.

It's depressing to feel like you're getting used.

"I often work with church groups, Wing. The ministers all tell me how useful traveling together is for binding the members of the church into a closer union, a deeper type of fellowship."

I had a sudden and increasing desire to drink a lot of booze. Maybe a quart of Jack Daniels Tennessee Whiskey would do.

"As a matter of fact," she said, "we once arranged for a tour group to be led by a genuine French choir director in the singing of religious hymns in a little church near the airport."

"Sounds interesting, Alice."

"Yes. They were Baptists. They said it made a lovely memory for them."

Maybe I could start taking heroin.

"You know, Wing, I just had a thought," she said eagerly.

"That's wonderful, Alice. What is it?"

She was getting excited now. "Just a minute," she said

194

putting her finger to her lips to 'sssh' me while she was thinking. "Listen, Wing. I bet we could get a list of the religious goods stores all over France. You could lead your congregation to see all the great churches—the cathedrals—*and also* you could take them to stores where they could buy marvelous Holy Objects. You know, the Bible, or maybe a silver cross of Our Lord, and prayer beads and religious candle holders. That sort of thing."

Maybe I could find a couple of women in leather bras to tie me down and beat me.

Alice asked me what I was thinking.

"Of salvation."

"What? Wing...are you putting me on?"

"What do you mean?"

"Do you *really* like the idea; does it turn you on?"

"I think it's a remarkable idea."

She settled back in the sofa, smiling with satisfaction. Taking a deep breath, she let out a contented sigh. "I knew you'd like it."

That just goes to show that sleeping with a person a few times can leave big gaps in your understanding of who they are and what they are about.

Alice is a nice woman in my opinion. Everybody has a job to do. We were each sitting there in our working clothes: she in hers and me in mine. Both of us were ordinary people, both of us just trying to do the best we could to make our lives mean something. She had her way, I had mine.

Alice sighed again, deeply satisfied, as though she had won something that made her happy. She sort of hugged herself.

"Yes, Alice, it's a wonderful idea, and I'll bring it up to the Holy Yessers, and see if they're interested in getting a group together."

"Then you will try to go?"

"We'll see what the future brings."

"Oh, I *like* you," she said as delightedly as though I was a dog that had rolled over at her command.

She sat back contentedly on the couch, like she'd just come home from the office and could relax. Seeing her sitting there, in her normal blouse and normal skirt, a very strange thing started to happen to me. Warlike feelings filled my chest. I took a deep breath, trying to relax, but that only seemed to add fuel to the fierce feelings that had begun growing inside me. I kept those emotions hidden behind a mask of coolness. But my feelings struggled to find a way to make themselves known, trying to find a way to burst forth into view. And they did. As I sat there, the lower part of my toga began to rise. My aggressive feelings were flowing into my dick, and I was getting the kind of erection a man could be proud of. There came over me a tremendous urge to reach out and put my hand on the back of her neck and push her face down into my lap and make her give me head like she was my humble slave and I was the Sultan of Swat.

I'd show her who the powerful one was.

She soon noticed how somebody's pecker was standing up under his toga like a new statue ready for unveiling in front of the post office.

"Oh, Wiiinng," she said like somebody'd offered her a box of chocolates.

"Yes," I said to this nice woman who wanted to send me on a tour of the religious goods stores of France.

"Maybe the afternoon *is* an okay time?" she whispered.

"Yes," I said to this woman who wanted to put me in a choir loft where recently vacationing Baptists had built themselves a nice memory.

Cutely, she snuggled next to me, and put her mouth to mine; her tongue was active like a warm snake. It was obvious that she was willing to fuck me now that her work was done, but I, as a matter of fact, would just as soon try to fuck the Holland Tunnel at rush hour. I would rather stick my dick out and challenge twenty thousand drivers fleeing New York than get involved with this woman any more deeply.

The dark-haired girl was right; women are too powerful.

They are too single-minded.

I'd have a better chance of surviving the cars.

There are few things in this world that will batter a man worse than screwing with a woman who tries to obtain her own security by manipulating him at the expense of his dreams. She'll drain him of his strength until all that's left of him is that he is a mass of quivering jelly.

On the other hand, my pecker was sending strong messages to my brain. "What's the harm..." my pecker was saying. "It might feel good to climb into something hot for a little while. What's the harm? What are you worried about?"

I kissed her real good and she seemed to enjoy it.

I put my lips next to her ear, and asked "Are you thinking what I'm thinking?"

"What are you thinking?" she asked.

I was thinking about shooting heroin.

I was thinking where a person could find tall women in boots to whip him.

"Hummm?" she said, and I noticed that somehow her normal blouse was now open to her skirt.

"Vegetables," I told her.

"What did you say?"

Held in by a lacy bra, her wonderful bosom looked appetizing.

"Vegetables. I'm thinking of vegetables, Alice."

"You're thinking of vegetables?"

"Vegetables are very good for you, Alice. They're healthy."

I started to get up, and she asked me to stay.

"Alice, come into the kitchen, we've got to get healthy."

I got up and headed for the kitchen, and she came after me, lowering the zipper on her normal skirt.

As a stalling tactic, while trying to think of something to do, I opened the refrigerator. She put her arms around me from the back, and I turned around to face her with a weapon in my hand.

I had a zucchini.

Her blouse hung loose, and she ground herself against me in a supremely sexual manner, and I laid the zucchini between us, resting it across the top of her exciting breasts.

"What's that for?" she asked.

"Are you hungry by chance?"

"Yeesss..."

I took the zucchini off her boobs and sent it down to our lower regions and started rubbing it against her.

"Ooooh, that's chilly," she said, "What are you doing?"

"Vegetables, Alice. Vegetables are very good for you. We're trying to stay healthy." While she rubbed against my erect zucchini, she lifted off my toga. With the toga gone, it was instantly revealed that my pecker was a traitor to my brain. She started to reach down for me, so I increased my work with the zucchini to distract her. I told her to sit and got her sort of slouching on a kitchen chair. Putting her hands on the zuc, I told her to work it in, and damn it all, she actually began doing it, moving her hips and licking her lips, and saying, "First the clarinet, now this."

"Go for it, Alice."

"You can make me do anything, you dirty dog."

Watching her, I was getting so horny myself I gave serious thought to replacing the zucchini, but I knew I should avoid doing that if at all possible, because the world must be full of better things for me to do, right? But it was hard to think of any at the moment.

"What about you?" the sweet woman said, her eyes at half-mast, "we've got to do something for you."

"Oh, I'll be all right," I said, wondering how.

She was going to be on me in a second.

Then I spotted it.

A cantaloupe.

"We got to do something for you," Alice said murmured, still zuccinying.

I picked up the cantaloupe.

"What's good for you is good for me." I opened the silverware drawer and took out a paring knife, which made me feel real nervous with my pecker sticking out there. The thought crossed my mind that without a dick a lot of my problems with women would be solved. But I had to be a man about this thing. Bravely, I cut a hole in the cantaloupe, and start to make love to it.

"Is that okay for you?" Alice asked with concern. "Is that enough, honey?"

Actually, it was a lot better than you'd think it would be.

"It's the seeds, Alice. If you twist it just right, it feels great," I panted.

The condo door opened.

Who cared? I was in love with my cantaloupe.

Daryl Spagnoff stood there shaking his head.

"You people are really weird."

Is *Yes* Enough?

Is *Yes* Enough?

Can *Yes* totally fill the human soul with contentment, with inner peace?

Yes, it can.

Yes, it does.

"But..." you may be asking yourself, "what should be done about the Big problems of modern Life? What about child abuse, violent crime, pollution, racism and poverty? What about War which is all of those things wrapped up in one bloody package?"

I am pleased to tell you there is enough power in *Yes* to solve all of those problems, too.

So far we have just been looking at *Yes* on a person-to-person basis, but now we can see how it is possible to apply it to the larger problems of society.

First, of all we must remember that those problems are acted out by individual people.

These people act alone, or they act in groups.

But that is of little importance.

What is important is their needs.

You must find out what people *need*.

And say *Yes* to it.

* * * *

Example

I had told the dark-haired girl to call me.

But that would be very difficult for her to do because The Holy Church of the Slippery Word was without a telephone. She would be unable to call directory assistance to get my number.

So I had a Holy Telephone put in.

Which left us with still another problem.

She still would have difficulty reaching me until she learned of the existence of our Church, or of my name, or my connection with the Church.

I had to get that information to her.

But how?

I meditated for a few moments.

And read the newspaper at the same time.

While munching my breakfast of lamb sausages and salad.

It was only a few moments before the Wonderous Creative Power of *Yes* flowed through the Eastern Window and filled my head with calm, quiet energy.

And then something mystical began to happen.

I began to dissolve.

I could feel myself flowing apart. I realized that I was turning into billions of tiny little dots like they use to make the pictures in comic books. *Each one of these dots was me, totally me, completely me.* My dots were flowing apart—flowing away from each other. I was like a balloon expanding. I lost the idea that I was one single man. I felt at *one* with everything. I realized that I was the *same* as the lamb sausages on my plate. I felt my *oneness* with the walls and furniture... And with the telephone I wanted the dark-haired girl to call me on. I felt wonderful, so at peace, so happy in my understanding that all the atoms of my body were brothers and sisters with all the atoms of everything else in the world.

I kept expanding and expanding.

I flowed through the walls of the condo and found myself—my consciousness—floating high in the air looking down at Laguna.

Below me lay that beautiful little town with its ocean and streets and buildings—with its plant life and animals and people moving here and there, walking, jogging, and driving around in cars. Each of those plants, animals and people had its own special concerns. The grass lawns were wondering when they were going to get their next meal, and wondering whether they would be served harsh chemical fertilizers or good old natural manure. The dogs were busy barking at cars and peeing on bushes and doing all sorts of doggy things. And the people were doing all sorts of people-things too numerous to mention.

What did they all have in common?

What did they all want almost more than anything else in the world?

Most of all, what they wanted, was to stay alive.

And was there any threat to all of their lives all at once?

Yes, of course there was.

Nuclear war.

As soon as I thought that—as soon as the Gift of Understanding flowed across all Eternity and lodged in my brain—I knew I had the answer.

Immediately all my atoms began to re-group, and I began to shrink back toward my former size like a balloon shrinks when you let the air out of it.

Soon I was sitting back in my chair finishing off the sausages.

That night I addressed the Holy Yessers telling them that for too long had we kept the Wisdom of the Wonderful Word within our group.

"It is now time," I announced, "for us to go forth and deliver our meaningful message to The Dogs of War, Part II."

The Dogs of War, Part II

Yes is kind and generous.

By practicing *Yes* a person gets great satisfaction through helping other people achieve what they really want.

Example

I had read in the newspaper that a very special type of exhibition would be taking place in near-by San Diego the next day. Lockheed Aircraft, and Boeing Aircraft, and General Dynamics and several other companies would be showing off some interesting new products.

War machines.

They would be displaying war planes and war missiles, and lots of other electronic death-dealing equipment designed especially for the modern warrior.

It promised to be a wonderful show.

About ten of us from the Church went to see it.

"What does your company really want to do with this thing?" I asked the nice fellow at the information booth of General Dynamics Corporation.

We were talking about the new Bat-Rat fighter plane—the Scourge of the Skies—the most exciting, deadly piece of aviation hardware ever invented.

A big model of it stood before us. It was sleek, swept back, with wonderful cannons and rockets in its wings and belly.

There was a big video screen near-by that showed what the Bat-Rat—Scourge of the Skies—could really do. We watched the tape and saw that the Bat-Rat was truly a great piece of equipment.

It could do *everything*.

It could fly faster than spit.

It could fly higher than God.

It could fly lower than bugs.

It could kill.

It could kill *anything*.

It had nuclear capability.

And puke-ulear capability.

It could turn on a dime and hand you back a dead body in change.

We were convinced. It was obvious that all over the world hungry lawns, and peeing dogs, and people who were busy doing people-sorts of things were easy targets for this beautiful monster.

We Holy Yessers gathered around the model, and I asked, "Do we all agree that the Bat-Rat is the best fighter plane at the show?"

"*Yes!*"

"Sure is!"

"Right on!"

We voted, and the vote was 27 to 3 in favor of the Bat-Rat. Toby Hanratty and Daryl Spagnoff voted for Lockheed Corporation's new fighter plane, the Rat-Fox Air Assassin.

"But airplanes are old fashioned," said Horny Harriet, and she voted for a Boeing missile system.

"What does your company intend to do with this airplane?" I asked the bright-looking fellow at the General Dynamic's big information booth whose name tag said he was Gary Carpingsneed.

Gary Carpingsneed stared at my creamy-white toga and at Bruno who was standing behind me like the Empire State building, if the Empire State building had moved from the East Coast to the West Coast and was wearing a jet black shirt open to the waist, and heavy gold chains from the ninety-first floor to the sixty-third.

Gary stared at our whole funny-looking group as though he was a public relations man who was reluctant to make enemies.

Who wanted everybody to be his friend.

Who was careful to avoid offending anyone even if they did look weird.

"We want to sell them," he told us as though we were respectable lawyers, dentists and accountants.

"To who?" Bruno growled.

"Oh, governments buy them. Our government may buy some from us. And perhaps we will be able to sell them to other friendly governments."

"Do you want to kill people with them?" I asked him as easily as if I wanted to know the time and had left my watch at home.

He sighed a bit.

He was a nice looking fellow with clear, intelligent eyes and well-kept hair, a good suit and pleasant tie.

"We only sell them. We build them and sell them." he said, looking around him as he finished talking—looking for a security guard, I guessed, or someone else, *anyone* else, who might get him out of this increasingly awkward situation.

"Well, then, as I understand you, your main purpose is to manufacture the best products you can, and then sell as many of them as you can so that your company can make as much profit as *it* can."

"*Yes*, I suppose that that's fairly close to it."

I turned to our group, saying, "He said *Yes*."

"Good for him," some Yesperson said.

"Excellent", said another.

"He's coming around."

"Gary", I asked him, "tell me honestly, do you believe you have the best fighter plane on the market?"

"*Yes*, we like to think so," he said with more enthusiasm than he had shown during the whole rest of the conversation put together. "We think its the finest military aircraft of its type in the world today."

"Well, so do we," I told him.

"We certainly do," said someone behind me.

"It's a hummer."

"But, Gary," I said, "it seems to us that you are failing to use all the means at your disposal to sell as many fighter planes as possible."

"You have a marketing tip for us?" he said like I was a hunchback offering him beauty tips.

"We certainly do. You realize, of course, that Lockheed Corporation wants to sell their planes, too. Lockheed is trying to take away some of *your* profits."

"That's their privilege," Gary Carpingsnead said like an economics professor at Harvard. "That's the way the American free enterprise systems works."

"But yours is the best plane!"

"I disagree," said Toby Hanratty strongly.

"But it is. By a vote of 27 to 3, Gary. We voted. Now why are you reluctant to use it?"

"Pardon?" he said.

"My God, man," I cried, "Think of how many more planes you could sell if Lockheed was out of business."

"What are you talking about?"

"Gary, forgive me for saying so, but you're being dense. What your company, General Dynamics, should do is declare war on Lockheed!"

"Oh, come on now."

"Gary, it makes sense, you're sure to beat them. You're got the know-how. You've got the best equipment. Fly over to Burbank and nuke 'em till they glow."

"Aw, shit," Gary muttered.

"I've said that many times myself, Gary," I admitted, "But have courage, man! *You* can boost profits. Those people are standing in your way. Who are they to take bread out of the mouths of your children? Bomb the fuck out of them. You people are making your money from war. You should eat the fruits of war."

"Please... get out of here."

"God, man, think of T.V. commercials you'll have. Actual footage of Lockheedians lying dead in the streets of Burbank. Gary, think! You can conquer the whole aircraft-manufacturing World. Every war monger on earth will admire you. Your planes will sell like frisbees."

"Guard! Guard! Could we have a security guard over here?"

"Why must you be half-hearted in your war business? Say *Yes* to War, Gary Carpingsneed!"

"Guard! May we have a security guard over here right now?"

Obviously, Gary Carpingsneed, an important representative for his company, was reluctant to act courageously.

The guards would be arriving soon.

We would have to act quickly.

"Accept your destiny, Gary," I begged him. "You must see that war against Lockheed is a logical, reasonable extension of your business."

"Get out of here!"

"Perhaps he's afraid," I said to the Holy Yessers. "Let's show him how easy it is. We must set a good example for him!! We'll declare war on Lockheed ourselves!"

"Yes!"

"Yes, we must!"

"For God, and Country, and General Dynamics!"

"Nuts!"

We moved quickly to the big model of the Bat-Fox—Scourge of the Skies. I sounded the call, "Man your battle stations," and "Clear for take-off".

All of us grabbed hold of the model plane (with Horny Harriet at the tail naturally) and pulled it off its stand and flew it across the convention hall. We ran with it like it was a battering ram. People saw us coming and dove out of the way crying:

"What the hell's going on?"

And "What the fuck?"

And "They're crazy."

And "Call the cops."

Courageously, we Yessers flew through the Boeing missile installation, toppling model rockets and knocking a piece out of the Boeing information booth. The Bat-Rat lost part of its right wing. But, magnificent aircraft that it was, it kept on flying across the floor—aided, of course, by the Enduring Power of *Yes* in the form of the brave Yesmen and Yeswomen of our Church.

We attacked our primary target—The Lockheed Rat-Fox Air Assassin—a model of which stood in front of the Lockheed booth.

We won.

The noble Bat-Rat flew into the Rat-Fox, and the Rat-Fox fell apart.

"You guys were right," admitted Daryl Spagnoff, who had voted with Toby Hanratty. "The Rat-Fox is a crummy plane."

"That's all right, Toby," someone assured him. "Everybody makes mistakes."

We flew the Bat-Rat directly into the Lockheed booth which had been abandoned by its defenders.

I grabbed one of the make-believe rockets that had fallen off our fighter plane. Leaping up on the counter of the Lockheed Information booth, I held that plastic bomb high above my head, and yelled out, "I've got a bomb here!"

My words echoed through the convention hall, and immediately I heard other words.

Words like: "He's got a bomb."

"They've got dynamite."

"They're a suicide squad."

"Hit the deck" and "Lemme outta here."

You can imagine how very quickly we Yessers had the convention hall all to ourselves. As the crowd was fleeing I yelled (and the rest of the Yessers picked up the chant), "We demand television coverage. We demand television coverage. We demand television coverage."

Crunch asked me if I wanted him to get me out of this one, too. I said, "I want to stay here for now, Big Guy. There's still work to do." And all the Yessers stayed with me. Bless them. (Except Daryl Spagnoff who split.)

Fortunately, luck was with us.

When you have *Yes* on your side, luck is always with you.

A local T.V. station had sent a camera crew to do a feature story on the exhibition for the afternoon news. They got a livelier story than they expected.

And we got our T.V. coverage.

Disregarding my fake bomb threat, fearlessly careless of their own safety, an attractive woman newsperson, and a fellow with a mini-camera raced up to get our story. This was hardly surprising. Newspeople always show up right away at such events. It's like they are little bees that are always flying around looking for the flowers of pain that bloom in our society. These little bees land on the flowers of pain and gather up some of the sorrow and take it back to their electronic hives. Then they broadcast it into our homes so that we can tune in the evening news and find out who got hurt and how bad, and wonder if we're next.

The newspeople and I did our work quickly because we wanted to get finished before the cops came to break up the party. I kept my remarks very brief so they would have to go over the air pretty much the way I said them. In each sentence I used the name of our Church so that the dark-haired girl would know who I was and where to find me.

It went something like this:

"We of the Holy Church of the Slippery Word believe that those people who make war weapons should use them on each other and leave the rest of us out of it."

We were a very interesting looking group. Me in the toga, and big Bruno, of course, and the rest of our people who were all smiling and very friendly looking. Very different from your average group of grim protestors.

Very photographable.

Lots of film was shot.

I could hear the cops coming.

But I knew we'd make the evening news.

The dark-haired girl would see me and know who I was and where to reach me.

She could reach me in jail.

The Forgiving *Yes*

We have all been hurt
Physically.
Emotionally.
At some time or other.
By someone.
We remember being hurt, and who did it to us.

That's the trouble: the remembering. Often the memory of having been harmed does more damage than the actual blow itself. We can usually repair the obvious damage we've suffered, but the feelings of anger and resentment toward whoever did it can linger on for years, for a lifetime. Such feelings can infect us, poisoning us at times, interrupting our moments of happiness and making us look and feel ugly.

To be happy and content, we must learn to forgive the people who've brought us pain.

How?

It's difficult, that's for sure.

Perhaps it helps to remember that everyone in this world is doing the best they can with what they've got. And, besides that, each one of us has hurt someone else—perhaps pretty badly. To *forgive* means refusing to see ourselves as innocent and the other person as guilty.

By doing that, everyone becomes equally innocent.

Everyone gets out of jail. *Yes,* by being forgiving we free ourselves from our own feelings of guilt, and open up ourselves to accept the same kind of love we are offering to others.

Example

The bars of the prison were painted the nastiest, dark orange you have ever seen. Chipped, and scratched, and ugly.

The police removed our group from the big cell where we had been kept like chickens in a cage, and they took us to a courtroom where a young judge sat like a block of black ice behind a high, desk-like thing. The judge set the bail at $500 for everyone but me.

For me, the bail was $5000 because I was the acknowledged leader of the group.

Everybody but me coughed up the bail money and went home. Since I had sent the Harvester sisters' check to Astoria, I had a lot fewer than $5000. Guards took me back to another orange-barred cell furnished with your standard hard bed with urine stained mattress, filthy chipped sink, and toilet without lid.

But that was all right with me, because the dark-haired girl would know where to find me.

But someone else showed up instead.

Astoria.

I was taken to the Visitors' Room, and there she was waiting for me on the other side of a glass wall.

So beautiful.

So lovely.

But she looked serious.

She is much younger than I. In her thirties. But, like me, she looks very youthful. Almost always, though, there is an air of tension about her. It's as though life is hard for her. As though she worries that she has to be careful and must always be on guard. It's as though she is afraid of something—afraid some pain or harm is just around the corner and might come to her at any moment.

But sometimes she melts.

Sometimes her fears seem to go away, and her face relaxes into the gentlest, most loving look that any man could ever hope to receive. Her mouth goes slightly open, turning up in a smile of happiness and trust, and her blue-gray eyes get crinkly and twinkly and seem to say, "I love you, I have always loved you."

But that look was missing now as she stood on the other side of the glass in the barren visiting room with pale green walls.

We sat opposite each other, ready to talk through a little steel-wire screen set in the glass.

She looked a little angry and sad, too. Her face was set in hard lines.

She spoke first.

"I lost my job," she said.

"That's all right, I've got one."

She ignored my announcement as though it was of little importance. "Doyle started firing people because of the recession. Construction has slowed way down, and builders were hardly buying anything from us. Otto Crumbly lost out on those two jobs he was bidding for."

"At least he got to have lunch with you."

She looked at me, annoyed.

I had to be very careful about what I said to her. She was so easily offended, and she often thought I was criticizing her when I meant something else. Then she would get defensive and distant and cold.

I told her, "It's strange Doyle would let you go. You work so damn hard."

That seemed to please her a little.

"Yes," she said, "I do. It's a crime." she said bitterly.

Silence.

"Thanks for sending the money," she said finally, and added gently "If you'd put a return address on it, I might have written you back."

"I figured you were better off without me. Or maybe I just thought that money was a poor basis for us to get back together."

She tossed her head a bit to rearrange her golden hair. She sniffled. Then her eyes began to fill with tears.

"What's wrong?"

She bit her lip and blinked away the tears. "I just feel sorry for you."

I doubted that, but all I said was, "I'm a happy guy. Things are going pretty well for me."

She scowled suddenly like she'd just bit into a sour grape. "Sure, You got a nice place here."

I shrugged. It would be too hard to explain to her that I had changed...that I had stopped worrying about things...that I'd decided to take life as it came to me and whatever happens is okay as long as I carry in my head as positive a frame of mind as possible.

"*What* are you *doing* here?" she cried out exasperated.

"Living," was all I could think to say.

"You're driving me crazy."

"I'm sorry."

I kept still although she looked as if she wanted me to say more. It seems the deeper a person gets into *Yes*, the less it becomes necessary to talk. You lose the need to explain, or to try to change people's minds. People can take you the way you are, or leave you alone. Whatever they want. It's okay.

"I suppose I should bail you out," Astoria said.

"You can if you want but I sort of hoped that that money I sent you would make your life easier."

She shook her head. Perhaps it's hard for her to understand me. She fails to realize how very much I love her. Or maybe she understands but refuses to accept it, because if she accepted my love then she would have to love me back. She would have to actually show me her love, and do loving things for me. She would have to live with me and share my life. And that would be very difficult for her to do because she is convinced that basically I am wacko.

She is mistaken.

I am as sane as a rock.

"It's all right, Storee. The lawyer that the judge assigned to me said I would either have to pay a fine or spend a little while in this hotel for outlaws. The lawyer said the fine would probably be the amount of the bail. So if you go bail for me, then your $5000 will go down the tubes, out the window. You'll be broke again. Of course, you can do what you want but I'd prefer it if you spent the money on yourself and the kids."

"The kids are with your sister in Connecticut for the summer."

"Then spend it on yourself."

"You're very generous." She said it as if she thought I was an idiot for giving so much to her when she was so reluctant to give me anything in return.

We sat silently, just looking at each other for awhile.

Finally, I said, "I love you."

She sort of gave a little snort, and looked up at me with hard eyes, as if to say, "What's the use of that?" or "What good will that do me?"

Then she said, "What am I going to *do* with you?"

"Come and live with me."

She shook her head again.

"I can support you now."

"How?" she said. There was both suspicion and curiosity in her voice. She looked coldly at me. She was being business-like and wanted to know what kind of deal I could offer her. That let me know that down deep in her soul she still cared for me, although she would have denied it like crazy if I told her. *Yes*, she still wanted to live with me. It was true, I could see it; she would come back to me if she thought it was *safe* to do so.

Poor girl.

She still believed there was such a thing as safety.

Of course, I knew better. I understood that safety is just a dream, and the more a person tried to be safe, then the more pain that person would have to suffer. You might be able to avoid the pain for awhile, but sooner or later it would come. And the later it comes in a person's life then the more it hurts.

So, naturally, I was reluctant to lie to her. Reluctant to tell her that living with me would be an easy existence.

But I did want to be with her again.

Have her close to me.

Put my arms around her, holding her close with her face snuggled against my neck warm in each other's affection.

I had to keep my voice as business-like as hers. "If you'll stay with me, I'll provide a home and food and enough money to live on."

"Promises," she said. "You're always full of promises."

I kept quiet.

"But when have you ever kept them?"

"I'll keep this one," I said, although it would have been hard to say exactly how I'd do so.

"How?" she asked coldly.

Well, that settled it. She definitely did want to know if it would be possible for us to get back together.

But what could I tell her?

That I was living in a borrowed condo?

That I bought my food with the small donations that the Yessers gave me?

I kept silent. It would be useless to try to explain to her that my old negative frame of mind had changed to a new positive frame of mind, and because of that good things just came to me like I was a magnet for good things.

"How?" she repeated.

And then a good thing happened.

The door opened and a uniformed guard came into the room.

"You two can continue this conversation outside. Somebody just put up bail for you, Wing."

I got up out of my chair, smiling. "Astoria," I said, "You've just got to have faith."

She looked puzzled.

"Wait for me outside, okay?"

She nodded she would.

A Good Thing

Life without love in it is an awful thing.
To regain a lost love is a wonderful thing.

Example

On the sidewalk in the sunshine in front of the jail house, Horny Harriet Harvester was waiting. She stood expectantly next to the front fender of a dark green Jaguar touring car. She wore a little old lady's dress: blue with white dots. Smiling sweetly, she asked, "Are you all right, dear?"

"Sure, I'm fine."

Astoria eyed Harriet suspiciously, her blue eyes darting up and down, examining and evaluating.

"Harriet, I'd like you to meet my wife, Astoria."

Harriet fixed her eyes on my golden woman. "Goodness, you're so lovely," she said, her voice full of affection and acceptance.

Astoria smiled almost shyly. You can usually please her by speaking kindly and complementing her.

"Wing has kept you a secret," Harriet said. "We're all surprised to find out he's married."

Astoria glanced suspiciously at me. "Well, he is," she said.

"Yes, I certainly am," I added quickly. "Thanks for springing me out of jail."

"Oh, please, dear. We're all so proud of you. Astoria, he's so courageous. We all love him."

"Yes, I see," Astoria said looking at me questioningly, wondering what was going on.

"He brings love into our lives." Harriet looked at me affectionately. "You poor man, was the food terrible in that horrid place? Do you want to get some lunch?"

"The food was okay," I told her, although I could only guess at it's quality because I had refused to eat any of it. Instead, I had fasted during the two days I'd been the Laguna's guest. "I'd love to have lunch with you, Harriet, but right now I want even more to talk with Astoria. We've been apart for too long."

"Of course, dear! You can drop me off at the office and take the car."

"Thanks."

"In fact, Bertie and I were thinking that you ought to keep it while Minnie is on her honeymoon," Harriet said, opening the rear door and climbing in.

I opened the passenger door for Astoria.

"You've got nice friends," she said under her breath, approvingly.

Inside the car, before starting the Jaguar's fierce engine, I looked at Astoria. She sat in supreme comfort—pleasured by the feel of the rich real-leather seats. As she stared straight ahead at the shining real-wood paneling of the dashboard, she seemed almost hypnotized by the luxuriousness of that expensive car. I could feel how much she valued luxury. She was born to live among fine, expensive things. She was most at home, most happy and content, when she was amid the toys that lots of money can buy. That is where she felt safest.

Why then had she married *me*? She must have known I'd have difficulty providing her with that sort of life.

It was quiet in the car during these moments while I was watching her. Finally, she looked at me to see why we were still sitting there. We smiled at each other. Her eyes got that crinkly, loving look. She seemed to be saying to me, ''Yes, this is where I want to be.''

Cock-a-doodle-do.
Let's screw.
In the morning light
In your cunt so tight
My cock will
doodle-do.

The Rock And The Butterfly

We have all seen butterflies dancing in the air.

They bounce from flower to flower in gardens and meadows.

And we have all noticed what happens when a person walks up to a butterfly. The butterfly flies away. It flees.

Why?

It does that because it's afraid. It's afraid of getting hurt.

But rocks are different.

When you approach a rock, what happens? What does it do?

It just sits there.

Yes, you've probably noticed that the vast majority of rocks refuse to flee when you walk up to them.

With these things in mind, you might someday want to spend a few hours watching rocks and butterflies. Almost certainly you'll see the vast differences between them. For instance, butterflies seem to spend most of their time trying to escape from things. They fear people, birds, lizards, spiders, dogs, cats, frogs, and snakes.

(And some people, you may have noticed, are afraid of these same things.)

(And, oddly, these same things are often afraid of people.)

(But hardly anything is afraid of a butterfly.)

As for rocks, on the other hand: birds, lizards, spiders, dogs, cats, frogs, people and snakes all fail to cause fear in their stoney hearts. Rocks are brave.

Why is that so?

Where do rocks get their courage?

It comes from their humility.

Yes. Rocks as a group have shed themselves of all their pride. You can search high and low, and here and there, but you'll have difficulty finding a proud rock. They refuse to view themselves as important things. It matters very little to them whether people throw them, or whether crawling things crawl on them. Whatever happens they just continue to do their best to cope with anything that happens to them.

Try this experiment sometime: go out in the garden, find a rock and pee on it.

Does it care?

Of course it cares, but very little. Getting pee-ed on is just one more thing a rock has to deal with. A rock takes life as it comes.

Now think of butterflies. Butterflies actually believe they're important. That's why they're always fearful, always feeling that it would be a great tragedy if something ''bad'' was to happen to them.

Try to pee on a butterfly.

See what happens?

You have to chase it all around the garden trying to get it wet. That's a difficult task for man or woman. Particularly a woman.

Why does a butterfly make life so difficult?

Why does it flee?

Because it refuses to accept your insulting actions, that's why. It's full of pride.

Try another experiment: sit on a rock.

What happens?

Very little.

But then...sit on a butterfly.

What happens?

The butterfly feels crushed. It's so humiliated it refuses to move. It just lies there refusing to even look like a healthy butterfly anymore.

Of course, some people will say that this is a stupid experiment. Most people believe butterflies are delicate, easily wounded things, while rocks are hard and tough to break. These people, of course, expect that if you sit on a butterfly it will die, and expect that sitting on a rock will change it very little.

But let me ask you this, if that's what you believe: what happens when a butterfly stays still and lets you sit on it?

It becomes a rock, that's what.

How can that be?

I wish I could tell you.

That's just the way it happens.

It's a miracle.

Butterflies flee: that's their nature, the way they are. Rocks stay still: that's the way they are. So if the butterfly stays still while some big ass is coming down on it, then the butterfly changes into a rock.

Like I said, it's a miracle, and it actually happens, although you might find that hard to believe.

Maybe this will help you believe it: remember that once upon a time that butterfly was a caterpillar, a type of little worm that crawled slowly along the ground. Then, it changed into a beautiful thing that could fly, could dance on the breeze. Well, that's one miracle, and I bet you'd have a hard time explaining exactly how that happens.

It's the same with me. I've seen butterflies change into rocks merely by sitting there, by refusing to be afraid. They lose their pride, and then they are rocks. All I can say about how it happens is that it's a miracle.

And it rarely happens.

Most butterflies fail.

They are full of fear.

Pride, remember, is just another form of fear.

A great deal of energy is wasted being fearful, wasted by refusing to take life as it comes. But the truth is: we creatures of the earth have only a limited amount of energy, so we pay dearly if we waste it. The butterfly darts here and there, always suspicious, always watching out for danger. By doing this it wastes its vital energy. On the other hand, rocks just sit there saving their energy. That is why rocks live forever, and butterflies die so young.

Example

Astoria is five feet eight inches tall, nearly my height. She is slender but solid; in fact her body has a certain heaviness to it. This shows in the way she walks, in the gestures she makes. Even when her movements are quick or sudden, they are also sort of weighty.

Astoria would like to be light and graceful. Sometimes she plays at it. Sometimes she will spin around, trying to twirl like a ballet star. I have seen her playfully flapping her outstretched arms while taking tiny steps across the room, pretending to be a flying swan. She laughs at herself when she does these things. She is pretending to be more graceful than she thinks she can be. She knows she's a bit awkward when she tries to get all the parts of her body moving together. She has doubts about her body and what it can do. She has rarely made big demands on it, seldom forcing it to high levels of performance. She would like to be graceful as a flying swan, but believes that she is clumsy, and so her playful pretending is a joke. Since she feels that being a swan is out of her reach, she becomes a clown. A clown-swan. But still she is the star performer in her own circus. And since she is the star, she is able to laugh at herself. These are the only times I have heard her laugh at herself.

But she does have true gracefulness deep within her. Once

when I was into yoga for a while, I persuaded her to do the stretching exercises with me.

She did and she changed.

She began to float as it were. Previously she had a sort of thumping walk, her heels hitting the floor like an elephant looking for its dinner. With the yoga exercises, she soon became graceful and light. But I went on to other things and she let the yoga slide away; soon she resumed that thumping walk with those lovely, long legs of hers.

Her thighs are long, and I love the way they wrap around my hips when we make love. I love the soft, downy, almost colorless hair that is on her legs. Bless her, when I mentioned that even her leg hair was beautiful to me, and it was a shame for her to shave it off, she said, "Okay, funny guy, if that's what you want, that's what you get." For me she stopped shaving her legs. "The hair's so blond anyway, it looks the same as if I shaved," she said.

And her cunt...I love it. It is coral colored, like if you mixed the color of a pink grapefruit and cantaloupe together. And, I love the smell of her womanhood. When things were going well between us, I used to go down there for a long time at a stretch. Nestled in her pubic hair. Her golden hair. *She* was golden. She was all different shades of gold at different times of the year. In the winter she was tall and pale gold; in the summer she tanned easily, and was tall and dark red-gold. Her hair in the summer was white gold, long with gentle waves in it, almost colorless, like moon-beams.

Sometimes I would awaken in the morning and look at her asleep, and wonder to myself, "How the hell did I get so lucky?"

Often we used to make love in the morning. That seems to me to be a sign of true affection when you see your lover beside you at the beginning of the day and suddenly everything else can wait because you want to be as close together as possible. Whatever went on the day before has been forgotten. Whatever is coming up later that day, that can wait, too. The sexual good feelings, the erotic satisfaction, the general horniness are important, but they're a lot less important than something else: they are less important than just being as close together as possible.

Yes, perhaps that gives an idea of how much a couple cares for one another, and what kind of love they share: making love in the morning.

Astoria and I were doing that when Daryl Spagnoff burst into the condo one morning three days after Horny Harriet sprung me from jail. We were gently humping and pumping away in a slow, controlled rhythm, feeling all of the deliciousness of it when we heard the front door open and slam shut.

Astoria's eyes, beneath me, popped open. She wrinkled her nose like she smelled something mildly bad. "Somebody's going to spoil our fun," she said playfully.

She had her arms wrapped around me and gave me a squeeze.

Immediately there was a tremendous swelling in my chest. It became an ache that rose up and made my throat feel thick. I felt a mammoth urge in me to tell her how much I loved her, to say how good—how deeply good—it was to have her back.

She was smiling up at me.

"I love you," I said.

She said, "I think you're the best pie in the sky." She bit me quickly on the point of my chin.

She makes me laugh.

I licked the tip of her nose.

Her nose is funny. It is very straight, without any bumps. Down the middle of it is a very faint, pale line which can just barely be seen. We have checked it out, she and I, and we've decided this line actually starts somewhere up in her hair. It's just slightly visible on her forehead and then it is more visible as it goes down the ridge of her nose and down the middle of that little piece of nose that separates the nostrils; and you can just barely see it on her upper lip. It is also there very faintly on her chin. We have joked that this faint pale line goes all the way down her body; we've traced it down between her breasts down to her belly button. One afternoon I spent fifteen minutes making her laugh, trying to trace the line into her pussy. We joked that maybe the line divides up her personality, and her life. Sometimes she seems like two people. I have always known that she loved me, but then she is hurtful, as though some part of her refuses to love me, wants to remain separate from me.

Does she want power?

Sometimes I think so.

Does she want to be able to crush me down when ever she wants, when ever she thinks it's necessary.

What good would that do her?

Besides, whenever we fight, or whenever the going gets tough, she just dances away from me, and I have to chase her, and she stays always just a step or two out of reach.

This line that divides her up: it stops at her pussy. We've looked down both legs for it, but all we found was a large, dark mole on the bottom of her left heel. Once during an argument, I told her that was where all her fucking brains had leaked out.

Comments like that did very little to heal the wounds we gave each other. They did very little to erase the line that divided her. Or divided us, who knows?

We needed help, I suppose.

Or did we?

Were we doing fine? Or what?

If we wanted help, who could give it?

Anybody?

Perhaps Daryl Spagnoff, who came into the bedroom of the condo with a black Labrador puppy under his arm?

Daryl has a big smile which is often made bigger by the dope he smokes. He has many friends and acquaintances, and rarely seems to work at any particular job. A generous fellow, he is always giving people things, usually that he has stolen.

"Hi, Blessed Wing," he said to me as I rolled off Astoria who was quickly gathering the blankets high up under her chin. "Hi, Mrs. Wing. Oh, am I interrupting something..."

"Sorry, Daryl, we had to leave you off the guest list."

"Mrs. Wing, we all enjoy the Master's sense of humor very much. We're all very glad you've come to join us. Here's a present..." He held the puppy toward us, a wiggling black ball of fur with a pink tongue and a black tail that whipped back and forth like it had a life of its own. The puppy noticed Astoria and immediately began yipping and squirming to get to her.

"For you." Daryl said to Astoria, "A present from all us."

"Oooohh! Thank you," Astoria said as the puppy leaped free of Daryl's hands and bounded into her arms. She tried to sit up and hug the pup, while still remaining modestly hidden in the sheets as the dog was climbing all over her, yipping and trying to lick her face.

"He's beautiful. You're beautiful, puppy." Astoria cooed.

The sheet around her worked free and Daryl got an eyeful of gorgeous tit. He saw, and gulped hard, and then looked at me to see if I had seen him see. I nodded to him and said, "Thanks for the dog, Daryl. He will enrich our lives."

"You're welcome, Master Wing. And I have something for you, too, but I forgot it in the car. Wait a sec." He ran out of the room. I left the bed and slipped into a pair of cut-off jeans and a yellow tank shirt, designed by Bruno, that looked like this:

across the back. I happened to be near the window (we were on the second floor) and looked down on the scene outside. A parking lot was directly below the window—the Jaguar was there—and beyond the lot was the street. There, at the curb, Daryl was reaching into the back of his old, wood-paneled station wagon which contained his surf-board and a much fucked-on mattress. My eye then went to the other side of the street, attracted by something. A person. A person was staring up at me while I was looking down at her.

It was the dark-haired girl.

Norleen.

How strange. How very strange.

I turned to look at Astoria playing freely, happily, trustingly with the puppy on the bed. Sitting bare-topped, she was waving one of my sandals under the puppy's nose, and he was jumping back and forth over her legs. He finally managed to clamp his jaws hard on the sandal. Astoria gave a wicked little laugh as he tossed his head quickly and wrenched it from her grasp. She laughed that sly laugh of hers; she enjoys strength and victories and aggressiveness. She looked up at me, giving me a huge grin and scrunching up her shoulders; her eyes got crinkly and were blazing with a moist inner light. "I'm so happy, honey. I'm so happy." she said.

I nodded and said, "Yes, me too."

She leaped out of bed and threw her arms around my neck. We spun in circles, dance-like, and came to a stop so that we were framed in the window with my wife's naked back to the street and me staring down at the dark-haired girl who was still looking up, and who could now see us both. "How strange," a voice said to me, a voice that came from far back in my brain. "How very odd that now when I have my wonderful wife back with me the dark-haired girl should become available to me also."

But my wife and I are bonded together for all time. I understood that.

How could the dark-haired girl force her way between us?

How could I open up and let her in, when Astoria and I are *one* in our love? Through all the pain we've had, our love has survived. The dark-haired girl stared up at us boldly.

I thought of the possibilities.

I remembered a New Year's Eve party when I had climbed into a dark closet with a woman I hardly knew and how soon that woman's talented mouth was sliding back and forth along my cock, and how she'd drunk my sperm like it was precious nectar while thirty feet away in another room Astoria was talking with our friends.

God, what a waste that was. My wife and I: so close but with someone else in between. Leaving that awful party, out on the lawn, at the start of the new year, I vomited and vomited: vomited so hard I thought my guts would come loose. Astoria just stood next to me, calm and quiet like she was waiting for the mail to arrive. Finally she asked, "Are you okay?"

Very little is okay, I wanted to shout at her; something is very wrong.

But I was silent. All that came out was some wine and the remains of a vile cheese dip.

"You want me to drive?" she asked.

For some reason what I said back to her—what popped out without my thinking about it—was, "I want us both to drive." It must have sounded crazy to her; she must have thought I was very drunk. She looked at me with pity, as though I was a very weak person. I climbed behind the steering wheel. My mind was as black as the closet where the stranger had given me head. What an awful way to start a year, I thought, and I made a promise to myself that it would get better, that Astoria and I would get closer together. As we drove away, Astoria sat leaning against the door on her side of the car as she always did, quiet, like she usually was.

Sorry, dark-haired girl, my wife is in my arms now and that's where we both want her to be.

Out on the sidewalk, Norleen, almost as though she had heard my thoughts, turned quickly and walked away. A couple of seconds later the condo's front door opened and closed, and Astoria made a dive back under the bedclothes, almost crushing the puppy who was sitting on a pillow happily chewing on a copy of *People* magazine that he'd pulled off the night stand. Daryl Spagnoff, grinning, handed me a parchment paper.

"I picked it up when I got the puppy his shots," Daryl said. "I bet you are missing this particular degree from your collection."

I looked at the university diploma he'd stolen for me, and said, "Yes, you're certainly right about that." Daryl had brought me a real treasure; it was the first of its kind I've ever seen. "Thank you very much, Daryl, I'm touched. Look, Astoria, I've just been awarded another diploma."

"What do you mean?"

"Well, I've just received my degree as a Doctor of Veterinary Dentistry. My D.V.D."

"What are you talking about?"

Then I remembered Astoria had yet to learn of my new enthusiasm for higher education. I explained to her I now was a collector of all types of certificates of higher learning.

"You've got to be kidding," she said.

"Education is a serious and important matter." I gestured for her to look at the walls of the room on which were tacked about forty diplomas, certificates, credentials, endorsements and similar documents of achievement including a City of Laguna license to operate a Chinese laundry.

"You've got to be kidding." Wrapping herself in a sheet she began walking around the room staring at all the papers that hung there. "I thought they were a joke. They've all got different names."

"Of course, they all have different names, Storee. They were originally awarded to different people."

"You could be arrested, for God's sake. That's stolen property."

I tried to put my arms around her, but she pushed my arms away and moved out of reach.

Being a citizen of the beach, Daryl could see the storm clouds coming. He said, "I better be going." He left the condo.

Astoria just stared at me. Finally, she said, "What's with you?" She shook her head. "It's like you've got holes in you. I mean, I look at you and there are holes...holes in you where other people have common sense. Stealing...stealing other people's..." She stopped for a moment, then burst out with, "You drive me nuts. Why do you do what you do? I mean, you're smart. You could do anything you want to." Then she yelled at me, "I want *us* to work out. I want *us* to be *together*. Do you understand?"

"*Yes.*"

"Do you really? Do you?"

"*Yes.*"

"But you always let me down. I mean, if you made up your mind to do something, *anything*, we would be rich. You get in and out of more scrapes than anybody I ever saw. You have the ability to talk to anybody. You know everybody's language. Politicians, priests, bums, everybody. Why do you always mess around? Why do you refuse to work?"

I kept quiet. I knew that even if I talked she would be reluctant to hear what I was saying. She was failing to understand.

"We could be rich," she said. "We could have a nice home. And friends. Important friends. The movers and shakers of the world could be our friends. You're as smart as any of them. They'd accept you. If you'd just be serious." She was making short gestures with her hands in front of her. Frustration. "Why? Tell me why?"

I wanted to tell her it was foolish for her to be so proud, but I kept quiet. I moved toward her to take her in my arms, but again she dodged away.

"Stay where you are," she told me and moved quickly farther off. I felt calm inside. My mind felt quiet whole and strong.

"You've got holes in you, Norris."

"Wing."

"Oh, that's so stupid. What does 'Wing' mean?" she said angrily.

Calmly, I told her, "Right now it means *me*. Tomorrow maybe it will mean something else and maybe I'll be someone else." I shrugged. "That's the way it is."

She shook her head and her face took on a defeated look. Her body sagged and she sat on the bed. The puppy, perhaps sensing she was hurt, clamored onto her lap, quieted down and lay still. Tears began to fall from her eyes, sliding in twin silver rivers down the sides of her nose and falling into the black fur of the puppy. She looked up at me, her head tilted in despair and in confusion as to what she could possibly do to make me understand. She was silently begging me to please do something that would take away her pain.

I knew I must avoid doing that.

She must accept the pain.

If I were to do that, it would be foolish. The pain is a gift. Should I distract her? I could tell her a joke. Or give her a funny line, or maybe make her a good promise. But the pain would still be there. Buried. Deep in her soul. All covered up with layers of fear. Say, *Yes* to the pain, Astoria. That's the only way to truly make it go away. Do anything else and the pain is just hidden. Drowned beneath layers of foolish hopes.

Hope is just another name for fear, Astoria.

She looked up at me with those lovely blue-gray eyes, all wet now. Her face was long and gaunt and pale, her mouth hung open. "Please," she said. "Please..."

I looked down at the parchment I held in my hand. Doctor of Veterinary Dentistry. Awarded to Michael P. Merkel.

"You are better than that, Norrie."

"Wing."

"All right, damn it. Wing. I'll call you Wing."

"Good." I whispered.

Suddenly, she bounced off the bed (the puppy leaped away) and yanked the parchment from my hand and spun out across the room as though she thought I would chase her, ripping the parchment into shreds as she fled.

She glared at me. "This belongs to someone else. Get your own. Get *something* of your own. You can do better than you are doing. Do it! Get us out of this mess, Norris or Wing, or whatever you want to be called. I want to live with you. I love you. You're my husband. Save us. I want to grow old with you. Save us, for God's sake.''

I could feel the tears rising in my eyes; she was hurting so much that I hurt too. When she saw my tears some of her anger left, and she sort of sagged. We fell into each other's arms, grasping at each other, and stood there rocking back and forth, and it was quiet for a long time.

She had buried her face in my neck and shoulder, and finally she raised her head and said, ''I want us to work out.''

Her words caused me to blink away my tears.

A memory popped into my head.

I remembered a time, several years before, when, although things seemed to be going smoothly in our lives, she had taken a lover. It was the second time she'd done it, it was the last time, the time I'd said, ''Aw, shit.''

We'd survived that crisis, our marriage continued, and—oddly—we'd hardly even discussed what had happened. Then about a year and a half later (as a matter of fact, it was on the night before the dinner party, which was just the night before I discovered *Yes*) she and I went on our evening walk and I asked her why she'd taken that lover, what had she felt at the time, what were the circumstances? I asked her to share her feelings with me as we walked along in the night.

She shot a quick look at me. She shook her head. ''That's my business,'' she said.

Now, with her in my arms, I again wanted the question answered. ''Why did you fuck what's-his-name?'' I asked her.

Storee looked confused for a moment, and then I could see she understood what I was asking about. She sighed as if it were a question she'd heard a thousand times.

''Honey,'' she said. ''Listen to me. Please. We've got a new start now. The past is past. Let it go. It's finished. Surely you can see that. A person learns their lesson, and then the lesson is learned. I know now I love you, that I've always loved you. I am going to stay with you. You are funny, and you are smart and I have a lot of respect for you, honey. Someway you and I, together, are going to work out our money troubles and any other trouble that comes along. And I know you love me, and that is all that is important.''

And then she kissed me.

Long and lovingly.

Too bad.

Such a shame.

So much pain in our past.

And so much pain still to come.

She had evaded answering my question.

She had said a lot of useless, hopeful words. She had avoided me. She had darted this way and that way, had bounced from one pretty idea to another, but refused to sit still and answer the question.

Why?

Was she afraid to look at herself?

Afraid of me?

I nodded to Astoria as though I believed and accepted her nice words, but I knew better and wondered why she had tried to snow me.

Was she, herself, confused as to why she had taken that man as her lover?

Had she ever tried to figure it out for herself?

If I had voiced these questions aloud, she might have said, ''You think too much.''

Maybe it was too embarrassing for her to remember those actions that she now regretted.

It hardly mattered, really, what the exact reason was for her evasion of my question. What was important was she refused to give me an open and honest answer. She had danced away from me, staying just out of reach. She'd wasted time, her time, our time; she was wasting her life, wasting our life together, committing the same errors over and over again. Almost certainly we would have a normal relationship for the next few weeks. She loved to lie in the sun and would probably be getting a wonderful deep red-gold tan. She would laugh and mingle with the Holy Yessers. She might even cook a few meals for me, which was something she always seemed reluctant to do, but maybe she would now, because of the infatuation and romance that was surrounding us like a fog. But the heat of life burns those things away.

It was obvious what she was going to do.

She would flutter around dropping butterfly shit all over me.

I only hoped I could behave like I was supposed to when the showdown came.

The puppy was chewing and swallowing some of the pieces of parchment that Astoria had thrown all around the room. I shook my head in sadness. "My new degree. My doctorate of Veterinary Dentistry. It's gone," I said. "Storee...?"

"What?" she said.

"Does this mean I'll be stopped from filling cavities in chickens' teeth?"

"You're a very silly person, Wing."

"I like it when you call me Wing," I told her, and I knew we were doomed.

Scrutiny

Spill your nuts upon the table
cloth, so that we may inspect them
closely, and choose the ones that suit us
best. Walnuts, almonds, cashews, or perhaps
those that hang between your legs.

Let's Drink to *Yes*

After hearing this story so far, can anyone doubt the Power of *Yes*?

Just think about it, a couple of months earlier I had been an ordinary bum, and now I was an extraordinary bum.

In early June, *Yes* had brought me to Laguna, and soon, while attempting to assist a black teenager, I had aroused the anger of two police officers (Kimberly and Gilford) who chased me into a homosexual bar where I delivered my first sermon, and, like many of the prophets in the Bible, I was attacked by disbelievers (Harold and his friends.) I was rescued by Bruno who urged me to share my wisdom with all humanity. Thus our Church was born. It enjoyed a small but immediate success. Although I asked for little in the way of material things, a number of interesting and attractive persons befriended me, easing my mind and comforting my body. Near the end of July, for the holiest of reasons, we Yessers held a demonstration at a military equipment exhibition in San Diego. This won for us a brief appearance on the six o'clock news which brought my wife back to me. Even the dark-haired girl had appeared at my window.

Let's drink to *Yes*, for *Yes* is mighty.

I even got my picture in the newspaper.

Example

"Bruno, how'd I get my fucking picture in the paper?"

Daryl had left, Astoria was in the shower, the dark-haired girl

240

had disappeared, the puppy was chewing on the leg of a table where the T.V. used to be. Bruno was eating a bowl of oatmeal across the breakfast room table from me.

"A reporter came by yesterday before Harriet sprang you from jail. I felt it was a good opportunity, Master."

There it was: my picture with Bruno standing behind me like Mount McKinley on page three.

"BEACH CULT SAYS YES TO PEACE"

By Frawley Yort.

The story contained much of what I'd been telling the Yessers about Acceptance, Cooperation and heroes.

"Did I get it right, Master Wing? I tried to tell Mr. Yort the way you would have told him if you were here."

The phone rang.

I had the impulse to let it keep ringing until the caller hung up and left me alone. What with Astoria and I making love, and Daryl coming with his presents, and the surprise appearance of Norleen outside my window, and fighting and making up with Astoria, it had been a very long day already, even if it was still only morning. I had the impulse to hide.

The telephone continued to ring.

I answered it, but instead of using my usual, normal voice, I talked in a foreign accent, making myself sound high and squeaky like an Indian from India just off the boat from Bombay. A quick-talking woman responded to my hello by announcing that she was Penelope Slick from *People* magazine. She asked to speak with Reverend Wing.

"He's having his morning rub-down, madam."

With a high, rapid voice she said she was calling from L.A. Her editor was sending her down to Laguna to interview Wing about his new church. "We need a picture of the big guy, too" Penelope said. She asked me to have myself call her back today for sure. This morning if possible.

Still pretending to be an Indian, I complained, "Perhaps

madam, but it will be very difficult. His schedule is very full.''

The front door opened without a knock first, and Joe Wagonewti, acting like he owned the place, walked in with a couple of strangers.

Bruno slopped another pound of oatmeal into his bowl.

Penelope seemed concerned that I might be lax in relaying her message to myself. Did I fully understand, she wanted to know, how valuable the national publicity might be to ''our cause'' and to Wing personally?

Joe was banging the cupboards open and shut behind me, asking Bruno how a guy could get a cup of coffee made around here.

Bruno grunted, annoyed. He thinks Joe has bad manners, and is suspicious of him.

I got up, and with the telephone cord trailing behind me, pulled the coffee can from a cupboard and started water heating on the stove.

I informed Penny that Reverend Wing had very little interest in money or self-advancement. ''Fortune is fleeting, madam, and fame a great burden.''

Astoria walked into the room wearing some beach stuff: a slit skirt (with flowery designs) that showed a lot of thigh; her halter bra had the same flowery print, and there was a white flower in her golden hair. She was a garden any man would want to visit. Wagonewti's friends looked like they were going to drop their teeth when they saw her.

Penelope expressed the doubt that I had ever even heard of her famous magazine.

One of Joe's friends looked to be in his mid-fifties, a slump-shouldered man with a long pale face and little, squinty eyes. The other fellow was younger, maybe thirty-five, a dark man who looked like he had come from some foreign country that got a lot of sunshine.

''Of course, we know your magazine, Madam,'' I said with

my Indian accent. "Just this morning our dog was eating a recent issue."

Joe and the dark man buzzed around Storee like they wanted to land on her flowers.

But the slump-shouldered guy just stood there as if his dick was on ice.

The water was starting to boil.

Penny wanted to know who the hell I was anyway.

Bruno's oatmeal was nearly gone.

"If I ever find out, my dear lady, I shall be most happy to tell you."

I hung up.

The dog was starting to poop in front of the couch.

"Storee...!" I said, pointing at our little fur ball. She scooped him up and ran for the front door, crying, "Wait. Oh, boy, oh, boy."

Joe said to me and Bruno, "Wing, I'd like you to meet my good friends here: Mr. Shifty Eddie and Fernando Clip."

Joe was talking more formally than usual, so I knew something was up, some sort of business deal was on the agenda.

Fernando Clip had a medium-expensive, dark blue shirt, light blue slacks—very color coordinated—and a thick gold chain around his neck. He wore a moderately expensive designer watch, and highly polished shoes. His hair was wavy with expensive razor-cut styling. On the other hand, Shifty Eddie wore jogging shoes, crappy polyester pants, and a sport shirt that probably looked good a long time ago with some other outfit. His eyes were calm, almost bored, while Fernando had an eager, interested look. It was obvious that in this deal, Shifty Eddie was the one who had all the money. It's mainly the strong people who dress the way they want without worrying about other people's opinions of their attire.

The phone rang again.

I nodded toward Bruno, silently asking him to answer it. He did.

Astoria came back inside with the dog.

Joe said that Shifty Eddie was considering making a significant contribution to my church.

Hearing that, Astoria's head bobbed up like a golden retriever spotting a duck.

"Give and ye shall receive," I mentioned.

Shifty Eddie nodded as though he'd had the same thought. Bruno was telling the caller that, yes, if the camera crew is here by two o'clock, they could set-up and the Master would receive them at four.

I wondered what the fuck was going on with Bruno and a camera crew? And with Shifty Eddie and a religious contribution?

The dog began nibbling at Storee's left toes. She, annoyed, sharply nudged it away with her foot. "What sort of contribution were you thinking of?" she asked Shifty Eddie while tossing her head and nervously brushing some of her blonde curls back behind her ear.

I thought it would have been better for her to keep quiet and let me talk instead.

Bruno was still speaking into the phone, telling the caller to check with someone named Marshall Merriweather.

Joe answered Astoria's question directly to me. "With your expanding congregation, you're gonna outgrow this condo place pretty soon. So Shifty can let you use some facilities he's got."

"That's very kind of you, Shifty."

Shifty gave me a quiet nod and was still.

Bruno hung up and smiled at me like he had another set of birthday golf clubs behind his back. He was so eager and full of good news, he looked ready to burst. His grin set world records.

"What sort of facilities?" Astoria wanted to know.

Joe again spoke directly to me. "A nice big room," he said, "and it's got a kitchen."

"We can have church socials," I said, as though that were a wonderful thing.

"Yeah," Joe agreed. "Say, could we get some coffee?"

Astoria jumped from the couch like her tail was on fire. Soon she was clattering cups and—for God's sake—saucers, putting them in front of the three visitors and me. I nodded with my head that she'd forgotten Bruno.

While she was bustling around, making a commotion, I used the time to ask Bruno who'd called.

"It was KOJO-TV, Blessed Wing. They're coming to do a feature story on you for the afternoon news program. A show called *San Diego P.M.*"

"Pretty marvelous, Bruno."

"Thank you, sir."

"Would you tell me what the fuck I'm going to say to them?"

"*Yes!*" said Bruno, grinning like a kite.

While she was making the coffee, Fernando Clip had his eyes on Astoria, watching her every move, with a look on his face like he wanted to offer her cocaine. On his dick.

Shifty Eddie sat quietly, almost bored, like he was waiting for Thursday.

Joe re-opened the conversation, "It's sort of a restaurant, Wing."

"What sort of a restaurant?"

"A disco restaurant."

"A disco restaurant?"

"Yeah."

"You want to give me a disco restaurant?"

"Yeah, Wing. Just to use for a while. You'll love it. It'll be great for you. A great meeting place for your church."

"Bruno, they want to give me a disco restaurant."

Bruno grunted; anyone could tell he had reservations about this restaurant.

But, then, he was always suspicious about everything anyway.

Astoria, on the other hand, had her ears up like an elk; she was finishing up making the coffee.

"Joe?"

"Yeah, Wing."

"Disco's dead."

"So's the restaurant," Fernando chimed in, laughing at his own joke.

"Look, Wing," Joe said, "I'm going to level with you."

Storee began pouring the coffee and Joe waited while she did it, and I used the pause to ask Bruno, "How come they want to interview me?" I stared at him right into his wide eyes, pinning him down because he has committed me to something I was going to have difficulty dealing with. Of course, I knew that I should accept the opportunity of going on T.V. to expand my business of spreading the Wonderful Word. On the other hand, my life was getting out of fucking control, especially this morning. It was beginning to feel like a landslide had started. Like the ground was giving way beneath my feet.

"You were gone," Bruno said defending himself, "and I felt that I was in a responsible position and it seemed to me that we had an opportunity..."

"A what?"

"If the newspaper was interested in you then probably T.V. would be too. Master, surely you can see that. It was a great opportunity and I, well, happen to know the producer of the show. Marshall is a very good, dear friend of mine..."

"Wing, Joe interrupted, "Let's get back to business. Mr. Shifty Eddie has another appointment to make this morning."

I nodded, "Sure" to Joe while thinking to myself that maybe Bruno had taken advantage of a certain type of connection. Maybe Marshall Merriweather was an old butt-fucking buddy from way back. Maybe it was a slow week on *San Diego P.M.* and Marshall could do a favor for a dear friend and, at the same time, fill up some air time with some odd people of local interest.

Storee had kicked off her sandals, and the puppy was chewing one. Clip was feasting his eyes on my wife. Joe was about to

246

feed me a line of horseshit. Astoria was pouring coffee all around and watching our conversation the way sharks watch tunas. It was meal time in Laguna.

"Hey," Joe said, "here's the deal. My friend, Shifty Eddie here, is a man of substance. But it is a fact of financial life that some investments fail to perform as well as some others. A while ago, Shifty Eddie bankrolled some associates who desired to open a disco down near the marina in San Diego. It is also a fact of life that as this club opened its doors the whole disco world fell over and died. So it happens now that Shifty Eddie is stuck with almost five hundred thousand dollars worth of equipment."

Astoria let out a soft whistle.

"...sound equipment, furniture, laser lights, and all that kitchen shit. And then, too, he's on the hook for the lease of the building."

"Sounds like a tough spot to be in," I said sympathetically, "How can I help?"

"Well, with business being bad now, and the whole economy being the way it is, Shifty Eddie has had difficulty finding anyone who's willing to take on such a big nut. It's very expensive to operate a store like this one."

"I believe it."

"Well, yeah, sure."

"Sure," I said.

"But if Shifty Eddie was to donate the whole thing to the religion of his choice..."

"Mine?"

"Right. Then he could write the whole mess off as a charitable deduction against his other income which is considerable."

"Oh."

Bruno interrupted to say, "I would think that it would be possible to write off these expenses as straight business losses. Why is it you need a charitable deduction?"

Storee scowled at Bruno like he'd been throwing flies in her perfume.

"Yeah, Bruno, sure..." Joe said. "The accountant got all this stuff figured out. They think we ought to do it this way."

"Oh," Bruno said.

I could smell money floating around this deal—these men were serious about something—so I told Bruno that the tax people were reluctant to let a person write off equipment unless it was actually being used and worn out.

As I said it, I wondered if it was true.

"That's right, Wing, that's right," Joe said.

Shifty Eddie nodded his pale face.

Astoria and Bruno looked slightly pleased that I understood these things.

The dog began relieving himself under the table where the T.V. once was. I gestured with my head, and Astoria jumped up saying, "Oh, boy, oh, boy." Holding the pup at arm's length in front of her she dashed outside.

"Say," I told the group, "I got an idea." I paused dramatically. "We could start a Holy Restaurant."

Joe beamed broadly and smiled and nodded at Shifty Eddie. "See, I told you he was smart."

"How about the menu...?" I said. "We could serve Lamb of God. Fillet of Soul."

Even Shifty Eddie smiled at that one.

"...we got Angel Food Cake. We got Devils Food..."

That got less of a response.

"Well, how about Garden of Eden salad?"

Astoria looked at me like she thought I ought to get back to business.

So I did.

The truth of the matter was that they were taking too fucking long to get their story out.

It was time to speed things up.

"Joe, Shifty, I know very little about restaurants. They give you a menu and you order. But actually running a restaurant is an entirely different thing. What I need is someone with disco-restaurant experience who can help me manage the place.'' I pointed my finger at Fernando Clip.

Joe said, ''Shifty, I told you, the guy is very quick.'' To me he said, ''Wing, sometimes you surprise even me. Here's the deal. Nano has been managing clubs on the east coast. Atlantic City, New York. This is going to be a turn-key operation for you. We're going to set up the whole thing. All you have to do is take over as owner, and, you know, promote the thing. Advertise, and get the customers in the door. You know what I mean? You'll own the club, and Nano will manage it for you. He knows how to buy all the supplies: the food, hiring the help, all that stuff. We'll take care of the liquor license.''

''What about seed money?''

''Fernando has funds to get you through the first few months of expenses.''

''Why me?''

''Like I said. Religious contribution for tax purposes.''

''Joe,'' I said, ''Hinduism has been around for thousands of years. Christianity has been around for thousands of years. Islam has been around for thousands of years. *Yes* has been around since June.''

''We're gonna take care of that, Wing. We're gonna register you with the Worldwide Church of Inspirational Faith. We send them fifty bucks and they send you back a charter that says you're a legal church. Yeah, that's right. Honest to God. You get this charter thing and you're a real church and the government tax shits got to leave you alone. It's been tested in court.''

''And you want me to front this thing for you?''

Joe nodded. ''A lot of religions are getting into legitimate businesses. It's a gimmick. The Moonies got stores all over the country.''

I thought for a few moments, wondering what was in it for me, wondering what sort of opportunity was coming my way if only I were willing to say the Wonderful Word.

"Joe, we got a problem. I only have one toga."

Joe shrugged. Shifty Eddie nodded, though, showing he understood immediately what I was getting at.

"Joe, if I spill Holy Spaghetti on it, I'm out of commission for the rest of the night."

Fernando laughed and looked at Astoria to see if she was laughing too. She looked puzzled. Bruno was paying strict attention to everything in the room. Shifty Eddie looked like he was asleep with his eyes open.

"I hear you, Wing." Joe said. "You can draw $1800 a month." Astoria's eyes widened, and she crossed her legs. There may have been times when I failed to bring home $1800 a year.

"You gotta be kidding, Joe." I told him. "What the fuck can you buy for 1800 bucks a month? I need more money than that."

"Jesus Christ, Wing, you think you're the Pope? You wanna get paid like the Pope, for Christ's sake?"

"Thanks very much for the offer, Joe. I only wish I could accept it."

Bruno grunted.

"All right. You can have two grand a month."

"$2400," I said.

Astoria's eyes were bouncing back and forth from Joe to me like she was watching tennis.

"I love you dearly like a brother, Wing, but leave some juice in the fruit. It's a bad idea to squeeze it dry."

"Fruit, bullshit. It's a fucking orchard, Joe. Let's be honest."

Joe sat back. He smiled. "I'm as high as I can go."

It was very quiet in the room.

Here's what I thought of: I thought of cashmere sweaters for Astoria. Maybe some of those expensive sneakers they make these days for my boy and girl.

"All right," I said, feeling like I had just sold my soul to the devil.

"All right what?" Joe asked.

"All right, it's a deal. I'll be very happy to go to work for you guys."

Joe seemed pleased with the outcome of our negotiations and began talking loudly and quickly. He joked about the waitresses we'd have, "We'll put 'em in tank tops like this thing you're wearing," he said, referring to the Holy Church of the Slippery Word shirt that Bruno had made for me. "Look, I'll tell you what," he said, "This is going to be a very big thing. You do your T.V. interview today. It'll be good publicity, be sure to mention the restaurant. Name it anything you want. I'll give Nano here your number and he'll call you tomorrow and take you by the place so you can see it. Right, Nano?"

Fernando Clip nodded and said, "You, too, Mrs. Wing. You come, too."

Astoria smiled like he'd handed her roses.

"Hey, that's great," Joe said, getting up. "We're gotta get going to our other appointments." Nano Clip and Shifty Eddie stood. "Here, Wing," Joe said pulling out his wallet. "Here's something to get us started." He pulled out a small pad of currency and started counting out hundred dollar bills. He stopped at ten. Then added two more. "Here's twelve hundred. Buy some more of those tank tops, and maybe get yourself a new toga or something."

"Hey, that's great, Wagonewti," I told him. "It's going to be good working with you guys."

Astoria's lovely eyes were wide and looked dazed like her brain had shifted into neutral.

"Damn right," Wagonewti said.

One by one, we all shook hands and the three of them exited.

After the door closed behind them, I went into the bedroom which looked out on the parking lot and the street beyond where I'd seen the dark-haired girl looking up at Astoria and me when Astoria was naked and we were, for a moment, happy. I wanted to see what kind of car they'd come in. Maybe get the license plate number. I wanted to know what was going on, really? Who knew?

I slid the window open.

There were footsteps on the pavement below as the three of them walked beneath my window, just out of sight.

There was a voice. Joe's.

"I like to lay some money up front to get a guy firmly into the deal...like get him obligated to me," Wagonewti said. "So, hey, what do you think? He'll do, huh?"

"Yeah, he'll be all right," Fernando said.

"What do you think, Shifty?"

There was a pause; Shifty Eddie spoke for the first time.

"He's a trouble maker."

To be or to fuck myself,
That is the question?
Is it better to continue taking shots from
    this outrageous world
Or to say, "To hell with it,"
And die?

The Verb: To Fuck

Surely, you've noticed the title of this book contains a word that's rarely used in polite society. It was difficult to decide whether to use that word, or instead just title the book *Yes!* Finally, the word was used because it is one of the two most important words in the world.

The other most important word is, of course, *Yes*.

These two words are linked together like left and right, like male and female. *Fuck* is the opposite of *Yes*, and like *Yes* it's a mysterious word full of meanings that are hard to grasp. Slippery meanings.

As a matter of fact, very few people, even among the professors who earn their living studying words, truly and fully understand this word.

What does *fuck* mean?

Is it merely an obscenity? A dirty word that refers to a physical act?

Well, for some people, perhaps yes, it's only that.

But for most people it means something more.

Come with me and I'll share with you what I've learned about this strange word.

Example

"Things are certainly going nicely," I said to myself one day early in my stay at Laguna before Astoria arrived. I was lying

255

against a beach backrest, gazing contentedly at the wonderful sea, thinking of the easy, comfortable life I'd begun to lead. The sun had warmed me completely, and I was too lazy even to dig my toes in the sand. "Ah, yes, I'm well-fed and well-fucked."

Then I thought how strange it was that I'd used the word fuck in connection with being comfortable. Normally, the word is used to announce angry or hostile emotions. A crucial and all-important question popped into my mind. "What does *fuck* mean?" I asked myself.

The crucial and important question drifted away. The day was just too nice, too accommodating, for heavy thoughts. But, like a mosquito that bites a poor tribesman in the jungle, my little question caused an infection in my mind and spirit that gradually began to plague me for an answer. At odd times during the following days, weeks, and years, I would ask myself such things as, Why do people say, "What the fuck's going on?" What's that mean? Why use *fuck* there? To an ever increasing degree I became obsessed with figuring out the meaning of the word. It haunted me, popping into my mind when I was in the shower, or eating, or even fucking. Like most people who run up against a question that baffles them I soon turned to a friend for assistance.

I turned to Alice.

I asked her about it one night while we were walking on the beach, our feet warmed by sand that retained some of the heat of the day. In her opinion, it was usually "lower class people" with poor educations who needed foul language to express themselves. My frequent use of the word puzzled her, she said, because I seemed to be educated and had "a way with words."

It bothered me that she would call some people "lower class" but I kept my annoyance to myself.

Why do people use the word at all, I asked her. She said, after thinking about it for a moment or two, that maybe it had something to do with "frustration." And maybe the people who used it were confused about their sexual identity, she said. The night was warm and pleasant; a three-quarters moon and a thousand stars provided all the light we needed. As we strolled along I wondered if Alice would be willing to fuck with me on the sand. (This was a short while before I showed her how good vegetables were.)

"I bet you've used it yourself, Alice, some time or other."

She laughed gaily, remembering a time when, yes, once she had. She told me her ex-husband was a very macho guy, a man who liked to publicly display his control over her. To her embarrassment he would order her around in front of other people, or criticize her. She said she'd accepted this treatment silently when it occurred, waiting until the two of them were alone to protest and to ask him to treat her with proper respect in public.

But he continued his ways and refused to change.

Finally, at a Christmas gathering at which both their families were present in large numbers, he loudly ordered her to do some little task, like getting him a drink, I think it was, and when she brought it he raised his voice so crudely they became the center of attention with everyone watching while he criticized her for getting it too slowly.

She stared at him a few moments, and finally said, "Well, fuck you." Alice grinned at me, looking guilty and happy at the same time. "He died, Wing. Literally. And everybody started clapping." Alice and I laughed together at the memory of her victory over the petty tyrant who'd tried to rule her. I thought to myself, Yes, everyone shall be free from those who abuse them.

But the real meaning of *fuck* was still a mystery to me, and I wanted to get to the bottom of it. "Alice, obviously there is a lot of anger tied up in that word. But why is the idea of anger combined with the idea of sex. Why do people scrawl on a wall, 'Fuck you'? What are they angry about, who are they really talking to, and what are they really saying? What do they want to happen?"

She agreed with me that this was a puzzle, and then her mind made an interesting little jump. She said, "What about when people say 'I'm so fucking happy' or say, 'That was fan-fucking-tastic'?"

"Yes, that is interesting," I agreed. "Those are very positive statements. What have they got to do with the idea behind 'Fuck you.'? Why can *fuck* be used to express feelings of anger, frustration, sexual confusion *and* happiness. And dirty shirts, too?"

"Dirty shirts?" Alice asked.

"Yeah, I got a fucking spot on my shirt," I said, pointing to a small strain of lamb chili on my gangster t-shirt.

She laughed and I wondered aloud, "What's the connection? How does it all tie together?" It mattered a great deal to me; I was straining for answers as though reaching for a world-shaking discovery. Alice stopped walking, and looked at me. So I stopped too and turned to face her. "You know why I like you, Wing?" she asked. "Most of the time I go through life like I'm watching a movie. With you I'm in the movie."

Alice and I got very close that night, but our discussion of what the word actually meant was postponed. The next time I saw her, she said that when she arrived home the following morning she'd spent two hours writing down what the word might mean. I'd really got her going, she said. It was the first time she'd ever been late opening her travel agency, she added. I was still curious about the meaning of the word, so I asked her to let me see what she'd written. (As a matter of fact, you know, it took me three years of thinking about it while working on this fucking sheep ranch before I finally came up with the answer.) It could be difficult for me to see what she'd written, Alice said sheepishly, because when she returned home from work and re-read it, she'd thought she'd done a poor job and burned it in her fireplace.

What an idiot, I thought to myself. You had to feel sorry for Alice because she had so little confidence in her own abilities, and was ashamed of her effort. "Alice, you were a big help to me when you brought up the idea of being 'so fucking happy.' It was a great contribution to the discussion and put a whole new slant on things. It expanded the whole idea of what *fuck* might mean."

I was momentarily irritated that her wisdom had gone up in smoke, but I realized that "*Yes*, I should accept it." Obviously fate wanted me to figure the rest of the puzzle out for myself. It was an opportunity. A challenge that I must meet alone.

Too bad, Alice.

Better luck next time.

The Banning of *Fuck*

I hope you love and cherish the English language as I do.

As a tool for expressing ourselves, it's flexible and powerful. And big, too.

There are over 600,000 Standard English words.

We have a great melting pot of a language that has accepted immigrant words from many foreign tongues. Among these hundreds of thousands of words available to us, there are two—and only two—that share a unique and curious honor above all others: between the early 1700's and 1961 these two Standard English words were the only ones left out of all dictionaries, and which were illegal to print in full, except in official reports and learned papers.

It seems the people who controlled the printing presses were ill-at-ease in the presence of these words.

The words are f--k and c--t.

The people who controlled the printing presses accepted other words that seemed to mean the same things: sexual intercourse and getting-it-on. Vagina and bush.

But they drew the line at f__ and c__.

Why did they draw the line at f**k and c**t?

What is it about these two words that makes the rulers of society, the executives and lawmakers, so nervous they hate to see ***k and ***t on a page?

And here's something else that's odd. It concerns the

professors in universities and colleges who dig into languages looking for new and interesting facts about words. Even these men and women who are so dedicated to their work always left f*c* and *un* out of the books they wrote, although they knew perfectly well these two words existed and were used by many people.

Example

The people who use these words most are soldiers. My father once told me that when he was a new soldier in training camp the use of these figures of speech was so common that the army put up a sign saying:

FOUL LANGUAGE IS BUT A CRUTCH UPON WHICH UNEDUCATED PEOPLE MUST LEAN TO EXPRESS THEMSELVES

It seems that the army officers agreed with Alice that the so-called lower classes need this word more than the so-called upper classes.

And it is certainly true that most of us become annoyed when someone who continually injects the ''f'' word into his, or her, conversation. Most of us are quite careful about using it in polite society. I remember a party, back when I was a young man, when a group of us fellows and gals were sitting around telling jokes. Some of the jokes were a little dirty, but it was all in the spirit of fun and everyone joined in. Everyone, that is, except for one fellow who'd been silent the whole while. We urged him to participate, but he declined saying the only joke he knew contained words which he was too embarrassed to voice in mixed company. We—including the young women present—requested he overcome his shyness, and contribute to the general merriment. Again he expressed his timidness. We suggested if he refused again we'd throw him out on his rear. Finally, he agreed to tell his joke, but only on this condition: when he got to the "f" word he would say the number 1 instead of the word itself. When he got to the "c" word he would say the number 2.

"Okay," we agreed.

"Well, it goes like this; there were a couple of French cocksuckers walking down the street..."

Say *Yes* to Confusion

At times, things come into our minds and refuse to go away. Now and then we become obsessed by something that has happened to us, some incident we are having difficulty putting behind us. Or perhaps it is a melody, a snatch of song we know is familiar but we've forgotten the title. The song keeps playing in our head like a record that refuses to be shut off.

Sometimes when this sort of thing occurs we ask ourselves, "Why am I thinking this?" Rarely do we take the question further though. Instead, we normally try to tune it out rather than find an answer.

It's a normal human response to retreat from confusion.

It takes a lot of energy to try to figure things out.

But I am here to suggest to you that perhaps it's worth the effort. Figuring out what is confusing us sometimes allows us to take great leaps forward in our lives.

Example

I was puzzled by the word *fuck*.

How could one word combine the ideas and feelings of anger, frustration, happiness and sexual contact, all in four letters.

Why did people with poor educations use it more than other people?

Why did soldiers use it more than anybody?

Why did the rulers of society, the executives, lawmakers, and opinion-molders feel so ill-at-ease with the word that they banished it from society as completely as they could?

And

mainly

why the fuck did I care about the word anyway?

All this was very confusing. These questions slid through my brain repeatedly during the time I spent in Laguna and continued afterwards. One day shortly after arriving at this ranch, I thought I'd found the answer. When I first began working here my duties included cleaning the bunkhouse and cooking and doing household chores, and while I worked, my mind would wander. One day while rinsing rice for the ranchhands' lunch, it came to me: *fuck* meant one thing at one time, and at other times it meant something else.

Sometimes it meant anger... as in "That fucking asshole."

Sometimes it meant affection...as in "You're the best fuck in the world, honey."

I was elated. At last I'd figured it out.

How simple!

Now I could forget about the whole thing.

And did I?

Yes.

But only for a very short time. Soon the question started popping back into my head again. "What does *fuck* mean, damn it?" Over and over it came, so I knew that my original answer lacked something. I realized that strange as it may seem, the word had only one meaning whether you were angry, frustrated, happy or whatever. Yes, it meant only one thing, but what?

Finally, one day when they had me digging a couple of holes for a new outhouse, I realized the necessity of getting some help figuring this thing out. It was then that I remembered that in universities and colleges there are professors who have developed a whole science for studying words. Like bone hunters digging into Egyptian tombs, these men and women dig into languages looking for interesting discoveries about words. Maybe they had already figured out what *fuck* meant.

"Life's great," I said to myself aloud as I finished digging the holes. "Whenever you're in trouble there's always someone who's had the problem before you and can help you out."

Another fellow and I began carrying the old outhouse to its new location over the holes I'd made. As we struggled with our burden, our knees bumping against the weathered boards, I recalled what I knew about the word-scientists. These people knew all the old languages—the ones that had fallen out of use. They even knew about the languages mankind was speaking when people still lived in caves—the tongues from which our modern languages had developed. They would be able to tell me all about the word that puzzled me, and I smiled to myself knowing I was God damn lucky to be living in a world where scientific people were interested in these things and could tell me the answer to my question.

It was spring and there was a lot of work to be done on this fucking ranch, helping with the lambing and sheep shearing. But even so, I quietly slipped away, hiding in a shipment of wool we were trucking to town. Once there, I jumped from the truck as we rolled to a stop, and made my way to the local community college, plucking wool off of my clothes as I went.

The librarian pointed me toward the dictionaries and reference books. The dictionaries told me what I already knew, that the word was obscene and referred to the most common sex act. Big deal. Eagerly, I moved on to the heavy books of the word-scientists.

It was then I found out *it was a mystery to them, too.*

What the fuck?

They were as confused as I was.

I studied the books earnestly, almost refusing to believe these people could let me down. But after hours of study the answer still eluded me. Looking at the wall clock I realized the truck would soon be leaving for the return trip to the ranch. Needing to act quickly, I piled six or eight large books on top of one another and hauled them to the xerox machine to make copies of all the pages having anything to do with the word *fuck*. There were more than a dozen pages, and at the end I had only one more dime left. I thought for a moment and came up with the idea of xeroxing the page with *orgasm* on it.

I missed the truck home; maybe it was waiting for that one last orgasm that made me late. How often that has happened to me.

Hitchhiking back, I fell asleep in the car driven by a stranger to whom I'd barely spoken, and we went sixty miles past my turnoff. As evening fell, I caught another ride back in the direction I'd come. I got off at the proper turnoff, a lonely one-lane road, and started walking. The world was closing down for the night. The crickets were chirping in the prairie grass, and in the chill spring air a couple of owls glided silently through the deep dusk, mouse hunting. Before long it was too dark to see them—so dark that two or three times I walked off the road and stumbled on the dirt shoulder, and tripped on rocks. It was about twenty miles back to the ranch; I arrived in the black, cold part of the morning, pleased with my adventure, although on the road I'd been afraid of the usual terrors of the night.

Lying on my bunk bed about a week later, reading the xeroxed pages by lantern light, I became acquainted with the word *fey*. It meant *doomed*, or *going to die soon*. It also meant *wildly giddy*, and *light-headed*. The word carries the idea of someone who knows deep down in their soul that their going to die soon and who cracks under the pressure, smiling crazily and laughing with a mad look in their eyes. *Fey* is related to *fuck*, the books said.

Well, this was all very fine, and good, and interesting.

Yes, but it did very little to explain why people say, ''I'm so fucking happy,'' if they, say, won the lottery. What has sex got to do with the lottery—except maybe if you win you have more time to fool around? And why do people say, "I've got an f-ing spot on my shirt," because shirts rarely, if ever, have sex. Could it be that the word was just an expletive, a little explosive sound that we use to add emphasis to our speaking? Is 'Oh, fuck' the same as 'Oh, phooey'?

Yes, in a way it is. But more people say fuck than phooey, so it's a good bet that the more popular word carries some special meaning, I realized.

"Hey, Jimmy," somebody yelled at me. "What're you doing?" He was one of the shepherds at the poker table at the far end of the bunkhouse.

"I'm reading."

"Yeah, well quit playing with your dick, and come on over here, and give us a chance to take some of your money."

Joining them, our poker playing ended hours later with me taking $15 of their money instead; I had to wait until the next night to continue my investigation.

It seemed very strange to me that the men and women who studied words as their life's work had done such a poor job of explaining *fuck*. They seemed to have a lot of ideas, and had given me some useful information, but the final answer was still missing.

I would have to supply it myself.

Good bye, my love.
It's time to go.

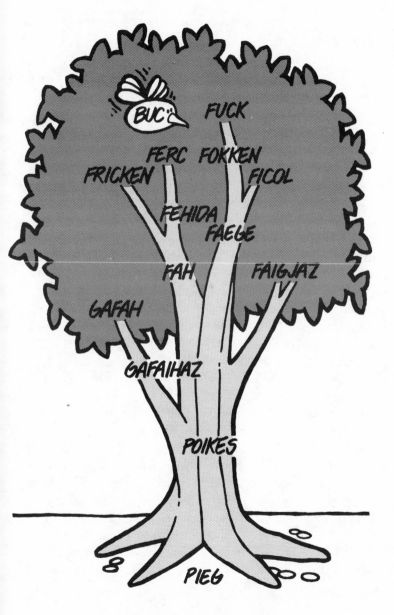

Fuck's family tree

Fuck's Family Tree

So that you may gain a full and confident knowledge of *Yes* it's necessary to relay to you some of what I discovered about *Yes*'s opposite.

This is what I learned from the professors who study words.

In the beginning there were very few languages in the world. As people spread across the earth new languages developed from the old ones. Hundreds of new ones were born.

In much the same way, a single ancient word might be the ancestor, the grandparent, to dozens of words that exist today in different languages.

Such is the case with the word *fuck*. All but one of the scientists believe that its grandparent was the ancient word *pieg* which means *evil-minded* or *hostile*.

That's certainly a fine beginning for a word that has become the most popular curse word of all time, right?

Down through the centuries *pieg* changed into other words: it changed into *gefah* (foe, or enemy) and into *fehida* (revenge) which in turn changed into our modern word *feud*, meaning a bitter fighting between families or individuals. Sure, it makes sense the two words are related. Fuck, feud. Us against them. Fuck them.

Another related word is *ficol* which turned into our modern word *fickle*, meaning a false lover, someone who makes out with other people: the sort of activity that Astoria used to surprise me with.

Finally, in the past few hundred years there have appeared a few words that actually sound like *fuck*. One is the Dutch word *fokken*, meaning both *to strike* and *to have sex with*. Another is the Irish word *ferc*, meaning *angry at*.

It turns out that the word *fuck*, itself, is a modern word, only a few hundred years old, but it has become popular and today 95 out of 100 people use it, at least occasionally, and 4 of the other 5 are lying.

Do you see the problem with all this?

Something's wrong.

Somehow the ancient word *pieg*, meaning *hostile, evil minded* developed into a word relating to the most personal and loving act that people do together.

But the word-scientists fail to tell us how the ideas of sex and anger came to be united in one word. In fact, they seem to be in the dark even about *when* the union came about.

Besides that, the ancient word *pieg* sounds very different from *fuck*. Anybody with an ear can hear that. So how can they be related to reach other?

One scientist, with a different idea from the rest of them, decided that Wonderword's opposite must have some other grandparent. As a likely choice, he picked the ancient word *buc* which meant a *point*, and *to pierce, to penetrate*. Considering the mechanics of sexual union, it's easy to see how the word *buc* might become a word for intercourse. And indeed it did. *Buc* became a lot like our word *screw*. It meant about the same thing. The problem is that anger, hate, and frustration are missing from *buc*, and, besides, it starts with a 'b' instead of an 'f'.

Where did the 'f' come from?

The word-people are silent on that point.

But I think I've finally figured it out. Here's how:

Example A

I was stumped.

Weeks went by.

Months.

Gradually, I came to realize that somehow *fuck* had just appeared in our language. Something had happened and— bang— there it was.

Baffling as this search was, there were a few chuckles along the way. One of the xeroxed pages contained examples of the word from the first times it appeared in print. In 1503, a poet named Dunbar wrote, "Be his feiris, he wald have fukkit." For a couple of days I'd drop that into conversations around the ranch. Somebody would say, "How you doin'?" and I'd say, "Be his feiris, he wald have fukkit!" The ranchhands started looking at me out of the corners of their eyes, so I figured I better stop before I lost my job. The truth is, I was hoping someone would tell what it meant.

In 1535, in a book titled *Satyre* was the line, "Bishops may fuck their fill and be unmarryit." In 1650, in *Percy's Book* was the line, "It made him haue a mighty mind to kisse and to ffuck." I hope Percy could screw better than he could spell.

In 1707, in the book *Fifteen Plagues Of A Maidenhead* was the line, "But I, a poor Virgin, am without a F---." It's the sort of problem lot's of guys would be glad to help her with. But, did you notice, this is the first time *fuck* started losing its letters.

There were dozens of these examples of the uses of the word: "Well, Lamelo," says Cidron, "while you're waiting to get married do you want to be entertained or educated?" "Well, Dad, what I really want to do is fuck."

I was stuck.

Forget the chuckles, the xeroxed pages were failing to provide the final answer to what the word meant all the time, however it was used.

The question went to sleep in my head like a bear in winter. It ceased to bother me although I knew it was there and would someday get up and rumble around in my brain, scratching and clawing. There was work to be done on the ranch; months more went by and my duties and responsibilities as a shepherd increased as my knowledge of the business grew. In time, I became fond of the work, taking pleasure in a job well done. One evening, comfortably tired after a good day's effort, I stood on a small hill looking west into the setting sun. The sky was painted in long streaks of purple and orange that glowed. Along the horizon, the distant mountains were black, except for the peaks which burned like flaming saw-teeth in the sun's dying light. Those mountains, I knew, were more than fifty miles away, yet the air was so clear I could see details on them—the valleys and ridges—as though they were much closer. All this fine scenery made me remember back to the time I'd lived in Los Angeles. The air had been so polluted that when you drove down Wilshire Boulevard, the Hollywood Hills were often hidden and invisible behind a gray curtain of smog, although those hills were only five miles away.

"Fucking smog," I said, remembering.

As soon as I said it I had the answer.

I knew what *fuck* meant, and when it was born.

Everything—the whole answer—was there. It came into my head and I had it.

As the days went by, the answer became clearer, and I figured out the solutions to all the other little questions, like why the word lost its letters and such.

What is *smog?*

The word itself, I mean?

It's a combination word.

A combination of smoke and fog. Somebody had put the two words together.

People had needed a new word to describe a new thing:

industrial air pollution. Smog is something that looks like fog but is dirty like smoke.

What is *fuck*?

It's something that looks like love but is dirty like hate.

It's a combination word, I figure.

Somehow the word *buc* (to penetrate, to have sex with) was combined with any of the 'f' words: with *fah* (enemy) or *fehida* (revenge), or with *feud* or *ferc* (anger).

That evening as I was standing on that hilltop, I thought of rape. In my mind was a murky picture, a vague image, of a person.

Maybe a woman.

Maybe a man.

Whoever it is has been harmed, taken advantage of, wounded.

This person feels helpless, powerless, violated. The deed has been done to them, and now they have to live with it. This person mutters the word for angry. *Ferc*. Then mutters the word for sex. *Buc*. Then says the words aloud. Ferc buc. Angry sex. Angry penetrating. Or maybe fah buc. Enemy sex. Six hundred years ago—in pain, perhaps in rage—the victim stumbles over the words, stutters, and ferc buc becomes fuc. Later a 'k' is added. *Fuck,* a new word, a useful word, had been invented. It describes the act of your soul being beaten, conquered and used.

Example B

As I watched from the condo window, Joe, Fernando and Shifty Eddie climbed into Joe's late-model Chevrolet and drove down the street out of sight. As I went into the living room, I thought about the job they's offered me. It was very quiet in there, as though each of us was waiting for someone else to start the conversation.

This day was getting screwier by the minute. Making love in the morning with Astoria had been nice, but then there'd been

Daryl's presents, Norleen's appearance, the fight with Astoria, and now Bruno had signed me up for a T.V. appearance, and out of the blue I'd been offered a strange but interesting job. And we were still on the early side of noon.

I felt hassled and my stomach churned.

"Storee, honey, I'm starved."

"Norrie, this could be a great opportunity."

"How do you mean?"

"Well, in a way they're offering you a job. If this restaurant was successful, you might even be able to start a chain of restaurants."

"Yes, you're absolutely right. But speaking of food, I'm real hungry."

She looked annoyed.

"Look, Storee," I told her, "it's very difficult to deal with you and with the rest of the world at the same time."

"Two thousand dollars a month!" she said.

"I'll take care of it," I told her.

Remembering the money Joe had given me, I pulled the bills from my pocket and peeled off six hundred bucks. "I'm going to take care of the business end of things, and I hope, maybe, you'll just use the opportunity to take it easy and have some fun."

She took the money I held out to her. But it failed to bring a smile to her face. She wanted something else, but kept her thoughts locked inside her.

"I was wondering," I asked her, "if you'd be willing to make me some breakfast. There's some lamb sausage in the frig. How about making me a couple of links? Maybe a little salad, too?"

"What am I a waitress?"

"I'll do it, Master." Bruno chimed in, seeing that Storee was holding back.

"I'll do it, Bruno," Storee snapped, as if she'd done it every day for years.

Turning her back on us, she went into the kitchen, and I

motioned Bruno to come over to the couch where we sat half-turned, facing each other.

"What do you think, Crunch? What's all this about?"

"Drugs," he said.

I would have preferred some other answer.

Trying to reject his idea, I told him, "Bruno, you know maybe they're legitimate, maybe they're telling the truth. It's possible they're just doing this to get a tax break."

"I believe you're mistaken, Master. It seems to me, you're psychologically hungry for it to be something legal because you're afraid.

"Bruno, two grand a month and a steady job would solve some problems for me."

"I understand that. But realistically think about what's being offered here. I believe you want the job so much you're blocking out your suspicions."

"Okay, Bruno, for the sake of argument, let's say you're partly right: Let's say they *are* engaged in some short of shady deal. Maybe the shady deal is this: maybe they actually bought the equipment for let's say fifty-thousand dollars. Or, wait a second. Maybe they stole all the equipment, but somehow they got sales receipts that show they bought the equipment for five hundred thousand dollars. Then they start writing off the five hundred thousand against some other income that Shifty Eddie has. Doing that sort of deal, Shifty Eddie could hide a hundred thousand a year from the tax people. What do you think?"

"Master Wing, I have always been in awe of your tremendous imagination."

Annoyed, I looked over at Storee. She was washing lettuce in the sink. The lamb links were sizzling on the stove. She looked over at me; her jaw was set firm and her lower lip stuck out a little.

"Hi, baby," I said.

She nodded at me without speaking.

Bruno sat calmly watching me, utterly patient, as though he was willing to wait there until the stars burnt out. It was irritating to watch him acting so differently from usual. I wanted him to act like the old Bruno. The one with a head like a gumball machine. He'd get an idea and it would come rolling out his mouth. Now he was pulling a switch on me, sitting there like a brick building while I was nervous like I had fleas all over me.

"Well, I think that they're legitimate businessmen, Crunch. It's like this: they recognize I am an intelligent person, and I work very well with people—with the general public—and they need somebody to run this business enterprise for them, and so they simply... they happen to... offer me the job."

Bruno nodded sympathetically like a doctor being nice to a madman.

"Dear friend, my teacher, I only wish I could support you in your hopes. You hunger to be in a position to provide material and emotional comfort for Astoria. I sympathize deeply with that. I had a similar relationship in the recent past before we met. But I believe your ambitions here are clouding your understanding of the realities of this situation.

"What? Have you been taking fucking speech lessons? '...clouding the realities of the situation...' What the fuck does that mean?"

"Master, are you forgetting my background in poetry? My training in poetic expression allows me to speak in brief and powerful images."

"What the hell was in your oatmeal this morning? Just tell me what you think, will you?"

He did.

He pointed out that recreational drugs are a fact of life in our society, and that San Diego borders on Mexico, a drug producing country. It would be a snap, he said, to smuggle narcotics aboard one of the pleasure boats that by the thousands use San Diego's harbor.

"Yeah, Bruno. So what? Get to the point, what's on your mind?"

He pointed out lots of deliveries are made to restaurants. Drugs could arrive labeled as, say, fish.

And go out in doggy bags.

Large amounts of cash, he reminded me, flow in and out of restaurants. Falsifying receipts would be an easy way to conceal drug money. Without fuss or bother it could be deposited in local banks.

"Furthermore, Master, as I understand the criminal mind, those sort of people often get into the tavern or restaurant business because it gives them a safe place to meet, and eat, and entertain business associates."

"Well, fuck you, Bruno. When I want your opinion I'll ask for it."

Rather than smiling at my attempt at humor, Bruno looked at me with loving kindness.

Who did he think he was anyway?

It was just like him to rain on my parade.

I shook my finger in Bruno's face. "I'm going to tell you something about yourself, Bruno. You're a suspicious, paranoid human being."

Bruno looked like I'd hurt his feelings.

"It's the truth, Bruno. You think everybody's out to get you. What's more you're trying to get me to think the same way. That's why you're trying to talk me out of taking this job."

Bruno started sputtering in protest.

"I understand you, Bruno. You're just like Astoria."

Astoria whipped her head around to look at me.

I was going to apologize to Astoria for suggesting she was a suspicious homosexual, but Bruno stopped sputtering, found his words, and said, "But Master, you're in error. I want you to take the job. I think you should."

"What?"

Astoria began opening cupboard doors and slamming them closed, looking for something which turned out to be the vinegar and oil for my salad.

"Yes, Master, this is a great opportunity."

"What the hell are you talking about?"

"Your job at the Holy Restaurant of the Slippery Word."

"The one with drugs on the menu, Bruno? Is that the one."

"Yes, Master, of course."

"The one with the cocaine omelets?

"It will be a great opportunity to win converts for *Yes*. We'll nourish their bodies and their souls. We'll win people away from drugs and lead them to a deeper spiritual life."

"You're nuts, Bruno. You've gone absolutely fucking bonkers."

"Try to understand, Master..."

"Me understand? You try to understand. Do you know what the drug business is all about? It's about broken lives. Kids with needles in their arms. It's about brains blown apart. It's about death."

I leaned forward, elbows on knees.

Bruno looked at me longingly, as though he wanted to reach out to me. I arose from the couch, thinking I should go somewhere or do something, but I was at a loss for direction, and so just stood there like a confused sheep.

Bruno came to my side.

God, it would be good to have a job.

Some place to go every day and earn my living.

I wanted to support my wife, and get my kids started off well in life.

Bruno, like some great bird of paradise, reached out his huge arm and put it comfortingly around my shoulder.

He said, "And Master, we *do* have our television appearance today."

Bruno tightened his arm, snuggly, affectionately. What the

281

hell was he thinking of anyway? Drugs. God damn it. I looked up into his face. He was beaming an enormous, eager smile at me.

Straightening up, I stared into his eyes. He gazed back at me eagerly; I put my hand on his shoulder to push him away.

"Try to understand, Master."

I pushed on his shoulder trying to get free.

He looked at me eagerly.

"You're out of your fucking mind, Bruno."

Turning me loose, he said, "Master, why?" with hurt in his voice.

"What am I going to say on T.V.? Tell me, what am I going to say?"

"Blessed One, just tell all the people what you've been telling to us chosen few. Speak to them of the Fiery *Yes*. Of Cooperation and a getting off people's backs. Speak of the health reviving benefits of Yesful meditation. Invite them to join us on our journey to the Cosmic *Yes*!"

"Aw, shit."

Storee brought my breakfast sausages and I looked down at them.

"Ah, double shit."

"So they got a little burnt."

Those two black things may have been sausages once, but only a lab technician could tell for sure.

"Thanks," I told her.

She brought the salad. She must have ripped up a whole field of lettuce; the fucking thing stood a foot high out of the top of a potato chip bowl.

"Do we have any goats around here to help me eat this?"

"I thought you were hungry."

"Yeah, I am. Thanks."

I watched her turn and walk back to kitchen where she poured herself more coffee.

I pulled myself together. It was easy. A snap.

"Crunch, baby, I want you to get me out of this T.V. thing this afternoon."

He looked at me like I'd punched his teddy bear.

Then I heard something.

It was in my head.

It came from deep in my mind, back where it's usually quiet.

It was like *Yes* being whispered to me.

I sagged inside as it became clear this message was telling me to accept this opportunity. I knew I had to, and gave in.

"Okay, Crunch, have it your way. I'll do it, but instead of this afternoon, have them come tonight. And... tell them, tell them that for the first time in history we're going to allow outsiders to attend our secret ceremonies and, what's more, they can actually film the sacred rituals of the Holy Church of the Slippery Word."

"Is that wise?"

"Yes."

He nodded in agreement, full of trust.

Saying *Yes* made me feel good again. I felt like my old self, like I was on a roll.

"Storee?"

"What, honey?"

"Will you give me a hand with something?"

"Sure," she said like she'd been waiting all day for me to ask.

"Bruno will give you a list of the Holy Yessers and maybe you could give everybody a call and tell them to be... I'm sorry. I mean *ask* them to be here tonight. Christ, I'm starting to sound like a fucking Boss. God, help me. Will you do that, honey?"

"Maybe this afternoon we could go take a look at the restaurant?" she said.

Was she bargaining with me?

Oh, what difference did it make?

As suddenly as my good feelings had appeared they started to dissolve. I could feel myself sinking. It was like a fog, like I had become surrounded by a fog that passed through my skin and made me soft. My eyes glazed over. Somewhere in my body, there was a sharp pain, as though a knife had penetrated somewhere.

I told her, "We'll see, Storee. We'll see." But in the dark spaces of my mind where there are voices without words, I was silently telling her, "Forget it, baby. You'll interfere with this restaurant business over my dead body. I'll let you into this deal when the man in the moon starts whistling Dixie...when the Russian army starts wearing Bermuda shorts."

"Plaid," she said.

"What?"

"For some reason I thought of plaid shorts," she said. "You know, bermudas."

I muttered, "Wow."

We stared at each other.

Finally I asked her again if she'd make the calls and she nodded, Yes. But she walked to the bedroom door and turned around like a fashion model and added, "After I get back from the beach." She disappeared into the bedroom.

The door of the condo opened without a knock first, and Horny Harriet Harvester walked into the room.

"Bruno, baby, it looks like you're going to have to make the calls for me."

Obediently, he nodded that he'd do it.

Horny Harriet looked tired and depressed, like she was convinced they were going to take away her license to screw.

Astoria, a beach towel around her neck, walked out of the bedroom, passing us without speaking. She wore a Walkman, the little headphones covered her ears, and she had the volume turned up so high that as she passed by us I could hear the harsh music she was pumping into her head. As the front door clicked closed behind her, a sudden image came into my brain. It was like a dream, like a vision. In this dream she was walking across a nice green lawn and right over a cliff. Tumbling like a rag doll, she bounced against the rocky side of the cliff screaming until she disappeared in the darkness.

"Bruno," I said.

"Yes, Master."

"Make your calls from some place else, okay?"

He nodded.

"And something else."

He waited.

"I want you to cut out that 'master' shit once and for all."

"But I must speak to you from my heart. You have brought me..." He searched for a word. "Hope."

Hopefully, I looked at Harriet, wanting her to tell Bruno for me to get the hell off my back. She opened and closed her mouth as though she had wanted to speak but changed her mind.

"You must accept your place and your *responsibility*," Bruno said.

"Go away, Bruno. Just go away."

"You can be of great help to the world, Master. You must be strong. You must keep your courage strong."

"Harriet, tell him to go away."

"Oh, Wing..." she said.

"Go away, Bruno. Make the calls."

Bruno sat still like a living mountain.

Harriet said, "You're being mean to Bruno, Wing. It's the first time I've ever seen you be mean."

"Harriet honey, he thinks I'm Jesus Christ. He *wants* me to be Jesus Christ. It's true, Bruno, right? Admit it?"

Bruno looked at me with pity in his eyes, like I was a bird with a broken wing.

"Bruno, I'm going to level with you. Being somebody's savior has very little appeal to me. Do you remember what happened to Christ? He had a very short career. They retired him early."

I got very little reaction from my dear bald friend.

Or from my dear lady friend with the horny hormones.

"It was fun, Bruno. It was fun playing our little game with the Church and the meetings, and parties and everything. But it's over now, see. It's finished, old buddy."

They just stared at me like I was talking Chinese at them.

Going to the bedroom door and turning around like a fucking fashion model I told them, "I'm going to take a shower now. You're offering me a very lonely job, Crunch... It so happens that I like people. I like to be around people. That's why I'm going into the restaurant business. I'm going to be just an ordinary guy with an ordinary job. You're wrong about the drugs. You're just wrong about that."

Bruno came across the room and looked down into my face. "You're courage will come back, Master. It will!"

I started to say the thing I usually say in such situations, but the phone rang and I just continued into the bedroom to answer it. Penelope Slick's voice came into my ear at high speed like cold needles.

"May I speak to Reverend Wing, please? This is *People* magazine calling."

"Yes. Yes. You may speak to Reverend Wing. You may speak to him when fucking hell freezes over. You may speak to him when Christ comes back to earth on a fucking silver cloud and the fucking Russian army goes into battle wearing plaid shorts. That's when you can talk to him. Get off the fuck off the line, I got a call to make."

I slammed the telephone down.

Everybody wanted a piece of me. Everybody wanted me to do this or that or the other thing. It was like getting fucked by a thousand dicks. I was through taking it.

I picked up the telephone and listened.

There was dead silence. The dial tone was missing.

The puppy came wandering into the room.

He sat in front of me

tilting his head

gazing at me with soft brown eyes.

I felt the impulse to slam my foot into his little chest.

"You're still there, Penelope, right?"

"Right," she said.

"Go away, Penelope. Go away."

"You talk different from the average preacher, or minister, Reverend Wing."

"You're wasting your time. I promise you that."

"I smell a story here. Something's going on."

"Go away."

"I could do you a lot of good. The magazine could, I mean."

"Forget it. I'm giving up the ministry."

"Come on, Wing, give a girl a break, do yourself a favor."

Horny Harriet came into the room. She picked up the puppy and sat on the bed, stroking the dog's shiny black fur.

I hung up on Penelope again.

I waited for Horny Harriet to notice how enraged I was.

But she was lost in a world of her own.

"If only Minnie would get back," she said.

What's the use, I thought. All anybody cared about was themselves. They were all wrapped up in themselves.

I sat on the bed, my back propped against the head board.

Was there any way I would ever get to lead a pleasant, ordinary life like other people got to lead? I was tired of the struggle, tired of the constant pressure to survive, of having to defend myself all the time, of having to be clever and happy-looking. It had all become too much of a burden. There had to be a way out.

"Is she still in the Caribbean?" I asked as though I cared.

"Oh, my goodness, we just found out she left there a week ago. She's in Hong Kong. We just got a obscene postcard from her. Here, I'll show you," she said eagerly. Hustling off the bed she trotted into the living room to get her purse.

Picking up the phone, I heard Penelope's voice squeak, "I can wait forever, Reverend Wing."

"You'll have to."

I hung up again.

Harriet trotted back, digging into her little-old-lady's handbag. She plunked herself by my side to show me the card Minnie had sent.

"My oh my, Minnie certainly has changed," I commented.

"Thanks to you, Wing," Harriet said lovingly.

There was something in her voice that made me look up, and what I saw in her face was a sexual gleam. A sexual hope is what it was. And at that very moment she was gently putting her hand on my inner upper thigh.

"Harriet," I reminded her, "I'm a married man."

"But you were married then, when we did it before."

"Yes. Yes, I was. But I'm more married now."

"It's because I'm old, right? That's the reason."

"Yes. Yes, it is Harriet. But it's also because I'm married. And also because I'm busy becoming a businessman. Frankly, I have been thinking about sex less and less all day long. I may be becoming impotent."

"Tell the truth, Wing. It's mainly because I'm old?" she said despairingly.

"Harriet, you were only slightly younger several weeks ago, and we did it then, so how can you blame it on age now."

"If only I could believe that," she said.

"It's true, Harriet. If I was single and out-of-work I'd rock your socks off."

"Oh, Wing, you're such a dear. I do so much love it when you talk like that. Somehow it makes me feel like a woman again. You know, you remind me of my Sam. What a dear man he was." She sighed. "I sure miss him. Oh, everything's going wrong."

"Like what, Harriet? What's wrong?"

"Oh, just everything," she said. "I can hardly ever get laid anymore, and down at the office things are just awful because the girl who took Minnie's place as bookkeeper is just a pest. She is just a pest, Wing. It's so hard to believe," Harriet said as she stood and straightened her skirt to leave. "It's hard to believe how awful it is to be getting old, and have trouble getting some action, and having to work with a pest bookkeeper."

I stood up too, waiting for her to go.

She leaned against me, burying her face in the hollow of my shoulder. Putting my arms around her, we rocked together like two orphans.

When we separated and she was leaving, I asked her to please come to the meeting that night.

"Of course," she said.

As the door clicked shut behind Harriet, I was already dialing the phone, asking the information operator for the telephone number of Winslow K. Smaggers & Associates.

At Smagger's office, a female voice promised to transfer my call to Norleen.

When she answered, I told her, "It's Wing. I got to talk to you."

Her voice was full of surprise as she told me, "I just called you."

"I've been sitting right here by the phone."

"Well, what are you, suspicious? You think I'm lying."

"Did I say that? Maybe you just dialed wrong."

"I know how to dial a fucking phone, Wing."

"Please, Norleen..." My voice went dead. "Could we skip the fighting? I need you. I need to talk with you."

It took her a long time to answer.

"Maybe," she said.

There was more dead air space in our conversation.

"You promised," I said.

"I only promised to call. And now we're talking. So talk."

For once I was empty of words, and silent.

"You make me nervous," she said. "Very, very nervous."

Everything made her nervous. That was obvious. Although miles separated us, I could almost see her face, framed by curls of shadow-black hair, her dark eyes alert, wary, careful, looking for threats that might be coming from any direction. Her firm lean body was ever-ready to tense up, ready to repel some sudden attack, or to attack something itself.

"Norleen, could we just meet for lunch?"

"I have something else going on."

I wanted to scream at her, "Come on, come to me, I need you."

But I kept it inside.

The words would just drive her away.

Then an idea came.

"Norleen..."

"What?"

"Maybe tonight. My group is having a meeting here. You could come to that, and afterwards we could have a drink, or some coffee or something."

She was quiet on the other end of the line.

She was so dark. So just-out-of-reach.

I gave up.

"All right. If you want to stay away...then stay away."

"Did I say that?"

"It's just that you seem reluctant..."

"Well, I'm wondering what I'm getting into."

"Your guess is as good as mine."

"I feel very vulnerable around you."

A light went on in my head, and I knew what I had to say next.

"Is there anything I can do to make you feel more comfortable about that?"

She was quiet for a moment or so, and when she spoke again the tone of her voice had changed a little.

"Well..." she said.

A dizziness came into my head. Something was happening inside of me.

"Norleen, is there anything that, maybe, you'd want me to do? Anything that might help you feel more at ease?"

The dizziness continued. It was as if a voice in the back of my head was saying something that had stunned the front part of my head, that confused it terribly.

Gently, as though she were asking me for a nice favor, Norleen said, "Well, you could stay calm."

I started to say something clever.

But the voice in the back of my head interrupted.

The voice in the back of my head was too faint for me to actually hear its words and understand the messages.

Stalling for time, I repeated the question, asking if there was anything I could do for her; my voice sounded to me—that is, sounded in my own head—as though it was coming from far away, almost as though someone else was speaking.

"Norleen, is there anything I can do for you?"

"Wing," she said, her voice now playfully gentle, "you're being silly. I just told you. If you just took it easy. That would help."

Listening to her speak, I could almost see her smiling.

"I'll be calm," I told her.

It was the most truthful promise of my life.

She would get from me what she'd asked for.

The voice in the back of my head was quiet now.

I felt a little sad because I knew I had failed to understand what the voice had been saying.

Norleen was quiet too, and then she told me, "All right, I'll come."

The telephone conversation ended with a feeling of warmth flowing between Norleen and me. She wrote down my address and I thanked her. We exchanged good-byes and that was that.

After the call, there was a weak feeling in my body, as though I'd been away on a long trip, and had just arrived back in town, tired.

Lowering myself to sit on the bed, the room grew hazy in my eyes. I slumped backward, lying on my back across the width of the bed with my feet dangling to the floor. Slowly I lowered the zipper of my cut-offs. Pulling out my whanger, I started to massage it gently. Gradually, the masturbatory rhythm grew faster. Visions of pornography played in my head. I fantasized this woman and that woman. Two men on one woman. Two women on one man.

Flipping over on my stomach, burying my head in my arms, I asked with hopelessness in my voice, "What's wrong with me?"

In the back of my head a voice said to me, as clear as a bell, "You're in love with your dick."

The answer surprised me.

Like water tossed over my head, I woke up.

I just lay there for a while.

Wide awake.

Alert.

Ready for business again.

That night, if the dark haired girl kept her promise I would see her for the fourth time.

Would it be the last time?

Arising from the bed, I went to the window from which I had seen her standing on the sidewalk, staring up at Astoria's naked back. I felt as though Norleen was offering me a choice. As though I would have to choose either her—out there in the street, a stranger in a different and difficult world—or Astoria with whom I had lived for so many long years. With whom I was so utterly familiar.

The front door of the condo opened and closed.

Someone had come in.

The light breeze floating in through the window washed gently around my face.

I sniffed at it like a careful rabbit.

I smelled something.

I looked quickly back at the calendar.

August 31, 1982

I smelled death.

The summer was dying.

It came as a very faint new smell.

The air had a certain crispness; it had that brisk needle-like quality that tattoos the inside of your nose when you inhale it. Many people notice this new crispness in the air during

September and October, and they associate it with cold, crunchy apples, and with the witches and goblins of autumn's holiday, Halloween.

Halloween is a celebration of death.

That year I smelled it early.

Death.

The end of August was the end of summer. The end of easy living. In the air I could smell the hard times coming. The cold. The snow. The ending.

The sun was still shining. The air was still warm. It might stay warm all through September, even into October. But the game would have been over for a long time by then.

While standing at the window, staring at the world outside, I saw Gilford Worthingglass and Kimberly Katz drive into view in their spiffy green cop-Dodge with its roof-top fright-lights and missing door handles inside. They parked on the street on the other side of the parking lot. Kimberly, riding shotgun, pulled a small pair of binoculars and stared at me with the intensity of a college boy shooting sorority beaver. With an idiot's grin, I waved at her like she was the Good Humorperson, and I wanted a 50-50 bar.

Behind me the bedroom door opened.

Astoria said "Hello" to my back.

Actually, she sang it.

"Hello"

Her voice gets sing-song when she's going to fuck your head. "How are you?"

She sounded like she was trying out for the opera team.

Turning around I saw her, and what struck me was how beautiful she was. Like a treasure, you know. All golden and warm, and somehow just out of reach. My shoulders and back started to tense up, like the springs inside my body were tightening. She was looking upwards a little, looking over my head instead of into my face. On her face was the expression she got when she was choosing her words in her mind. Getting her ammunition ready.

I was scared of her. Even before we started talking, I feared this battle that was coming.

"I'm going to write the kids in Connecticut," she said.

She sneaked a quick look at my face to check me out, then lowered her gaze to the floor, waiting for me to respond.

"That'll be nice," I told her. "They'll probably want to hear from us. Hear that we're back together again." She had some new freckles on her face, brought out by the sun after only a few days on the beach.

"That's what I was thinking," Storee said. "I'll tell them that we're all going to live here now that we both have jobs."

?

Jobs?

She had a job? What did that mean, she had a job?

This was the first I'd heard about it.

In the old days—before *Yes*—I would have gotten very, very excited and very angry that she would have made such a move without us talking about it first. My style—before *Yes*—was to jump up and down screeching like an enraged chimpanzee. However, since the Wonderword had entered my life, I'd become much calmer.

"Pardon, Storee? What did you say?"

"I'm going to write to the kids and tell them about my job."

"What job is that?"

"Alice Angsterlobe is giving me a job in her travel agency," said Astoria, like she was telling me the sausages were a little burnt. "It's a sales job."

"Alice Angsterlobe?"

"You know her," she reminded me.

"Yeah. She's good on the clarinet." I said.

"So maybe she'll perform at the office Christmas party."

"Yeah. That would be nice."

"I'd like to take the car," she said

"All right," I answered.

There was dead air between us.

"Storee, listen, I got this restaurant thing."

"So?"

"You've been working hard for years. I was sort of hoping it might be nice for you to take a good long vacation. We'll have enough money for the time being. Maybe you could rest up."

"Who knows if your restaurant thing will work out, Norrie," she said evenly, like a telephone operator telling you the line was busy. "You always seem to lose your jobs."

She turned her head away again to keep from looking at me directly.

"Yeah, something always seems to happen, huh?"

Storee nodded as though I was finally getting the message.

"Baby, this morning you were telling me that you wanted us to work out."

She gave me an angry look. "Are you threatening me?"

"It's just that we probably have a better chance if it's just me working for now."

"Forget it," she said. "I'm taking the job."

Yes, yes, she was. I could tell. The best thing to do was to accept it. I went to the chair and picked up my toga. "All right, baby." Slipping on the toga, I looked in the mirror, adjusting my clothes like a Roman getting ready to go to the circus.

Her voice became sing-song again. "You'll see. It'll work out for the best."

"Yeah, Storee. You're right. You're probably right."

She nodded like she agreed.

She asked me where I was going.

"Fernando Clip called. He wants to take me down to the restaurant this afternoon," I lied.

Her eyes narrowed like a boll weevil whose cotton field had just gotten sprayed.

I asked her, "That sort of bugs you, right?"

"Hey, look, I'm glad for you," she said. "Two thousand a month is a lot of money. A lot of money."

"It's just a start, baby. I know I can make a lot more than that. We can be on easy street. We can be fat, believe me."

Instead of answering me, she went to the closet and with jerky movements took out slacks and a blouse. Reaching behind her, she pulled the string on her halter bra with the exotic flowers on it, but she held her hand to her bosom keeping the halter in place as if it was against the law for me to see her well-known tits. She disappeared into the bathroom, shutting the door behind her.

Through the closed door, I asked where she was going. I wanted to get away from her before Gilford and Kim left, otherwise I would be delayed in my plans.

"Alice's," she said. "I've decided to start work today."

In a raised voice so that she could hear me over the water she was running in the sink, I called, "It would be nice if you'd just say, 'Congratulations, honey. I hope you do well with your restaurant thing. I hope it all works out for you.'"

Silence, except for the running water.

I waited for her to speak.

Continued silence.

She turned off the water.

I opened the door.

She had her slacks and blouse on, and was brushing her hair with long, determined strokes. I stood behind her and a little to one side, so that in the mirror our heads appeared to be just inches apart. There we were, both blond and nearly the same height, in the prime of life, blue-eyed and dead serious.

A matched pair.

Two sides of a coin.

I felt the urge to give her a sermon.

A lecture.

A little free advice.

Instead I asked, "This morning after those guys left you said you thought this could be a great opportunity. Maybe we could start a chain of these things. What happened?"

"Maybe I'm Hitler," she said.

What a stupid thing to say. How could anyone say a thing like that? She must be wrong. What the hell did she have in common with Hitler? She could be pretty mean but she had a long way to go before she reached Hitler's class. Right?

"Norris," she said.

"What?"

She turned around and looked me up and down.

"Why do you wear a dress?"

Confusion Vanishes!

There is a piece of stage-wisdom among stand-up comedians that goes like this: you can get an audience to laugh at a thing three times, but the fourth joke, about the same thing, will fall flat.

Well, here's the fourth chapter about *fuck*. What's more, later on, there'll be a fifth chapter that wraps everything up. If you're tired of this subject, if you've had all you can take, then you can skip Example A and go on to Example B, which continues the story of what happened to me, Astoria and the Yessers.

You can take the easy way out if you want to.

But perhaps you'll be missing some information that might help you deal with the world better. One of the great things about being human beings is that we can learn new things and add them to the vast amount of knowledge that we already have inside of us.

Sometimes that knowledge is buried deep within us.

Often it will take great effort to bring it to the surface.

But when you do manage to answer a question that's been bothering you, then other questions often get answered automatically, almost by themselves. Things connect in your head and become clear. Confusion vanishes. You feel wise and capable. You feel like a good person.

All this happens because you were willing to work on your problem, even though it was hard.

* * * * *

Example A

My search for the meaning of fuck took quite a long time.

That was odd because once the answer came it was so clear it seemed I'd known it all along.

Fuck is death.

A particular kind of death.

It's a worse death than just having your body cease to function and start to rot. Instead, a person is split, and part of them killed. What's harmed is the spirit or soul. Sometimes this includes the body. But usually the victim keeps on living, but injured.

The injury comes through penetration. The word means to penetrate in a selfish manner. To fuck someone is to invade into their life and use them for your own purposes and satisfaction, ignoring who they are and what they need. A person to whom this happens often feels as though they've lost something. Lost a part of themselves. They often feel wounded and empty.

When I realized this, certain events and conversations took on new meanings. For instance, I remembered Alice telling me about the Christmas party where her husband pushed her around once too often. She finally said, "Fuck you" to him, and told me, "He died, Wing. Literally." I realized she was right. He'd been bossing her around, making her do this and do that, interfering with her own image of herself as a worthwhile person who deserved respect. So she fucked him back. Her words pushed into his mind, penetrated through the macho armor he wore. As soon as she stood up to him, the bully who'd pushed her around for so long was conquered. He died and was replaced by a poor man on his way to losing his woman.

I remembered the other thing she'd said: about how the people who used the word most were likely to be "poorly educated, frustrated and sexually confused."

How smart she is, I think.

It makes sense.

The less education a person has, the less control over their lives they have, the less respect they get, the more vulnerable they are to getting interfered with, invaded, used. The more likely they are to scrawl "Fuck you" on a wall.

It was easy for me to imagine a man, say, who feels this way, who wants to be a father and have a family, but is having much difficulty earning enough to support his wife and children. It's got to make him feel less of a man.

Or to imagine a woman in a similar spot. Perhaps she has the brains and ambition to grow, but a male-dominated society hinders her from developing in the ways she wants to.

It was then I realized why Norleen had said "Fuck you" to me when I said golf was a man's game. She wanted to play and who was I to tell her she lacked the balls for it.

How embarrassing; and I was only trying to be friendly and make conversation.

Then I realized there's a major problem when the information stored inside us comes bubbling to the surface: sometimes we wish it had stayed buried. Sometimes it's embarrassing and hard to accept. For instance, I understood why Quentin had said "Fuck you" to me at the end of our basketball game on the night before I discovered *Yes*. It mattered very little to Q that I was trying to change him into a better person. What mattered to him was I'd invaded into his private life and tried to change him into the sort of person I would be more comfortable around. Sure, Quentin certainly understood he had some problems and he could have been a more successful person. We all know that about ourselves. But he figured that was his business, and he felt I should leave him alone, and resented it when I interfered.

(To fuck is to interfere with.)

But I was trying to make a new man of Quentin. I wanted the cowardly part of him dead, and wanted a brave new Quentin to be born.

Why did I want that?

Probably because I was a coward myself.

How did Quentin feel?

He felt like saying "Fuck you" and throwing the basketball down the street, that's what.

What he meant was "Fuck you back."

How different it was with Dulcinea the next night, the night I discovered *Yes*. Instead of trying to form her into a new person I merely shared my knowledge with her when she asked me a question. Obviously, giving information and then getting out of people's way so they can make up their own minds is a good idea. With Dulcinea I'd cooperated; with Quentin it was combat. I'd been respectful with Dulcinea, and felt much better about the way the thing had turned out.

So even though some of the things I remembered and figured out were embarrassing to me, and made me look like a fool, I felt wonderful, over all. So what if I'd made mistakes, I'd also figured out the origin of the word *fuck*, something that hundreds of well-educated professors had failed to do. And now I was armed with knowledge that would prevent me from repeating the stupid mistakes I'd made throughout my life. I would eliminate *fuck* from my actions. Now I would stop interfering and be able to get along with people much better.

Believe me, that felt great.

Example B

Astoria had asked me why I wore a dress. She stared at me coldly as we faced each other, there in the bathroom.

Frankly, the question made me nervous.

More and more ill-at-ease.

Sort of panicky.

Backing away, keeping my eyes on Storee, I exited the bathroom with increasing speed. She looked surprised as I flipped the door shut, putting a barrier between us. Across the room to the window I fluttered with my toga flapping behind me. Pushing open the sliding glass as wide as it would go, I began to climb out. Gilford and Kim were still in their cop car at the curbside, as if waiting for someone. Desperately, I swung my legs, then my body, over the window sill. Turning onto my belly and sliding further out, I hung for a long moment by the length of my arms over the pavement one floor below. Hanging there, it occurred to me my ankles in my sandals would snap when I hit the cement.

But happily there was a flower bed below, and so my ankles were only sprained a little, and the pain felt wonderful.

Half-limping, half-trotting, I hustled over to Gil and Kim, and without waiting for an invitation, I popped open the back door and slid into the back seat, telling them, "Winslow K. Smaggers place, and step on it."

A wire-mesh screen separated the front seat from the back. On the other side, Kim and Gil just sat watching me like it was a hot day in Mississippi and they were waiting for the corn bread to rise. They were half-turned in their seats, staring at me.

"Okay, you guys, I'm going to confess," I told them. "I know you've been waiting for this for a long time, trying to pin something on me. But I'm ready to crack now. I'm ready to spill the beans."

Without speaking they just stared at me, watching me like a couple of alligators on the banks of a muddy river.

"The pressure's getting to me, guys. I'm getting in too deep. You want to know about Shifty Eddie and Nano, the Clip, right?"

Gilford gave Kim a knowing look.

"Okay. I'll tell you. But we got to get away from here."

I gave them Winslow K. Smaggers address, and said if they'd take me there I'd tell them everything they wanted to know.

Gilford gunned the engine like he was warming up for the Daytona 500.

But then he slid the car smoothly away from the curb like we were on gondola ride on an Italian canal.

I laughed.

I laughed a lot.

It felt so good to have escaped from Astoria.

They looked at me like I'd lost my buttons.

Kimberly started the conversation. She was very professional in her handling of the situation, looking at me with her clear dark eyes, and speaking in an relaxed tone, as though she'd done this a million times and knew exactly what was what.

"Things are going to go a lot better for you when you're on the right side of the law," she said. "We're here to help."

Her voice was wonderfully soothing.

Tired, I laid down on my back on the back seat.

I thought I saw pity come into her eyes.

It's all right, Kim, I thought. Pity me if you want, but there are still some tricks up my floppy sleeve.

Could that possibly be true, I wondered?

Did I have an limitless supply of cleverness?

Could a person continually dodge life's bullets forever?

Kim said to me gently, "Looks like you're at the end of your rope, Wing."

Gil said, "You're playing with the big boys now. Shifty Eddie's out of your league."

"Yeah," I told them. "It's like you step into mud, and you just keep sinking and it turns out to be quicksand. You just keep sinking and sinking and pretty soon it's up to your chest and hard to breathe."

"You want to tell us about it," Kim said.

What was there to tell?

We were all silent for a while, the car hummed as we moved along.

Finally, I asked them, "Shifty Eddie's in the narcotics business, huh?"

Gil said, "Very funny."

Sitting up, I leaned forward, resting my forearms on the back of the front seat, pressing my nose against the wire screen, and gazing at Gilford's reflection in the rear view mirror. He looked good. Very healthy. His eyes were clear and hard, his moustache trimmed thin and neat. Good square jaw. Short sideburns. His dark hair was neatly combed. Beneath that sharp-creased tan uniform he almost certainly had good solid muscles. He looked firm and satisfied. From the rear view mirror, he smiled at me like a contented rock.

My gaze sank down. I noticed that on the car seat between them was a black vinyl folder on which someone had fixed a decal: a football helmet with a silver, five-pointed star on it. Below the helmet were the words:

DALLAS COWBOYS
AMERICA'S TEAM.

Looking up again, I saw that Gil was still observing me in the mirror.

Kim looked at me. "You know, Wing, you're hard to figure."

"You're very nice too, Kimmie," I answered, meaning it, feeling very sentimental about these two good people whom I was probably seeing for the last time. "It's very nice how you wear just a little bit of eye make-up, and how clear and clean and healthy your skin is. You have so much energy, and you try so hard to do your job just as good as you can do it."

"Thanks," she said, accepting the compliment gracefully, more gracefully than I would have expected. "The whole department here is very dedicated. You could be of some real help to us. Officer Worthinglass and I were talking about how you could be a valuable source of information for us."

"Kimmie, I know very little about narcotics, and even less about Shifty Eddie, and more than I want to know about Fernando Clip." (From the street signs I could tell we were nearly at Winslow K. Smagger's office.) "But, Gil, if you'll pull over and let me out I'll tell you what I do know. And then I'll be pretty much finished with everything."

Gil and Kim exchanged meaningful looks. Pulling the car to the curb, he cut off the engine.

"This is what I know. Most of the people you see every day are concentrating on making themselves feel good. Particularly the men. Some people take narcotics. Some masturbate. But the intention is the same for both. Some to go to fast-food places and eat death burgers. Some people drink, and some people smoke. Some indulge too much in physical exercise. Some sit around watching television. It's all the same. Especially for the men. Men are acting like cunts for themselves. The women encourage them to do it and then hate them for it," I said. "Shifty Eddie and Fernando Clip are trying to open some sort of nightclub near a San Diego marina. A friend of mine thinks they might be involved in the narcotics business, but that's just a guess. They wanted me to be the front man. Go fuck 'em, guys."

After I stopped talking, there was silence for a few moments. They just stared at me, as if waiting for me to continue.

Gil said, "Is that all?"

"Yes, let me out."

They refused.

Gil and Kim wanted more information. They asked for specific details: what sort of operation was Shifty Eddie running, who else was involved, what sort of narcotics were in the deal and had I seen any? They had a hard time believing I'd already told them everything I knew. When I pointed out that somebody had stolen the inside door handles of their car and would they open up for me so I could leave, they refused again. Kim's voice got low and friendly; her words came stealing toward me like Indians in canoes at dusk. "Wing, we're your friends, we're going to help you get out of the trouble you're in."

"You got it all, baby, you already got it all."

"Look," Gil said, "you could get your butt hauled in for booking right now, you understand that?"

"What do you want, Gil?"

"What do you know?" he barked.

"Only hearsay."

"What hearsay?" he said.

"Well, I hear that Masters and Johnson, the famous sex researchers have said that 95 out of 100 American men beat off."

"Oh, Jesus Christ..." Gil bitched.

He was upset.

"Do you ever masturbate, Gil?" I asked him in a friendly manner.

Gil seemed reluctant to tell me. Instead, he gave a low whistle—like he was trying to keep his cool—and he glanced at Kim shaking his head.

Kim just sat there watching us both, looking interested.

Since they were silent for a moment I took the opportunity to turn the situation around and I asked Gil for some information. I asked him if it would make him feel good if I answered his questions as fully and truthfully as possible. He said, yes, and I told him that was a fine word. Kimmie, in response to the same question, answered, somewhat suspiciously, that she too would have positive feelings if I helped them in their investigation.

"See, what I mean?" I asked them.

"You explain it to us," Kimmie said.

"You guys just want to feel good. It hardly matters at all to you how I feel. You're taking advantage of me, you're using me to make yourselves feel good."

"We're just doing our job."

"Yeah, but you're fucking me. You're holding me in this car when I want to leave. You're calling me a liar when I say I've already told you everything I know. And you're threatening me with police actions if I refuse to cooperate. You guys are supposed to be public servants, but you're taking advantage of me. You are abusing me."

307

"We got a job to do," Gilford said.

"You are making yourself feel good, at my expense. You're fucking me instead of taking care of me. When you deal with people, each person should get something good out of it."

Gilford started the car as though he was going to drive off to the jailhouse.

"Kimerbly Katz, do you know that Gil probably beats off. That's the truth. Masters and Johnson, the famous sex researchers, found out that 95 out of a 100 men whip it, and four of the other five guys are liars."

Kim nodded like she knew it all along.

Gilford started the car rolling.

"Instead of taking care of business, these guys are taking care of themselves. Instead of using their hands to do work, they're shaping their hands into cunts. Instead of servicing women, they're servicing themselves. Think of the Dallas cowboys, Gil?"

Saying that may have annoyed Gil. He hit the brakes and pulled the car to the curb. Turning on me, he was nodding his head furiously, demanding, "What about the Dallas Cowboys, Wing?"

"They beat-off, Gil. All those he-men football players beat off. Did you think they were taking care of cows like cowboys are supposed to do? What if all those Dallas Cowboys surrounded this car right now, and the windows were open a little bit, and they all decided to beat off into this car. God, you'd be swimming in sperm, it'd be up to your eyeballs and in your nose. You'd be drowning in it."

"You disgusting pervert," Gil said.

"You'd be helpless because they could rip you limb from limb if you objected to being a sex object."

Kimberly, perhaps because she was out of the line of fire, looked faintly amused and interested. Safe.

Gil jumped out of the car. Wrenching the back door open, he said to me, "You get out of the car, creep."

I hopped out. Gil said some more things to me. But I failed to hear them because his words were lost in the noise of the traffic and the wind whistling in my ears as I ran down the street.

Winslow K. Smaggers & Associates was located in a faintly familiar, low, brick building in front of which I paused for a moment to compose myself and collect my wits. Had it only been this morning that Astoria and I had been interrupted in our love making by Daryl? That seemed to have taken place a hundred years before. Was it now only a little after noon? I had the feeling that it would seem like years longer before this day was over.

I walked into the building.

A short, plump young woman with a few pimples and enormous breasts was sitting at the reception desk. She smiled sweetly and buzzed Norleen for me. After a few moments she said Norleen must be away from her desk, and she'd go find her. Waddling away she disappeared into the interior of the building. My quick inspection of the top of her desk revealed two airline tickets which—God damn it—were in the name of Winslow K. Smaggers and Norleen Winkowski. (So that was her name.) That son of a bitch, Smaggers, was getting in my way, it appeared. I told myself I'd kill him if I had to. They were leaving the next day for Atlanta and the return date had been left blank. How could she do this? I wanted to get away with her this weekend. I had to prevent her from going. How could she fuck anybody else but me? The plump receptionist had only a few seconds head start, but time was wasting so I followed her, wandering down the corridors of the office suite.

Winslow K. Smaggers may have had Associates, but that day the offices were deserted like everybody was on assignment in a foreign land. Then: I thought I heard low voices. As I headed toward the office from which they seemed to come, Norleen suddenly came through the doorway out into the hall and gave a start when she saw me.

"Christ, I thought you were a ghost," she said.

"Just me, baby. It's sort of quiet around here, huh?"

"What are you doing here?"

"I was in the neighborhood and I thought maybe we could go to lunch."

"Sorry," she said, "I got to get ready for a trip tomorrow."

"Gee, I was hoping we could do something on the weekend," I said, hoping that she would tell me that she was only going to be gone for a day, and be back on the weekend.

"Sorry," she said, "I'm going to be out of town. Say, are you all right?"

"Yes, sure. I feel great. Tell me, if you would, how come you have to work so much? Like on the weekend?"

"Who said it was work?" Norleen said.

I wanted to get down on my knees, beg her to stand by me; *please, baby, it will be so painful to be here alone.*

But just by looking at her I could see her mind was firm, determined; she was going. She watched me closely, with calm intensity. If I were to push her, she would get angry, and maybe refuse to see me again. I was on thin ice.

How could I reach her? Make her see?

She asked again if I was all right? "You promised to calm down," she reminded me.

"Yeah, I feel great. Hey, did I tell you I got a job offer this morning? It's been a remarkable day so far. I had a heart-to-heart talk with a relative who just got into town the other day, and some real nice friends of mine just gave me a ride over here. We were talking about football and the restaurant business and stuff. It's been a great day so far. Hey, you know, I'm going to be on television tonight; you're going to be there like you promised, right?"

She was nodding Yes, when a man came through the office doorway into the hallway. Instantly, I knew it was Winslow K. Smaggers, and I was stunned. Speechless. How could it be?

He handed her a file folder; she introduced me to him, and I shook his hand like I was a mechanical man. Norleen was saying she would walk me to the front door, but my eyes were riveted on Smaggers, and his eyes were dead on me, each of us taking the measure of the other man. I was definitely sticking around until I learned his story, and said to Norleen, "See you later."

She wandered away.

He and I stared at each other.

You know what he was...?

He was *old*.

He was older than fucking me?

(And remember that I was 57 at the time.)

(Although I looked about 33.)

For god's sake, his hair was *white*.

That was bad enough, but he had a crew cut. A thin, white-haired crew-cut, for god's sake.

And he wore glasses. Glasses like they had in the nineteen-fifties, those big, black framed glasses, like he's looking at you through portholes.

I turned quickly around and saw Norleen's cute little body disappearing around a corner like a teenager going out to a movie. *She* was going on a fucking weekend with *him*.

Why?

Old man, young girl?

Why?

He turned and went into his office, with me following, determined to get the real story and to prevent this immoral, dirty sin from occurring.

His office was small and plain, all business, a place where a lot of work could get done. He went around behind the desk, and what surprised me was that on the desk was a good size pile of zucchini. They were great looking squash of various sizes: dark green, and seemingly firm and fresh. I eyed the zucchini, and I eyed Smaggers. He eyed me, and he eyed me eyeing the zucchini.

311

I was ill-at-ease so I did what I always do: started talking.

"That's a lot of zucchini, Mr. Smaggers," I said smiling.

He nodded.

"Zucchini supplier to the world," I said charmingly.

But he was hardly charmed at all; in fact he sort of reminded me of Mr. Shifty Eddie the way he looked at me as if waiting for me to say something worth hearing.

"You a ... a gardener?" I asked.

"Yes," he said. "I enjoy gardening. I wish I had more time for it."

"Oh."

He just stood there looking at me.

"What do you do with a lot of zucchini like that?"

"We use them. Give them away. Some we sell."

"Oh. Hmmmmm."

"We usually have a lot this time of year."

"Hmmmmm."

It occurred to me that this conversation was out of my control. It was a strange sensation.

"Well, are you interested?" he asked me, nodding at the pile.

"Oh, I like zucchini," I said hurriedly, surprised by his question.

Maybe he was going to give me some, I thought; but then I realized that he'd said he sometimes sold them.

Then, deciding that, *Yes*, he was going to give me some, I faked being polite and offered to buy them. "How much?"

"Twenty-five cents a piece."

I was disappointed to realize he was going to make me pay for them. "Sounds fair," I said.

"I try to be fair," he answered.

He watched me with steady eyes as though he was willing to deal patiently with me—using as much time as necessary—even though he had a lot of other work to do. I thought of Norleen and his going away with her.

How to stop them?
Violence?
Ridiculous.
Con him? Persuade him?
Where would I start?
What were they up to anyway?
"Well?" he said.
"They're nice zucchini."

He had me stopped cold. It was one of those times when you just run into a person who stops you in your tracks. It would be a waste of time trying to con this man.

I relaxed a little, and it was then I realized something that surprised me. I realized Mr. Smaggers was very tired. I almost expected him to sigh and let his shoulders sag. But watching me steadily, he remained as he was, a man in the last quarter of his life, a businessman working his way through one of the thousands of wearying afternoons of his adulthood. He remained alert and polite, dealing with me, a minor interruption in the progress of his workday. I realized he had lived a long time and done all right for himself; anybody could see that. And he knew with absolute certainty who he was. It would be a waste of time trying to fuck his head.

"I'll take four if it's all right with you."

He nodded that was okay with him, and reaching down behind his desk he pulled a brown paper grocery bag into view, and motioned for me to select the zucchinis of my choice. Choosing three medium ones, and one large one, I handed them to him and he stuck them into the bag. While lifting the hem of my toga and reaching underneath to fish the money out of my cut-offs, my mind returned to the subject of the trip he and Norleen were going to take. I'd pretty much given up the hope I might prevent it, but it would be nice to know some of the details; I wanted to know what the two of them were up to, although wanting it made me feel like a peeping Tom, like I was looking into someone's bedroom window, prying, sneaking. It embarrassed me, like trying to listen to hear if your parents are screwing, but still I wanted to. Then I was even more embarrassed because I realized that I'd left my wallet at home. My pockets contained only a scattering of coins. Dragging them out, counting them, revealed there was only 95 cents. I dropped the coins into his outstretched hand, figuring that to a man like him the extra nickel, the nickel that I was short, would mean very little, and he'd give me the wonderful green zucchinis at a small discount.

He counted the money, and without bothering to look at me, he opened the sack and withdrew one of the zucchinis. He put it back in the pile. Handing me back 20 cents, he said, "We're even now."

The way he said it made me understand that he refused to be short-changed. You get what you pay for with Mr. Smaggers.

"I figured it was only a nickel," I said.

"A nickel's a nickel."

It was like running into a brick wall. Smaggers was too much for me. I felt like a child. Obviously he was a man who—besides possessing an impressive pile of zucchini—was also going to possess the girl of my dreams and fly away with her to Atlanta. I could argue or complain or coax or throw a temper tantrum of some sort, but it would be useless in preventing them from flying away. They were as good as gone.

Good-bye, Norleen.

I wondered if she would tell me when she was returning.

Or maybe kiss me good-bye.

Then I thought of Astoria.

Maybe I was wrong about Astoria.

Maybe that situation could be saved.

It was worth making one more championship effort for. That's what I'd do. After all, we were married.

The possibility of loneliness hit me.

For a moment, dizziness swarmed through me like butterflies tugging my head sideways.

It would have been nice to sit in a chair, but I knew that my interview with Mr. Smaggers was finished. It was time for each of us to go about our separate business. He walked around his desk and accompanying me the few short steps to the door of his office, politely and pleasantly seeing me out.

Alone, I walked down the hallway like it was the longest hallway in the world. Entering the reception area, I noticed the plump young woman with pimples and big breasts was absent. As I approached the desk, the idea occurred to me of snatching the airline tickets and fleeing.

But then something caught my eye.

On a wall behind the desk, hanging off to one side.

Winslow K. Smagger's college diploma.

Now was my chance.

But it was hard to move.

Something was holding me back.

And then my chance was gone.

I had company.

Waddling back to her desk came Pimplyboobs, the receptionist.

I thought of hitting her for some money, so I could buy the extra zucchini Smaggers had taken back.

"Could I borrow a nick..."

But it became impossible to finish the sentence.

The words stuck in my throat like nails.

I *saw* her and choked. It dawned on me that she was a human being and deserved more respect from me. Guilt burned in me. How shameful it was to think of her as Pimplyboobs, just Pimplyboobs, the Receptionist.

Smiling at me with a soft look that barely made creases in her chubby cheeks, she waited nicely for me to finish my request. Her body looked like pillows on an over-stuffed couch.

Changing my mind, I reached into the paper bag and withdrew the big zucchini while asking her, "Would you accept this?"

"Huh? What's that for?"

"It's for you. I'd like you to have it. Just because... Just because you're *you*, let's say. They're very good."

Reaching out, I took her hand. It felt warm, like a place a dog has been sleeping. I put the big thing in her palm and wrapped her fingers around it.

She became sort of tense all of a sudden, looking at me stiffly as though she were afraid to move, as though she thought she might be in the presence of someone slightly off his rocker.

"Thank you," I said. "Thank you."

Sort of dumbfounded, she stood there with her arm outstretched holding my zucchini while I skipped out the door, happily. In my brain were swirling odd thoughts about farmers, and about how it was the end of summer now, and all over America crops were being harvested.

Go For It

If You womp me,
Dear Daddy,
It'll be
   just one more ache
In a life time
Of many mistakes.

But I'll be happy,
Dear Pappy,
There were balls in my pants
   When life dared me
   And scared me and
I took a chance.

Working Your Way Back

Everybody gets down-hearted sometimes.

Saying that, I'm only telling you something you already know.

But what else I want to say—what this book wants to say —is that by approaching your problems in a Yesful manner, accepting your hardships as gifts, you will work your way up toward glory and contentment.

And it is possible to work your way all the way back, even though the cards seem stacked against you, and the rest of the world seems to hold all the aces.

Example A

I was very depressed. The initial happiness that had bloomed inside me, when I stood on the hilltop and finally discovered the meaning of *fuck*, faded quickly. Soon afterward all the pieces fell into place, and I had a full understanding of the word. I realized that *hate masquerading as love* was more than just a thing that happened between individual people. Perhaps it started out that way, but hundreds of years had passed since then, and now it was a constant part of everyone's world. *Fuck* had become an institution.

It's become a part of everyday life.

It's so much a part of everyday life we've mostly come to forget it exists. We tune it out in the way people in cities ignore smog even as it penetrates their lungs, injuring their health and shortening their lives, stealing their energy and limiting their potential.

But there it is. Fuck is. Happening all around us, and to us. People penetrating into our lives, interrupting us, interfering with our progress, leaving us partly dead.

People close to us may do it: friends, lovers, associates, spouses, and parents. Yes, the list even includes people who love or like us.

Besides them, there are others. People we barely know, and strangers, too. Even people who pretend to serve us. *Especially* people who seem to serve us. The executives and lawmakers, for example. Yes, the same type of people who led the way in banning the word from our language for several hundred years.

These people, these power people, I realized, just act as though they have our interests at heart, just act as though they care for us and about us. But it's mostly an act with shallow, greedy feelings behind it. They are concerned with their own power. With keeping it, and increasing it. That's all.

I thought of examples of this in everyday life. I thought of the way we're robbed of our humanity, of our wholeness, of how we're split into pieces.

To our employers, our bosses, we are mainly tools for producing money profits. We are eyes and hands to keep their equipment running. We are tools to be discarded when our usefulness has passed.

To the manufacturers of fast-food deathburgers, we are just mouths and wallets. Rather than feed us in a health-giving manner, they pump advertising into us, tempting us to swallow any shit they care to serve.

To advertisers, we are consumers. Those smiling fuckers on T.V., and those charming fuckers with cheerful voices on radio, behave as though they have our interests at heart, behave as though they are our friends. They give us cheap imitations of intimacy.

But in their minds we are only partly human.

To the advertisers of rings we are only fingers.

The sellers of aspirin want our heads to throb so they can sell us medicine.

The tourists bureaus of a thousand recreation areas all urge us to come see their particular attraction. We are pulled this way and that, so that it is difficult for a person to even have one single personality. Everyone wants us to do this and do that.

They feel free to pump their messages into us.

Pump, pump, pump.

Into us.

They treat us like cunts.

When I realized that, I understood why, besides f***, the word c*** had also become illegal to print with all its letters.

Then my mind drifted back to the xeroxed pages I'd copied at the community college library on that day I snuck off the ranch and rode to town in a truck load of wool. I remembered that wonderful sentence from 1707: "But I, a poor Virgin, am without a F---."

Alas, she had only a short time to wait.

In the 1700's the speed of the world had begun to pick up, and soon just about everybody was getting fucked. The Industrial Revolution had just begun, and the owners of factories—the Captains of Industry—had begun to rule the world. The Machine Age had begun in the 1400's, about the same time as the word *fuck* was invented. It was then that the first crude factories were set up. Seduced by the promise of an easier life, people left farms and country-life to come to the city to work in factories. But by the 1700's factory life was well on its way to dominating human life. The Captains of Industry got into the habit of fucking their workers real good. Too good. The workers rebelled. They rose up, like a bunch of pricks, and formed labor unions. That's why, in much of the world today, factory owners pay workers a decent wage.

In India and China the rebellions took the form of actual warfare.

But, despite the gains of labor unions and other groups of ordinary people, the world has steadily become more and more impersonal since the time of the invention of *fuck*. Shallow, greedy relationships have become increasing normal as the years have gone by. Just as gunpowder was invented around the time of the word *fuck*, so now we have long range missiles. The age of the mass fuck is upon us.

Thinking about gunpowder—which allows one person to kill another at a distance without any human contact taking place—led me to think about soldiers, and why they use the word so much that the officers—the executives and lawmakers of the military—once put up a sign trying to shame the men out of using earthy language. Soldiers lives are intimately connected with *fuck*, and that's why they're addicted to the word. First of all, they are on the receiving end of it more than anyone else in the world. They get it from all sides. Rules, regulations. Officers getting on their butts all the time. Soldiers are used like puppets. They're told where to sleep and when to eat. Do this, do that. It must be hard to feel like a human in such a world.

Second of all, they're job is to penetrate into other peoples' lands and other peoples' bodies, severely limiting other peoples' potential for breathing.

Besides that, the fucking enemy wants to kill them.

After thinking of all these things and coming to these conclusions I was very tired. I'd traced *fuck* all the way back from the basketball game with Quentin to the invention of gunpowder, and had solved several mysteries along the way. I'd learned I myself was a fucker. On top of that I had the awful feeling that the whole world was standing in line to do it to me.

It seemed to me, then, that we individual human beings must make a choice. A person can deal with the world like a respectable man or woman; that is, they can fight for the right to live without the interference of others. If you do that, there's a good chance you're going to die, like so many of the Chinese and Indians when they rebelled.

The other choice is that a person can go along with it, accepting getting fucked. And if you do, then the fuckers will take care of you, and feed you, and give you money for clothes and an occasional vacation. The institutions of society are designed primarily to pacify people, to keep them docile, like cows. Like sheep.

I thought of sheep. And about God, the Good Shepherd.

What does a shepherd do?

Raises sheep.

For what?

For slaughter.

When I realized this I was in the bunkhouse, looking in the mirror which hung over the dresser upon which lay the photograph of the Yessers and me and Astoria and the dog, on the beach.

Example B

Outside of Smagger's offices, the mid-afternoon sun was bright to the point of being blinding. It took a while for my eyes to adjust. Some of the automobile drivers passing by were turning their heads, staring at me, making me realize how peculiar I must look wearing my toga here in the middle of town. Suddenly I was so tired of being different. Pulling the toga over my head, taking it off, I crushed it into a small bundle, and grasping it firmly, I began to run. I ran in an easy loping pace down the street until reaching the highway along the ocean, and there turning south I continued on. Running out of breath, it became necessary to walk, but soon, catching my breath, I was running again, shirtless and intent, like any of the ordinary joggers that you see trotting along the roads of our country. Moving, keep moving, was the idea. After being so close to losing control, perhaps the running would help. It was the only thing I could think to do. Soon the sweat was pouring off me. I ran for a long time—for almost an hour—although slowly at times, barely progressing at all, but constantly pushing onwards, sometimes having to walk. I continued south on the highway towards Mexico, and at one time had to stop at a park across the street from the beach. The park had a nice green lawn with benches and mothers with baby carriages. I drank from a fountain, the water icy on my lips and steaming face. In the bottom of the catch basin of the fountain was a clam shell.

Clam.

Bearded clam.

In high school, that's what we used to call girls: bearded clams.

Astoria.

She deserved a good time.

She was my woman, you know.

She deserved a good time.

I knew that. Knew she deserved a good time.

Wanted to do that: show her a good time.

I took her to a restaurant, once a long time ago.

Paid attention to her.

She talked, I listened.

Nice dinner, nice restaurant.

Outside afterwards, we were walking down the block to the car. She was smiling, she was grinning. "It was a nice dinner," she said.

My arm was around her shoulder, her arm around my waist.

Delight was in her eyes, she grinned at me like an imp.

"I want to show you something, honey," she said. Taking my hand in hers, she brought it up to the lapel of her little blue jacket. "Feel this material," she said. She had my thumb and finger on each side of the material, my thumb on the inside and my finger on the outside of her jacket. Holding my hand in hers, she moved it up and down, feeling the material. What the hell, I'm wondering, what's she getting at?

I was confused.

Then I realized that she's got my hand brushing against her breast; she's moving my hand up and down so the back of my thumb is brushing her nipple. Her nipple is up and hard like a diamond. She's aroused as hell, she's standing there grinning like an imp as she has me secretly feeling her, as she is telling me how excited she is as a woman, and thanking me for being her good man that night, as people stroll past us on a downtown sidewalk.

…in the catch basin of the water fountain the clam shell lies where maybe some child left it.

Clam.

Bearded clam. Besides that, we used to call girls "hair pie". Back in high school.

…the pores of my body, as I resumed running, were all open and pouring sweat. The salt of it got in my eyes, burning them. Wiping them with the back of my sweaty hand was of little help, but I refused to stop moving unless it was absolutely necessary, and I ran through red lights at intersections, rather than waiting on the curb for the light to change because I felt that if I stopped running something dreadful might happen.

Running southward still, Laguna was behind me now. After another hour had passed, or so, it might have been expected that the heat and the exercise would have had a great deal of effect on me, drained me, but perhaps I was beyond all that, because I felt fine, if I felt anything at all. A bus was coming up behind me, it's diesel engine laboring as it approached. When it was very near, I had the impulse to fling myself sideways, in front of it, beneath its wheels. Instead, I continued a slow jogging sort of trot, deep into the afternoon. The only thing that was important now was to keep going. Even when it became necessary to slow to a walk—I must have traveled for two hours by then—I kept moving, until finally even walking was too much of an effort. Sitting, at last, in the shade of a tree, I grinned wickedly to myself, knowing that I had gotten back to normal. I'd survived; my mind was okay once again. The pressure of Astoria and Norleen, and my teeter-totter existence had almost gotten to me. But now it was possible to smile because I felt safe. Arising, walking onto the beach toward the ocean, I thought how good it would feel to be in the water. Dropping my toga at the shoreline I ran jerkily through the surf, lifting my knees high to prance through the water, and plunged in and swam away beyond the breakers.

How far could a person swim, I wondered, if a person were just to swim outwards toward Japan and China?

The thought brought a shudder to my body, and hurriedly I turned and with almost frantic strokes swam thrashing through the water toward shore. It took a long time to get back through the breakers until at last my feet felt the grainy comfort of the sandy bottom.

Leaving the water, moving back to my discarded toga on the sand, exhaustion overcame me, and I collapsed on the warm cloth and fell asleep blanketed by the comfort of the afternoon sun. It must have been about two hours later that the on-shore wind which picks up in the late afternoon, propelling sailboats and cooling off the town, gradually chilled and awakened me. I rolled over, sat up, wondering what time it was. The sun had dropped close to the horizon formed by the gray arc of the sea. Some of the sand that clung to my face and chest and legs, and that had gotten into the curls of my hair, fell from me as I stood and walked back to the highway. Standing at a street corner, realizing there was too little money in my pocket for bus fare, I wondered how to get back to town. It was then a young woman, maybe just a few years out of high school, stopped her

325

convertible at the signal. We eyed each other. I nodded in the direction of town. She smiled and mouthed, "Sure." She may have thought she was going to meet a good-looking guy and maybe have an adventure, but she was mistaken. For her sake and mine, I only grunted a few answers to her questions; we finished the short ride in silence and she was glad when I got out. Watching her drive away, I thought about how easily good breaks came to me, like catching a ride so easily, always helping me or saving me in the nick of time.

Up the steps of the condo I went, and opened the door feeling strong and in absolute control of my life.

The living room was crowded: Astoria, Bruno, Chester Grooch & The Orchestra, Horny Harriet, and Toby Hanratty and his darling wife Darlene who had a half-empty bottle of California Spritz in her hand. As I entered they all looked toward me expectantly like I was the pony express rider in from Abilene, Kansas. Then suddenly everyone had something to say: Bruno began telling me that Marshall Merriweather and the T.V. crew were setting up in the rec room; Astoria was saying it looked like I'd gotten some sun, and how was the restaurant? (Remember, I'd lied to her, saying Fernando was taking me there that afternoon.) Horny Harriet wanted to speak with me, she said. Chester & The Orchestra told me that tonight's soloists would be Bing Crosby and Tina Turner. He asked if he could wire The Orchestra directly into the T.V. recording equipment to get higher fidelity. Toby sat grinning like an idiot and Darlene offered me a drink from her California Spritz.

Hugging Darlene and taking the bottle from her hand, I thanked her, told Astoria the restaurant looked okay, and said "Sure, let's talk," to Horny Harriet. I suggested to Bruno that he handle M.M. as best he could. We'd start the services about 8:30 PM as usual—okay? Yes, we agreed. I told Chester that high fidelity was a wonderful thing, the higher the better, and he should check with the T.V. people about how to get wired. Having eaten only Astoria's lettuce and cremated sausages, I wished someone would think to offer me dinner, but they were silent on that point so I just grinned back at Toby like it was somebody's birthday and that person was going to get everything a person could wish for. Bruno and Chester Grooch were about to go to the rec room. I suggested that Toby and Darlene go with them; they said they would. Toby arose from the couch and Darlene laid down and passed out. My stomach ached, my head felt light, and suddenly I had a moment of panic: I had lost my zucchinis! Where the fuck were they? Then—remembering—I hurriedly felt my back pockets. Thanks to God; they were there, one in each pocket. Reaching down, I whipped them out like Marshall Dillon in Dodge City. They were more rubbery and flexible than your average Colt .45, but remember they'd been on a long run, and had been swimming, and crushed against the car seat of a nice looking, young woman just a few years out of high school whose head I had left completely unfucked. With the zucchinis in my hands, I calmed down, and asked Harriet what she wanted to talk about. She looked hesitant and concerned.

She is such an endearing person. When God made her, He did so without putting one mean, nasty bone in her body.

I asked Astoria, "You all right?"

"Fine," she said.

"Good."

"Just fine. I was wondering where you were," she said.

We stared at each other like there were vast distances between us—like we were on opposite sides of the Grand Canyon and we were both out of mules to take us to the other side.

"How's Alice?" I asked. "How's the job?"

"Fine," she said. "Just fine."

I thought of Shifty Eddie and Fernando Clip and the cops. I thought of my brief interview for a position as a zoo keeper back on the day I discovered *Yes*. I thought of playing basketball with

327

Quentin and tearing the skin off my thigh.

I told Astoria, "Good, good."

She and I were down at the bottom of the barrel again, covered with rotten apples and pig's knuckles and shit. Covered with veal scallopini made of chicken thighs.

"What can I do for you, Harriet honey? What's up?"

She looked at me hesitantly. Then at Astoria.

She nodded toward the bedroom door.

"Harriet, be serious," I said jokingly.

"Oh, Wing," Harriet said, "I just want to talk in private." Turning to Astoria, "Would that be all right, dear? I just need him for a little while."

"Sure," Storee said to us, sounding more confident than she would have if she'd known that Harriet had the world's best portable lemon squeezer.

Harriet and I ducked into the bedroom.

She sat heavily on the bed, and for the first time I realized something was terribly wrong. Some great sorrow had come into her life. My heart went out to her. For the first time she looked truly old. Her skin was pale, loose and wrinkled; her eyes were downcast. Lifting her head, she gazed up at me. She must have realized how weak she seemed, because she tried to straighten herself up. I was about to sit beside her and put my arm around her to help her, to comfort her, but she started to speak, so I stayed put and let her get it out. When she spoke she attempted to sound like her sister Bertie, business-like, pretending her heart was made of cement.

"Wing, Minnie is flying in tomorrow, and..." She paused and began having difficulty talking.

"Yes, go on."

"Well, we've all spoken by phone... In a phone call to Minnie... And it's been decided..."

"What is it? You can tell me, Harriet."

"If I had had a son, Wing. I would have liked him to be like you."

328

I thought of us in bed that time.

She must have guessed that, because she snapped, "Oh, you're being silly, Wing. Forget the screwing, I only meant that a mother would be proud to have a son like you. You have great talent and great ability in you. And such a good heart."

Some of the cruel things I'd done came back to haunt my mind.

"Your trouble is you think you have to be a hero, a he-man." You'd be a lot better off it you'd just remember you're a human being like everyone else. If you'd ease up a little."

Rather than give her my speech on heroes, I just said, "Yes, maybe you're right."

"What you say and what you think are often two different things, my boy. Oh, what's the use?" She arose from the bed, and came to me, and put her arms around me and hugged me, her head pressed against my chest. Then she stood back, straightened herself and said, "We're moving, Wing. We're going away."

A lump grew in my throat, and I bit my lip.

Her voice had much finality in it. She sounded like this would be the last time we would ever see one another.

She was such a lot of fun.

She had so much life in her, so much energy and spark.

Besides that, something else, something deep within me, was trying to express itself. I felt tears rising in my eyes and wondered how much... It had been such a long day... How much a person was able to take. Fortunately, just as I was getting real low, the Wonderword came to my rescue. I told myself that whatever happened *was good*. I gave Harriet the best smile I had available.

Harriet said, "I know. I'll miss you too." She puffed herself up trying to stand tall and began talking to me, a little bit stiffly like she was handing out diplomas on graduation day. "You're a good man, Wing. The things you talk about are very confusing to me, but I know you're an honest person."

"Thank you, Harriet..."

"And Astoria, she's a lovely, good girl."

I nodded, *Yes*.

"But I think she must have had an awfully difficult time living with you all these years."

We both laughed a little at that.

"You're so strange."

"You're a little different yourself, beautiful."

She smiled although she wanted to be serious.

"I want you both to be happy," she said.

"We're happy."

She paused and said, "Well, there's something missing, Wing."

I nodded that she was right, and kept quiet hoping that maybe she would be able to tell us what the missing ingredient was.

"I think I can help," she said, and started rummaging through her over-size, little-old-lady's purse. She withdrew a large envelope. "Here," she said.

Peeling back the flap of the envelope, I pulled out a thin stack of engraved papers. There were eight of these sheets, all covered with fancy printing in various pale colors. It was ornate printing with swirls and flourishes. Each paper had a large sheet of coupons attached like sets of over-sized stamps from the post office. Across the top of each splendid sheet was a name like: 'City of Dallas" and "City of Los Angeles" and "Municipal Water District of Muncie, Indiana."

"They're bonds, Wing."

Yes, they were.

"Do you like them?"

"It's too much, Harriet. Please take them back."

"Please accept them, Wing.... It's what you need."

Oh, sure. Like I needed a ride from a girl just out of high school.

I should have walked.

"Everything I need, I have. Believe me, Harriet."

"Maybe you do. But your wife needs this security."

I wanted to shout to her: I'm clean. I'm free. I've lost it all, Harriet. Let me be. Just let me be. Let me fly.

Instead, I counted. The sheets added up to about five hundred thousand—that is, one-half million—dollars. Wow.

I stared at them for a long while.

The people in the other room were making more noise than before.

The rock music was loud.

Gradually, it started to dawn on me that I was rich. *We,* Astoria and I, were *rich.*

"It's too much, Harriet."

Ignoring my protest, she started rattling facts and ideas into my face, while I was thinking: I'm rich. I can buy Shifty Eddie's dead disco, if I want to. I can start my own dead disco. Astoria and I can have matching dead discos.

Anything... Anything suddenly had become possible...

"Now these are *municipal* bonds," Harriet said. The average interest they pay is 13%. That means that each year, twice a year as a matter of fact, you will get checks totalling about $65,000. That will go on for fifteen years more or less."

She showed me the different maturity dates on some of the bonds, saying when that date on each bond arrived I would be paid the face amount of the bond: $60,000 or $80,000, or $20,000 or whatever that particular bond happened to be worth.

Like a third grade teacher, she beamed at me, "Do you know what's really wonderful about these bonds," she asked. "The sixty-five thousand dollars you get each year is completely tax free. By law... It's perfectly legal. The money's all yours." Her sweet face broke into several thousand wrinkles of happiness. "So you can spend it *all.* Buy Astoria a nice house, Wing."

Part of me wanted to jump up and down, yelling, "Yippee."

Money like this could buy a couple of people a lot of space.

On the other hand, another part of me understood that these eight pieces of splendid paper would make only the flimsiest of bridges across the Grand Canyon. The answer was somewhere else. Or was it.

Should I accept them.

Yes?

Of course.

"You're screwing up my life, Harriet. For the first time I'm getting close to some final answers."

"Stop thinking of yourself, damn it, Wing. This is more serious than that."

"I'm thinking of everybody. Believe me."

"That remains to be seen," she said. "In the meantime, you just accept these, please," she said firmly, "and see what good you can do with them."

I fingered the splendid pieces of paper.

"It's a half a million dollars, Harriet."

"Well, with inflation like it is who knows how much half a million will buy in fifteen years."

"Oh, sure. It might only be worth three hundred thousand."

"That's so true, Wing. It's this damn government spending. But remember, all this money is tax free."

"Harriet, how can you do this to me? I've worked so hard to get here, to get myself down to zero. I'm nearly empty, and you come at me with this..."

I almost added, "Let me die in peace."

Brushing aside what I'd said, she stepped up to me and put her arms around me, hugged me. "Give them to Astoria," she said. "She'll know what to do with them."

Oh, yeah?

Fat chance.

It was more likely that I would grow feathers than I would turn these over to Storee.

"When are you leaving, Harriet?"

332

"Tomorrow."

"So soon?"

She smiled weakly. She got back to business. "There's one other thing, Wing."

"What?"

"You must avoid telling anyone I've given you these bonds."

"Why?"

Harriet remained silent, looking guilty.

"Do Minnie and Bertie know you're doing this?"

"It is my money, and we sisters have agreed we can each spend our own money any way we like."

"Yes."

"But you see... Our father, Cyrus Harvester, the Third, refused to realize that women are just as capable as men in handling money. He thought we'd just waste it, or throw it away."

"I wonder what ever gave him that idea?"

"I'm afraid Daddy was old fashioned. You see, in his will he appointed a bank trustee who looks after most of our financial affairs, even though we are perfectly capable ourselves. In fact, that's why we went into the business, you know: to learn how to handle money. Well, anyway, this bank trustee is a very old fogey of a fellow; he makes life very difficult for us sometimes. Why, Wing, if he were to find out I'd given you this money he would just have a fit. Honestly, I believe he's beginning to think I'm getting old and senile. I'm afraid he might put me in an old folks' home.

I shuddered. It would be horrible for this wonderful woman to be shut in with a lot of half-dead people watching Mindy and Mandy's T.V.

"I'm going to give you these bonds, but I'm sure he would object."

"That's certainly hard to understand, huh? Why should he object to you giving away half a million dollars?"

"Exactly, Wing. I'm glad you see it my way."

"I was joking."

"Well, this is serious. You are supposed to keep this a secret from everyone except Astoria. Put the bonds in a safe deposit box at a bank. And whenever it's time to cash in a coupon just tear one off the bond and take it to any bank and they'll give you the money." Harriet started to say something, but I heard Astoria just outside the bedroom door talking to someone.

There was a knock.

Power surged into me.

I knew what I must do. An angry energy filled my chest and flowed into my hands which tensed into fists. This lasted only a moment, this strong emotion, and I concealed it from Harriet. She stopped speaking in mid-sentence as I quickly slipped the bonds back into the envelope. Making a sssh-ing motion with my finger to my lips, I urged her to be quiet and thanked her, saying, "Harriet, I know you're doing this because you want to help us."

"I do," she said.

Bending, I hurriedly slipped the envelope under the bed.

She was puzzled by my hiding them.

"Let me tell Astoria about the bonds when the time is right, okay, Harriet?"

"Then you'll keep the bonds."

"I've always wanted to have a large sail boat."

Harriet smiled sweetly, happily.

"Even more than that, I've always wanted Astoria to have a comfortable and happy life."

"You will keep them then."

"Maybe."

"You're suppose to say 'Yes'."

"Yes, I am," I said. "That's true. I *am* supposed to say *Yes*."

Harriet hugged me affectionately just as Storee came into the room. She looked like she wanted to know what was going on.

"I have some serious news, Astoria. Harriet just told me that she and her sisters, Bertie and Minnie, are going to move away."

Astoria's face softened and said, "Oh, that's too bad. You were the first person I met when I came to Laguna."

"I'll miss you, too, dear." She put her arm around Astoria's shoulder and they started moving toward the door. "But we'll write to you from Miami, and occasionally we'll all fly out to visit you."

They left the room, talking, and I sat on the bed wondering about how strange life is. But there was little time to wonder, because the evening meditation was about to begin.

Amazing Space

The world is a wondrous place, an amazing space that's filled with the most fascinating things. Do you feel this way, too? Speaking personally, I'm dazzled and delighted by the endless flow of life around us. Life in all its imaginative and extraordinary forms fills me with awe and deep respect for the creative mind of Nature. Far from feeling that we human beings are of little importance, small specks in an enormous universe, I feel privileged to be a part of it all, privileged to be able to see with my own eyes the astonishing variety of life that Nature has invented. So many different kinds of life! So many beings and things and processes making their journeys from birth to death!

How great and powerful we human beings are, to be allowed to witness such magnificence. What an honor it is—what an honor I feel—just to watch the everlasting parade of growth that forever happens all around us, and inside of us, as the various forms of life work out their destinies.

Thank you, God.

Example
There was music coming out of the rec room as I approached. Backed by a symphony orchestra, Laurel and Hardy were reciting *My Country 'Tis of Thee*.

Stopping in the doorway, I saw Chester Grooch & The

Orchestra in a corner of the room. While The Orchestra played, he stood speaking with a couple of strangers (one of them in a glowing pink shirt) who probably belong to the T.V. production truck parked outside.

Darlene Hanratty was lying on the pool table at the far end of the room, a bottle of California Spritz clutched to her chest. Other T.V. people—a mini-cam operator and sound person (one woman, one man)—were deep in conversation with big Bruno near the fireplace, which was dark. Behind me, the sun was setting, but in the room the lights were still off, so the room had a warm, dusky feeling, like a dark fog was settling in.

I saw all this from the doorway where I'd stopped like a dead soul reluctant to enter hell.

Turning away, I trotted back towards the condo, and dashed up the steps, through the front door, into the bedroom, and grabbed the telephone. The information operator gave me the phone number of N. Winkowski, but the rings just sounded endlessly in my ear. Finally I hung up, deeply concerned that she and Winslow K. Smaggers had left early on their trip together.

She'd promised.

Would she keep it?

While descending the front steps of the condo, going back to the rec room, I tripped. The toga floated out from my sides like wings as I vainly tried to regain my balance. Waving my arms awkwardly, I lurched sideways and fell, clipping the black metal railing with the left side of my forehead before landing, in a sudden stop, with my head on the bottom step and my legs stretched up the stairs behind me. Lying still, I watched the blood run along the bridge of my nose, and saw it drip in little red zeros onto the pavement just in front of my eyes. It hardly hurt at all; it felt sort of good in fact. I jumped up like it was Christmas, and ran with flapping toga back to the rec room, where the devoted Yessers were alarmed at my injury. All twenty or so of them gathered around me, concerned that I be properly tended to. Commenting on the wound—which was small—I said, ''Well, you have to expect things like this.'' Bruno shooed most of them away and tended to me at the wet bar.

Darlene was motionless in the same position I had seen her earlier, the California Spritz clutched to her bosom like a stuffed animal. I wondered if she might be dead. Bruno dabbed a cool, dampened towel on my brow, washing away the signs of blood. Someone came up with a Band-Aid which Bruno taped to me. While he attended my injury, I listened to the T.V. people and some of the Yessers, as they resumed their conversation, which I gathered was about the Viet Nam war. At the far end of the room, a T.V. was on, tuned to an exhibition football game which, from where I sat, looked like a xerox of all the other football games that had ever been played. Several Yessers gazed intently at the screen.

Chester Grooch & The Orchestra began to play slow, wavy music that might remind a person of ocean swells passing through their head. This was the signal the services were on their way to beginning. We church-goers had formed the habit of sort of easing into our devotions, rather than having some formal beginning. For a while the music would play, getting us in the mood to share our joy with one another. Already the fumes of burning vegetation wafted through the room as the first marijuana and hash bongs were ignited. Astoria and Alice Angsterlobe were huddled in a corner, probably doing business, dreaming of increasing sales, higher profits. Storee still wore the Walkman, although now the earphones were loose around her neck. But she still had tape running, I could hear it faintly across the room—hard rock & roll, guaranteed to put you in a world of your own, alone. Someone lit a candle, then another. Against the far wall the huge red cushion, on which I sat during service, was illuminated by the candle glow like a soft throne. Horny Harriet was deeply in conversation with Toby Hanratty and

Daryl Spagnoff. The door opened and Joe Wagonewti entered the room, followed by Fernando Clip who scanned the room like an eel looking for a blond swimmer. Horny Harriet put her arm around Daryl's waist as that small group warmed up toward the evening. Joe and Fernando came lumbering in my direction like thirsty cattle.

I waited; it was all there was to do.

The T.V. people: Marshall Merriweather—his shirt glowing in the dusky light—and the two mini-cam operators were in total agreement in their discussion about the Viet Nam war. Without doubt, they told each other, T.V. coverage had hastened the end of the war because nightly the American people had seen the horror of the conflict on their own home screens and had been repulsed by the violence, savagery and wasting of life and money, and they had finally demanded our withdrawal of our soldiers from the ugly conflict.

Joe and Nano were coming at me like green berets through the jungle.

I had the strong feeling someone should tell the T.V. people that their coverage of the Viet Nam War had prolonged it. The war was a good drama with a huge cast of interesting characters. It was the stuff T.V. is made of: conflict and violence. If it had been different—if it had been an ordinary war, one which just sent home dead bodies and crippled young men, and was reported with the old-fashioned way—with photographs, radio and written reports—then people might have tired of it quickly. But Viet Nam came to us in living color, on tape, sandwiched between commercials for Hamburger Helper and mouthwash and other doo-dads of little importance, like any other T.V. series. Yes, by any measurement, you'd have to say Viet Nam was a hit show; it lasted ten full seasons and had many spin-offs. As wars go, it was more expensive than most, but, for sure, the people got more for their money than ever before. It lasted two and a half times longer than any other American war, which was a sign of how popular it was. After it was over, the producers turned loose all the soldiers—the veteran actors—and treated them very badly. But that's the way it is in T.V. Hardly anybody gets a new show once the old one is cancelled.

After the war was over and done, many people complained about the ending. And, many people said they hated the show the whole time it was on.

People are reluctant to admit how addicted they are to violence.

The room got very black indeed. All the images, all the people, became different shades of darkness. I heard sounds dimly, softly, like they were coming at me through thin mattresses.

"Wing, what the fuck..?" Wagonewti said.

Deep in my own thoughts, I began to laugh and laugh. I had suddenly realized I was dying. I said so, out loud, to myself, laughing, "I'm dying, man, I'm dying."

"Let me do it for you, you bastard." Wagonewti said. "What were you doing in a cop car this afternoon?"

Joe was being pushy. He was often pushy, I realized. Then, looking around the room, I realized that everyone in sight was doing things I'd seen them do before. A sense of hopelessness came over me.

How could we get anywhere if everybody stayed the same, if they repeated the same activities over and over?

The television people were comfortable in their jobs, and talked of the importance of their industry, and—therefore—of themselves.

Everybody was doing the same things as always.

Astoria and Alice were taking care of business, involved in the same lonely self-interest they had always indulged in. Chester Grooch & The Orchestra continued to roll out waves of the oceanic music that had always obsessed him. Bruno was attending to me, just as he had done from the moment we met.

He looked confused. He was still a poor morbid fellow, a true believer, who lived two falsehoods at once: believing that the world is a rotten place and that I, the object of his devotion, was somehow a special person.

Soon I would be gone.

What would he do then?

He would do the same things as always, probably.

The door opened.

I waited for the dark-haired girl to come through.

Instead it was a middle-aged woman with enormous red plastic eyeglasses perched on a nose a parrot would envy. Her hair was chopped short like a porcupine with a crew cut. She was coming toward me, and I knew that her voice would sound like dentist drills at three o'clock in the morning. It was Penelope Slick, and you had to hand it to her, she was persistent. She was digging like hell for a story for *People* magazine, just like she always did. Sure.

Wagonewti said, "You gonna explain it, Wing? Because I am very serious about this."

"*Yes*, Joe, you are."

The Fabulous Word, would stick by me, I knew, until the end and beyond. It was comforting.

It was all very frightening.

Toby Hanratty, who's mother refused to breast feed him, who's darling wife, Darlene, lay on the billiard table continuing the endless pickling of her brain...he was talking to one of our recent converts to *Yes*, a brand new Yeswoman. He was staring at her bosom.

The little dog, over near the dark fireplace, was eating the August 31 edition of the San Diego *Union*.

Daryl Spagnoff, Horny Harriet...

Everybody was doing the same as always.

The same goddamn things they'd always done.

"Bruno..."

"Yes, Master."

He would always call me Master.

Where was the dark-haired girl?

It was easy to imagine that she had screwed up every opportunity she ever had for deep union.

My mind was growing as dark as her hair, as dark as the puppy's nice coat.

"Joe and Nano here are very angry at me."

Bruno eyed them in a way that made them ill-at-ease.

Chester Grooch & The Orchestra were raising the sound level; the waves were getting bigger, crashing over the piers and wharfs and rock jetties.

The door opened.

There stood the dark-haired girl.

She looked wonderful, so wonderful.

She looked so feminine to me.

Across the room, Astoria looked up from her intense conversation with Alice. She stared at the open doorway, and then at me.

Sure, she loved me.

Too bad she had refused to trust me.

Her eyes narrowed, as she stared across the gloomy room wondering what was up.

What would happen if Astoria had trusted?

Would she have died?

Yes, she would.

But she was going to die anyway.

Everybody dies.

"Bruno, if Joe or Nano try to leave, or try to interfere with me..."

Astoria resumed her conversation with Alice.

"Yes, Master..."

"Kill them."

"Yes, Master."

The dark-haired girl walked into the room.

She looked this way and that, trying to make out things as her eyes adjusted to the gloom.

A man could drown in her.

It was time for the services to begin.

I went to my red cushion over against the far wall, and sat down. The Holy Yessers began to be seated, in chairs and cross-legged on the floor.

Except for Darlene.

My mind was black as the tar that paves the wide road to hell. A sense of tragedy filled me like thunderclouds fill Wisconsin skies. This would be the last time we Holy Yessers ever got together. As we looked at each other—with them waiting for me to speak—I realized that this sort of thing, this talking, was the same thing I had always done. I laughed. How funny. Just a few moments ago I had been thinking badly of these people, and now I realized that it was *me* who constantly did the same goddamn things I had always done. It was me who took advantage of people, me who conned them, and gave so little in return. Astoria, and Bruno, and the convertible-driving girl just a few years out of high school: I had promised them so much more than I delivered.

This thought made me smile.

It was as though I had discovered a great truth.

The dark haired girl, sitting across the semi-circle from me, smiled back.

Somebody had already started passing around the Holy Collection basket. Like most churchs and sects, we collected money from our believers. For a basket, we used a Chinese coolie's hat, a cone shaped thing such as stooping Chinese men and women wear when they are calf-deep in muddy water, harvesting rice. When the hat reached Norleen, she held it for a moment, then set it down in front of her. From her large floppy purse beside her, she withdrew a folded paper, about four inches square, and dropped it into the hat, which she then passed to the next person.

For some reason, Chester Grooch & The Orchestra stopped playing, and Astoria's voice sounded out in the silence, continuing the conversation she was having with Alice. Realizing she was interrupting the services, she stopped speaking. She stared at me for a moment or two, then coolly said, "Excuse me," as though we were strangers in a supermarket bumping carts.

Over on the other side of the candle lit room, Harriet sitting beside Daryl, accepted a hit from his hash pipe.

Bruno had seated Joe and Fernando on the floor with their backs against the wall, far from the door.

The coolie hat was set in front of me.

Taking from it the dark-haired girl's folded paper, I carefully opened it to find that it was Winslow K. Smagger's college diploma. It had been awarded to him (and now to me) by the University of Chicago in 1944. It was a degree in Mathematics. Ah, good. Now I'd be able to add things up.

Too bad it came so late.

I looked at Astoria. She was speaking to Alice again.

The dark-haired girl approached me. She moved gracefully, limber and fluid. She came down in front of me, kneeling and sitting back on her heels with her back very straight and up-right.

Shaking her head and speaking in a low voice, Norleen said, "Very bizarre, Wing. This all looks very bizarre."

"Yes, it's nice, huh?"

She shrugged .

"Thanks for coming."

"I said I would, so here I am. Besides, Winslow asked me to bring you that."

"The diploma?"

"Yeah. Actually, I had a lot of things I wanted to get done, but he wanted you to have it."

I knew she was lying. I was certain that she was very attracted to me. Attracted by my good looks and clever mind. I probably had impressed her a lot that day on the beach when I got the cops off her tail by decoying them away with false promises of marijuana and cocaine. (I smiled, remembering how angry Gilford had been when we got to the police station and the joint I'd tossed him turned out to be a Pall Mall.) Sure, Norleen was a very proud person, and wanted to hide the fact that she was interested in me. That was probably why she'd made up the story about the diploma. I knew she'd stolen it for me.

"Why'd he want me to have it?"

"How should I know?" she said, irritated. "He asked me how we'd met, and I told him I caught you trying to steal his diploma."

"That should just make him mad."

"Ah, quite to the contrary; Winslow has always got his temper under control. He said that if you wanted it that much you could have it, and he asked me to bring it to you."

I hated it when she called him "Winslow" so familiarly.

"Do you always do what he tells you."

Norleen scowled at me.

I looked away.

I looked down at the diploma and opened it again.

"He also told me to tell you that when you ran out of zucchini you were welcome to come back and see him."

This news puzzled me, which must have showed because Norleen said, "How should I know? Maybe he likes you."

Norleen was a very strange person for making up a story like this, and I was trying to think of a polite way of telling her so, when we heard a rustling sound beside us. We both looked up to see Astoria standing next to us. Ignoring my motioning for her to sit with us, she put her hands on her hips and remained standing.

"Norleen, I'd like you to meet my wife, Astoria."

"Hi," Norleen said cheerfully and openly, like they were sisters.

Astoria refused to recognize the dark-haired girl was even there. Instead she looked at me tensely and said, "Perhaps you should remember you are the father of two children." With that she spun around and bounced away toward the door to the rec room.

I jumped to my feet and spread my arms widely, my toga fanned out like wings, pure and creamy white. "Wait," I cried out.

The T.V. camerawoman, quick on the job, turned her mini-cam on me. The guy assisting her held a sound boom over my head just out of camera sight as they recorded my performance. My arms were outstretched to all our congregation. Startled by the noise, they all quickly turned their attention to me. "Tonight is special. There is something for us to share. Tonight I am going to share with you everything...."

Astoria, from the doorway, raised her chin at me, full of pride. For a moment she held her pose, then turned her back on us and left the room, going out into the night alone, clamping the Walkman's earphones firmly over her ears as she went.

Without calling to her, or even hoping that she'd come back, I began my final sermon.

"Holy Yessers, hear me...

"We hear you," somebody said.

"We're all ears."

I told them, "For thousands of years, even from before the dawn of history, the greatest dream of all Mankind has been to be able to fly..."

"Fly me to the moon," someone crooned.

"Yes, that was the dream, Holy Yessers. Yes, it was. And now Mankind is able to fly, but I want to ask you this: What good has it done for us? Flying? Has it done us any good?"

"Yes!" some of the crowd affirmed.

346

"Sure!" someone called out.

"Fly me to the moon," sang the crooner.

...an odd feeling began to grow in my body, but I ignored it and continued...

"Well, of course, you're right," I said, confirming their affirmatives. "It used to be that people had to stick around home all the time. But now, if you or I should suddenly want to go to New Zealand or Peru, we can go by airplane. That's much quicker and less trouble than traveling by canoe. It's hard to canoe to Peru."

...the odd feeling in my body seemed to be gathering itself mainly behind my eyes...

"But, dear holy Yessers, my friends, my loved ones, my family, my selves, let me ask you this. Why have people always wanted to fly? When the first cavemen and women looked into the sky and saw the mighty turkey buzzard soaring above them in magnificent flight, why did they say, 'Gee it would be great to fly like a turkey buzzard.'?"

...I waited for the Yessers to respond, but, strangely they had fallen silent, and seemed to be looking at me in a weird way...

"So let us ask ourselves," I suggested, "Why did all these cavepersons stay home instead of flying somewhere nice on vacation? Was it because there was a traffic jam on the way to the airport? Or because all the flights were showing movies they'd already seen? Or because they were tired of having some cabin attendant—some stranger—ordering them to fasten their seat belts?"

...things were getting very bizarre. Besides my audience becoming strangely silent, I—who usually spoke so perfectly easily—was having trouble getting my words out of my mouth. What's more, my eyes felt moist...

"Yes," I told them as best I could. "Those were the real reasons cavepersons stayed home. Particularly the last one. The truth is: most cavepersons deeply resent being told to fasten their seat belts. In fact, everybody deeply resents being told to fasten their seat belts.''

...I sucked in my breath. Besides having trouble talking, I realized that the room contained fewer Yessers than it had a few moments ago. Some of the Yessers must have left. Even more strangely, as I watched, a couple others got up, and made their way toward the rec room door. But like any good performer I went on with the show....

"Why? Why do they resent it, you may ask?" I gave them the answer immediately. "It's because *they already have their seat belts on*! And they're having such a hard time *getting the fucking things off*."

...the T.V. camerapersons were gone, and with them Marshall Merriweather...

"Do you understand?"

...I waited in vain for a response from the Holy Yessers...

"What would happen if we all released our seat belts and wandered free? Like I did when I came to Laguna?"

...even Bruno had gone. Joe and Nano, Harriet, Daryl, Toby...

"Oh sure, we all get scared. We become afraid. Fear, like a little devil, hisses whispers in our ears..."

...someone had even carted off Darlene...

"Fear will urge us to eat too much.

"To sleep too much.

"To smoke a cigarette or a joint.

"To fuck a stranger."

...the room was empty except for the puppy and the dark-haired girl, only they remained with me. Her face shone in the golden candle glow...

"What happens when you refuse to listen to the whispers of fear?"

...in the distance I heard someone crying...

The dark-haired girl said, "Wing?"

I nodded.

Again, she spoke, "Wing, are you all right?"

I was sort of surprised to find myself sitting again on my red cushion. I thought I'd been standing.

She was kneeling by my side, and asked again, "Are you all right?"

"Yes, of course," I said.

"It's just that you were so silent. And the tears..."

"Pardon?"

"Well...you were crying."

"I was speaking," I said. She looked puzzled, so I added, "You must have heard me speaking?"

"Just crying, Wing." Her voice was gentle and understanding like that day on the beach with the soldier. Her eyes were dark and calm.

"I was telling everyone about Fear, and about seat belts and shit like that."

"You started talking about flying. And then you just stopped saying anything. And then you started crying."

"What was the last thing I said?"

"You said, 'It's hard to go to Peru in a canoe.' "

Oh, my God, I thought, my whole message was lost. It's flying around out there in space. Everyone missed it. "Well," I said to myself, "if that's the way it is, then that's the way it has to be."

There were just the two of us now, sitting next to each other like rocks on a desert.

I scooted on my red cushion up close to her side and reached out my arm around her shoulder, and hugging her a little, said, "Thanks for coming."

"Is the blonde really your wife?"

"In a manner of speaking, yes."

Norleen smiled, shrugged.

I looked down and closed my eyes. A moment later it was surprising to feel her firm hand on my head tousling my curly hair. "It's going to be okay," she said. "You'll be all right, Wing."

I loved it when she called me Wing.

"You're just a little stressed out," she said.

The room was still except for some scraping noises the puppy was making as he chewed a chair leg. I studied her face and was calmed by the look I found there: in the candlelight all the tension had vanished from her. She gazed at me with soft warm eyes and an expression of peace that told me she was content to be right where she was. I thought it strange she should be like that at a time when I was so weak. The stillness with which she sat there, and the tiny smile that played around her lips were magnetic to me, drawing me toward her.

She waited.

Gosh, she was attractive. She wore a little, loose knitted vest of this pale violet color; it was tied with a couple of little thongs. A very feminine little thing. I liked it. Beneath her little vest she wore a silky, dark blouse that picked up candle glow. She was even wearing a skirt, dark too, that hung loose from her hips to down around her knees, giving her a womanly sort of look, a softness, like she was maybe somebody's loving wife, like she might be a young mother with a kid somewhere.

Just seeing her caused me to relax.

She was still.

Gradually, I came to feel she was sending me some sort of message. She seemed to be waiting for me to do something.

Almost in a spirit of puzzlement—as though wondering what she should do or say—I reached over with my left hand and took hold of the thong holding her vest together, and pulled. The halves of the vest fell open. I watched them do it, then looked into her eyes and saw the same steady look of warm amusement. I was sure I saw some sort of affection in them.

How could that be?

I reached to the silky blouse, to the little pearl-colored buttons that held it closed. Slowly I loosened them, one by one. Soon, her breasts, braless, stood firm and beautiful before my gaze.

I said to her, "You love sex, huh?"

She put her finger to my lips to sssh me. She drew the back of her hand along my cheek caressing me. We kissed softly. "Hmmm," she murmured. I bent down and gently kissed her nipples. She put her hands behind my neck and held me to her. She kissed the top of my head.

She murmured, "I'm glad you like me."

The candles flickered and time faded away. Her eyes full of beauty and kindness, looked down on me. Her smile, tiny and playful, flickered around her mouth.

It's a mystery to me how long we were like that. All I know is that I awakened to hear the dog whimpering. He stood by the door, wanting us to take him out to pee.

Norleen gave a little laugh.

"What do you think we ought to name him?" I asked.

"It's your dog," she said.

"How about Muggs?"

"Your dog."

"Muggs it is then." She shrugged, and I said, "I know, it's my dog."

"Right," she said.

"Say, would you be willing to go for a walk on the beach. I think Muggsy needs some exercise."

"Sure," she said.

Her being so agreeable was sort of strange.

"First I'd like to go back to the condo to change out of this priestly garb," I told her.

"Sure, okay."

I wondered if I could get used to it. Her being nice.

* * * * *

351

Back in the condo, stopping at the bedroom door, I said it would just take a second to change clothes.

"I'll be here when you get back," she said, understanding that I was concerned that she might leave, duck out.

We walked Muggs until he did his thing, and then brought him back to the condo, left him there, and set out on our own, the two of us, hand in hand, looking for fun and adventure.

We drove the speedy Jaguar south down the main highway, south toward the Mexican border. For some reason that was a mystery to me when I did it, I decided to stop at a beach that was new to me. There was a long, deep parking lot that stretched alongside this beach. Pulling into one of the entrances we rolled along the blacktop until we saw a station wagon in the glare of our headlights. I turned the car into a space about seventy-five feet from the other car. In the dark, it was only a dim outline. I switched off the lights and we rolled down our windows. The night was warm as red velvet. The air washed around us; it made a person's muscles loose. The warmth was like oil, so that you moved in the night with a kind of easiness, as though you were floating out in space. What a fine California night. The air was full of sex and the possibility of violence. The black-haired girl and I sat half-turned toward each other.

She was more at ease than I'd ever seen her.

"Well, what shall we talk about?" I asked. "Real estate?"

She had been looking at me too calmly, and it made me a little nervous because it was hard to tell what she wanted and what she was after.

Relaxed and easy, she said, "Oh, Wing, you're so fucking hopeless."

She slouched with her back against the door, looking at me, with her lips parted and mouth open slightly.

"Baby, I can handle anything," I told her. "By the way, I like it when you call me Wing."

"Of course, you do," she said in a friendly manner, "You're an idiot."

"Well, that's true, too," I agreed.

"It's all right, she said. "*Most* men are idiots."

"What makes you think so?"

"Men get things wrong all the time," she said, adding that we men need women to let us know that we're men. "I bet you love oral sex," she said. "I bet you just love it."

Excitement surged through me like electricity. In my head were visions of what she could do. I could almost feel her hands on me, and see her mouth lowering toward my prick.

But I kept my face expressionless and said, "Pardon?"

"You heard me," she said teasingly. She repeated her question. "Do you like oral sex?"

"You mean, do I like to talk about it?"

She looked puzzled, then laughed. "You're funny. I might even get to like you."

"So tell me about oral sex," I asked, wanting to get back to business.

"I bet anything you thought of me giving it to you, rather than you giving it to me, right?" She laughed.

She had me there.

"Men want to be reassured all the time. They need it," she said. Her voice dropped low as she did a funny imitation of a man, "Hey, baby, get down on that big thing, huh?"

I laughed, she sounded so "manly".

"Hardly any men I know know how to use their cocks, Wing. And that's the truth. Almost all the time they're using them wrong."

I thought of Bruno and Marshall Merriweather taking turns pretending to be women, and pretending to be men for each other. Getting shit all over their dicks.

I thought of myself in the closet on New Year's Eve with the stranger.

"So how should they use them," I asked.

"You're the man, you figure it out."

We just looked at each other, easy and smiling.

God, life felt good at that moment.

Me and her together at last.

A voice in the back of my head spoke to me. It said, "Be of service to her." I smiled. How nice it was having this mysterious voice giving me good advice. "Be of service to her."

I can do that, I thought. *Yes*, I will.

"But for God's sake," the voice warned me, "keep your head. Try to keep from drowning in her, will you, bozo?"

I tingled with excitement, like low voltage electricity was being pumped through me.

I was happy.

It had taken so long to get to this point.

Thoughts of dying crossed my mind.

Even though I was happy.

What must happen right now, I knew, was that I had to make this as much fun as possible.

Relaxed and at ease, I leaned back against the car door, facing Norleen. Casually, I slipped my sandal off and lifted my bare foot and rested it against her thigh. She turned her body to sort of face me, so that she, too, was leaning against her car door.

Casually, like dipping my toes in water, I slid my foot onto her dark blue skirt, right over her cunt.

"Ooooh," she said.

"Uh-huh," I said.

Slowly my foot began to rub, press, massage her pussy through her skirt for a few silent minutes. This got a favorable reaction from her, judging by the way she said, "...oou..." Slipping my foot under her little skirt, I rested my toes against her crack and gently applied some pressure in a pleasant sort of way.

"So tell me, Wing...," she asked calmly like we were standing around after church services, "are you happy at home?" At the same time she spoke she started moving her hips deliciously against my foot.

"Very happy," I said evenly, like answering someone who asked if my lamb chops were cooked right.

"Ummmm," she sighed, like she'd just taken a good lick of ice cream. "Why are you doing this then? I mean why would you want to if…"

I worked my toes under her panties which were damp and warm.

"Perhaps you're right," I said. "I'll stop in a minute."

"It's okay," she said, "It's all right with me." She was trying to act casual but I could tell that she wanted me to rub her pussy forever, that she wanted the delicious contact to go on and on. She began rolling her hips back and forth, her breathing got heavier and heavier, but she kept her face very blank. It was as if she thought that if she let on how much she liked it, then it would be taken away from her. As though she feared all the pleasure would vanish, and she wanted it to continue forever. She blew out a long stream of breath and inhaled deeply and talked to me blankly as though we were both waiting for a trolley.

"Have you been a preacher for long?" she asked.

"Forever," I said.

She said, "I see."

"Do you like it?"

"Yeeessss," she breathed.

"I mean, the preaching."

She could barely hear me. The ball of my foot covered her fur, my big toe was rubbing her clitoris. My leg was straight out, stiff against her, and she was twisting hard in pleasure and sexual hunger.

I asked her, "Do you live in Laguna?"

"Anywhere you want," she said under her breath.

I pulled my foot away, and she went, "Oooh." Reaching for her, I brought her gently up-right on her knees and turned her so that she was kneeling on the seat with her forehead resting on the back of the seat. My hand went to her cunt, rubbing it, and it was all running with juice, and she was squirming rhythmically against my one hand while my other hand went to her tits, full and round like a young she-goat's. She rolled her forehead side to side on the seat back and mumbled. "All right, all right, do it, do it."

"You got it, you got it," I said, massaging her pussy and rolling her nipples between my fingers.

"Oh," she said. "Put it in. Put it in."

"Right," I said. "Sure." I said. "It's time, right? It's time to get fucked."

She moaned, "You can have anything you want."

I took my hands away. She looked at me wildly. I popped open the car door, got out and moved quickly to her door. She jumped out of the car to meet me. Our bodies pressed against each other. We were trembling like we'd caught some disease together. We held onto each other, shaking like our circuits were shorting out. "Come on," I said to her, and led her away clumsily with our arms wrapped around each other, each of us with our hands on the other. "Come on, it's time now," I said. In our stumbling walk we crossed the parking lot toward the station wagon we'd passed on the way in. Her hand was rubbing hard on my fly. My hand was on her; her skirt pushed up over my forearm, my fingers moving in her cunt. We stumbled toward the station wagon. "It's time to get fucked," I told her.

We stood there, ten feet from Daryl's car, and we could see the two people inside, on the mattress, fucking hard, with the woman underneath. She had her feet held high with her thighs pumping back and forth against Daryl's hips. They were really getting into it; she was straining like mad. Norleen rubbed my dick through my cut-offs and mumbled with her mouth against my ear, "What are we doing?" Inside the car the straining woman pressed her foot against the window, pressing her sole against the glass, so that we could see, so that everybody could see, the black mole, the dark birth mark where all her fucking brains had leaked out.

"Is that the way we do it," I screamed at Astoria through the glass that separated us. "Is that how?" I screamed.

Norleen got a look in her eye like a hunted animal, and got behind me, out of the line of fire of my rage.

Astoria and Daryl together twisted their heads and stared at me, their mouths dropping open in surprise.

"Stay here, Norleen," I screamed. "Keep tough. Look at them." I picked up a rock that was maybe the size of my fist. Astoria brought her face near the window, peering at me in disbelief. We stared at each other. Everything in the world stopped, motionless; then I cocked my arm back to hurl the rock through the window into Astoria's face. Her mouth opened in a silent scream but when the rock stayed in my hand, her face sagged. She looked, for a second, sorry. I started shaking like it was cold. From behind me Norleen put her hand on my arm; my arm dropped and I held the rock at my side in my sweat-damp hand. Confused, I turned to look at Norleen. She seemed strangely calm, as though she were only watching a movie somewhere. I tilted my head as though asking her, What should I do?

"This is very bizarre, Wing," she said.

She was refusing to provide a clear answer to my question. I knew I had to be good to my dark-haired woman, but I was in the dark about what else was right to do. I turned and stared at Astoria and Daryl. They both looked worried and he seemed to be getting ready for a fight; cautiously he moved free of her. I saw his glistening wet dick slide out of her, and I gulped. The pain tore at my heart. Astoria, at this moment, must have seen the confusion on my face. She sat up, sat on the mattress, with her legs sort of tucked under her. My God, she was suddenly calm. She had read my face like a book. What she saw there was my worry and hurt. She smiled faintly. She did. She smiled! My confusion swirled in my head. Astoria was smiling. She was feeling her power. She had the power to hurt. She could hurt me, and she did, and she smiled and she held her head up in a cool, haughty way. Her smile was saying to me, "I'll show you. I'll show you who has the power between us."

Astoria and I stood there looking at each other for silent moments until I felt the dark-haired girl behind me. Norleen wrapped her arms around my waist and pressed her tits into my back, and ground her loins and belly against my butt.

Astoria's smile sort of froze.

The dark-haired girl's hands dropped down and started massaging my dick through the cloth of the shorts.

The smile left Astoria's face.

Norleen put her lips near my ear, her hands still rubbing me in full view for all the world to see. "Do you want to make love to me in front of your wife? You can do it."

From behind me she reached around and lowered the zipper of my cut-offs, and pulled my cock out, like a bar of iron. My pants dropped to the ground and she held my dick like we were alone and had been doing this for years.

Astoria said something hurriedly to Daryl. He sat there looking awkward, as though having difficulty deciding what to do.

Norleen and I stood sideways to the car. Face to face. She put her arms lovingly around my neck and stood on her tip-toes. I snuck a last glance at Astoria. She seemed frozen, refusing to believe, rejecting the idea that I'd do this to her. Suddenly she snapped some words at Daryl. I bent my knees somewhat, and Norleen got a little higher on her toes, pressing against me. Reaching down, I glided my dick into her easy as cream pie. I hoisted her up on me a little and we started pumping, and it felt slick and good.

There was a commotion in the car. Maybe Daryl climbing into the driver's seat.

My dark haired beauty was wrapped around me like a monkey on a pole. She was pumping away and doing her part. I yelled in happiness, "Okay, okay, all right, all right."

The engine of the car blasted alive as Daryl over-revved it in a effort to get them out of there quickly. Oddly, I noticed I still had the rock in my hand. This distracted me from the business of screwing. I wanted to smash the glass that separated Astoria and me before she could get away. I wanted to pound the rock into Astoria's face; I wanted to beat Daryl until his whole head was a bloody pulp.

The tires spun. The car, in reverse gear, leaped backward. Daryl hit the brakes, he shoved it into first gear. Turning on the lights, he caught our fucking bodies in the white beams. The lights swept across us as it passed close by, shooting gravel against our legs. Norleen and I, like a two-headed animal turned our heads together to watch it flee toward the parking lot entrance. We lost our balance, tumbled to the ground. This halted our sex. The car, in the distance, in the black night, stopped briefly at the entrance to the street. The brake lights blinked red for a few seconds, and then the car turned out onto the highway and disappeared in the endless stream of flowing automobile lights.

In the silence, I realized I still held the rock in my hand. Norleen was lying half on top of me. I thought of hitting her in the head...of smashing the rock into the back of her head killing her.

Instead, off-handedly, I tossed it away, as though we were relaxed, sitting around taking it easy. What the hell, we were in this together, Norleen and I. I laid my hand on her cheek, and brushed her hair gently and kissed her mouth. "You were wonderful, just wonderful," I told her softly, and we kissed again, slowly like we had forever ahead of us.

"You, too," she breathed, bringing her mouth to mine, our tongues playing together like friends. I pulled her on top of me to get her off the rough ground. With my arms wrapped tight around her, and our mouths kissing, we went back to making love. She was fine and warm. The pleasure built and washed through us and exploded in us.

Afterwards, we laid still for a while, of course. Finally, I pulled her skirt back down over her bottom to keep it from getting cold. She slid off me, and sat on the ground beside me. She giggled.

"What so funny?"

"We sure took care of that marriage."

Sitting up and grinning, I could feel the pebbles and grit biting into my ass. "Yes, we certainly did."

One Thing Leads to Another

Fuck leads to *Yes.*
That's the truth.
It's the main truth in the universe.
After fuck comes *Yes.*

Example

Norleen and I went for a long walk and talk on the beach. We walked with our arms around each other, and spoke in low tones. How different it was from the time we'd fucked out in the ocean hanging onto the inner tube, when afterwards she refused even to touch me, that day when she had saved all her positive feelings for the Dog Of War, Part I. This night, we murmured to each other how much we liked one another, and how satisfied we were with everything, and how fine the night was. After about an hour she said she had to go. Reluctant to have her leave, I asked if she would stay with me, instead of going off with Winslow K. Smaggers.

Half-angry, half-joking, she said, "Oh fuck, Wing, quit trying to change my mind. You know better than that."

We were down near the water's edge.

It was then that she told me she wanted to go home alone.

When I asked her what she meant, she said, she was going to go for a swim, and when she came out of the water she wanted me to be gone.

"How will you get home?"

"That's my business," she said.

Suppressing the urge to tell her I felt responsible for her safety, and that I wanted to be sure she arrived home without harm, I merely said, "Okay."

Then I had an idea. I suggested we would swim out into the ocean together, and we would part there in the water, and individually make our way back to shore. That way, our parting would be sort of equal.

"Oh fuck, Wing, you're so goddamn dramatic. Just go."

"All right."

She turned and walked without hesitation into the waves. Looking at her going to the sea, watching her back retreating with her dark head held stiffly as she walked away, I finally understood something essential about her I'd missed before, something I'd failed to understand all the time I'd known her and thought about her. Seeing her walking away from me, I understood that, more than anything else in her life, she hated being a woman.

She turned to face me just as I was thinking that.

She was about knee deep in the water and shouted back to me, "Leave my purse where we parked the car. So I can call somebody."

"Sure," I shouted back, wondering which somebody she was going to call.

After returning to the car, and placing her purse where she might most easily spot it, I drove back to the condo.

The light in the living room was on. Horny Harriet was asleep on the couch. In front of her, on the coffee table was a note saying, "Wing, please wake me when you get in. Harriet." Instead, I went to the kitchen for a glass of water. Hunger clawed at my stomach. My last food had been Astoria's incinerated sausages. But there were still things to do, and if I ate I probably would go to sleep or have too little energy to finish out the events that had been set in motion. Hot water from the tap soothed me a little bit. Sipping it quietly for about ten minutes was restful and brought a certain peacefulness to my mind. I began thinking about Norleen. I wondered if maybe Norleen hated being a woman because all the men she knew were so weak they made a mockery of her womanhood.

There was a sound of movement in the living room, and Harriet came around the corner into the kitchen. Without introduction or explanation, she said, "Be easy on her, Wing. We all make mistakes."

"Be easy on who, Harriet?"

"You know very well who. Astoria."

It turned out that what had happened was my wife had approached Harriet for help. Daryl had driven her to Harriet's home and Astoria had asked for shelter for the night. Harriet's kindly wrinkled face looked up at me tenderly, pleading with me to be gentle with Storee. I told her hurting anyone was a very ugly thing, and that hurting Astoria was the worst thing I could think of.

Harriet patted my arm and said, "Good."

"Everything is good, Harriet. Did you talk to her?"

"Yes..."

"Well, tell me..."

"I told her about the bonds."

"Oh, boy," I said.

"It was the right thing to do, Wing." Harriet assured me.

"It might help if you told me what you told her, Harriet."

"It's funny. She just asked me if I was kidding. She looked very confused, and like she was calculating how she should get out of her mess. In fact, I told her, 'Honey, I can see that you and Wing are in a mess,' and Astoria said, 'For sure. That's for sure, Harriet.' She's such a pretty girl, Wing. And a nice one."

I agreed.

"Wing, do you know you frighten that girl to death?"

I laughed.

"You do. She's frightened by lots of things in life but mostly by you. That's why she acts the way she does."

"How does she act?"

"You know better than I. I'm sure you love her, Wing. And she loves you. Very much. But you scare her shitless, dear. You have refused to be her anchor in life. She loves you but finds you impossible to understand. She feels vulnerable to everything, but especially you. Why do you do it to her?"

"What?"

Harriet ignored my question and went on to say, "You know you're too tough for her to compete with. If you ever get in a real fight with her she's going to lose everything she's got. Stop fighting her, just take charge."

"What did you tell her, Harriet?"

"I told her I had given you the bonds and that money was going to be like a door that would open up a whole new life for the two of you. I told her you were reluctant to accept them but for her sake you would."

"How can you be so sure of that?"

"You'd do anything for her, and you know it."

"Almost anything, Harriet. There is at least one thing I'm going to stop doing."

"What?"

"For now, just tell me what else you told her, if you would."

"Certainly, I told her that she should put her faith in you."

"Pardon?"

"You know, like you're always telling everybody. I told her to say "Yes" to you.

"It surprises me to find out you've been listening to what I've been saying all these weeks."

"Well, maybe I have. Anyway, I found myself telling Astoria she should start trusting you. She should get very, very open to you. She should open herself up and take a big chance on you.

I told her the last thing in the world you would ever want to do is lose her, and if she put all her trust in you and absolutely avoided all competition with you—sort of got out of your way—you'd begin to trust her. I told her you'd probably get yourself in gear and make something of yourself.

"Yes, that's very good, Harriet. What did she say?"

"Well, let me, see. Astoria said....oh, yes, I remember, she said, 'I'll think about it.' Yes, that's it, she said, 'I'll think about it.' Yes, that was funny. She said that, and then just stared at me, stared at me with this sort of angry look."

"Yes, go on."

"Well, she just was sitting there quiet and I sort of thought I had offended her, which was the farthest thing from my mind. So I said to her, 'Astoria,' I said, 'You've got lot's of money now. Some people would say you are rich. And you are, I told her. I said, 'You have someone who loves you and whom you love. And now you have money. You two can have a lovely life together if you will just learn to put down your defenses, honey.' That's what I said."

"What did Astoria say there?"

"She said, 'I'll think about it.' "

Well, there was very little that needed to be said after Harriet told me that. It sounded like the same old Astoria: tight-lipped and playing everything close to the vest.

The door chimes rang. They rang repeatedly, shattering the silence that surrounded us. As the chimes finally died away, there was a pounding on the door. We just stared at each other, Harriet and I, motionless. The chimes sounded again, and there was another fit of pounding on the door. It seemed the craziness of this mad day and night was going to continue. There was another round of chimes and pounding, and this time they were followed by a voice—Bertie's voice—demanding Harriet open the door.

"I know you are in there, Harriet. I saw your auto and you had best open up this door immediately, Harriet Harvester. And I do mean immediately."

Harriet looked away from me. Embarrassed and nervous.

I let Bertie in.

"Shame on you, Harriet. You are most irresponsible." Bertie said, bursting into the room, and heading directly toward her sister.

Harriet lifted her chin defiantly, "I did what I thought best."

"Thought? Thought? When have you ever *thought?* All your brains are below your waist."

"Who's to know? Harriet pleaded. "It will be our secret."

"You are a foolish old woman, Harriet."

Harriet looked down at the floor, and said quietly but with great belief, "Wing needs the money. I want him to have it. I want Astoria and him to have it."

"I'm afraid your wishes are of little importance when weighted against the larger issues here."

"Who's to know, Bertie?" Harriet cried out. "What possible difference does it make?"

Softening a little, Bertie looked with pity on her sister. She said "I'm sorry, Harriet." Shaking her head slowly, she added, "Dear, surely you can see your plan will fail. Wing and his wife...particularly, Wing...."

Harriet bit her lip, and nodded.

Bertie looked at me, "Mr. Wing, I'm afraid I must ask you to return the bonds."

I nodded.

"Then you will give them up?"

I smiled, and looked at Harriet. "I know you want only the best for us, honey."

Harriet smiled weakly.

"As I understand it, Bertie," I said, "Those are bearer bonds. I mean whoever has possession of them can cash them without having to prove ownership. So I could just hang on to them if I wanted to."

Bertie swallowed hard. "Yes, that's correct."

I said this partly to worry Bertie, to make her feel bad, to pay her back for being nasty to my friend Harriet. But mainly I was stalling for time, trying to figure out what was going on.

Then suddenly I understood and was surprised it had taken me so long to figure things out.

"Yes, of course, Bertie, you can have the bonds back."

Bertie sagged with relief. Going toward the bedroom, I said, "They're in here; I hid them under the bed." But at the door I stopped and asked, "Bertie, before I turn the bonds over to you, would you tell me something?"

Bertie said, "Yes," and Harriet nodded.

"Tell me what your real names are."

Bertie looked at me suspiciously, and Harriet said. "Oh, I just love you." She beamed her lovely smile at me, and said, "We *are* really sisters, you know."

"Sure." I said. "Of course, you would be."

"Our family name is Pook. Bertie's real name is Geraldine Pook. I'm Millicent Pook."

"And Minnie?"

"Minnie was originally Virginia."

"How fitting."

"Yes," Bertie said. "So now you know."

"I suppose so. It was just a guess, that's all. Here's another guess. The first bonds you ever stole were issued by International Harvester Corporation."

"Yes," Bertie said. "They were the 4-1/2%'s of 1974."

Harriet added, "Then we moved out here and changed jobs and our names in honor of our first successful theft."

"I see," I said. "And now the police are after you; you think somebody's caught on to your game."

"Yes, if you must know," Bertie said. "I'm sure the

Securities & Exchange Commission, and the FBI will conduct a thorough investigation. They're sure to investigate you, too, because of Harriet's connection with you."

Harriet looked at me hopelessly. She sighed, looking weepy. "I tried, Wing."

"Harriet, you did the best you could. You should remember the immortal words at the saintly Mahatma Gandhi. 'Total effort is total Victory'. Thanks for trying." I went to her and put my arms around her little shoulders. She tucked her head against my chest and said, "Poor Astoria. She needed it most." Harriet dropped into silence; but her thin body began shaking, and she pushed away from me and looked up at me with a fierce, angry look. "It was that damn pest bookkeeper, Wing. I told you she was a fucking pest."

Bertie said, "Harriet, that's quite enough."

"It was her, Wing. Bertie would steal the bonds, and I would route them through a phony stock account and then Minnie would do some shifty bookkeeping to make it look like some other office in the firm had lost them."

Bertie said, "Harriet, please hush up."

"Oh, Wing's all right, Bertie. You worry too much, that's your trouble. It dries you up inside like a prune."

Bertie looked startled, and Harriet continued. "That's why the firm refuses to allow relatives to work together, you see. To stop deals like this. But we fooled them until Minnie went on her honeymoon, and we got this awful new bookkeeper who took over Minnie's job and turned out to be a damn, nosey pest."

Bertie said, "Harriet, you must stop talking. You're just going to cause more trouble."

"How?"

"The police are going to be over here very shortly talking to Reverend Wing, and the more he knows about it the more likely the police are going to think that he was involved in it."

Harriet nodded as though at last she understood and agreed.

"It's all right," I said to them. "Everything is turning out the way it is supposed to. We are creating something wonderful here. You feel sorry for Astoria and me, but you should remember it was I who helped Minnie to release herself from the fear of men and fear of intimate involvement, and so she went away on her cruise. Because she went away, the pesky bookkeeper came, and now Astoria and I are released from the burden of all this money, and so we can now concentrate on finding out why she and I keep fucking up each other's lives. We have this chance because I helped Minnie to be free and go away. So, truly, I had a big hand in helping to lose this money. This whole affair has a wonderful sort of circular beauty to it."

Bertie looked and shook her head. "You are a very strange person, Wing."

"Yes, thank you, Bertie."

At that, there was a long pause in our conversation as though we had reached a point where everything that could be said, had already been said. Finally, Bertie broke the silence.

"Reverend Wing, perhaps you should give me the bonds now. Harriet and I must pack, meet Minnie at the airport, and then catch a flight to Miami."

Probably going to catch a bus to L.A., I thought, and leave from there for Venezuela or New Zealand.

Or Peru.

"Certainly, Bertie," I said.

In the bedroom, they stood by, watching while I knelt beside the bed and reached underneath, feeling around.

My hand grabbed something.

A ball of fur.

Muggs nipped at my hand. I grabbed him by the leg and dragged him out. In his mouth was a shred of paper that said *Phoenix Arizona Redevelopment* on it.

"Oh, my God," Bertie said.

I flipped up the bedspread and the two sisters dropped to their knees on either side of me. With our tails in the air, we peered beneath the bed, staring at the mess of confetti—the scraps of paper that Astoria's pooch had left uneaten.

Harriet said angrily, "That fucking dog!"

Bertie snapped, "Must you always think of intercourse?"

"Bad dog," Harriet said to the poor pup that was crawling to hide in shame under the night table.

"Harriet and Bertie, do you have enough money for yourselves?"

"Yes, of course we do," Bertie said. "But that is hardly a sufficient reason for you to feed your dog the most expensive meal in history."

Harriet looked disappointed at me. "Really, Wing, you have screwed up."

"Stop speaking of intercourse, Harriet," snapped Bertie. "I am quite tired of it, and you are getting on my nerves."

I gathered a couple of handfuls of the scraps of the bonds and set them on the floor in front of us. We all sat on the floor in a circle, sort of staring at them.

"He must have eaten most of them," I said.

Harriet observed that, indeed, it was an awfully small pile left of the five hundred thousand dollars.

The night was ending. Looking out through the eastern window you could see the sky was lighter. I thought how happy Astoria would have been in a home of her own. I could see the joy she would have had on her face when she was decorating it, the excitement she would have in her eyes when she showed me new things she had bought for it. She would have had pride in entertaining her friends there. She could have had a stronger sense of her place in the world. She would have had a feeling of security. A home for us and the children. Slumber parties for Dulcinea. A place for Quentin to sneak out of at night.

Now it was gone, her anchor in life.

Did it matter? We sat there on the floor, the Pook sisters and

I, gazing up through that eastern window which was now lightening with a new dawn. It was the same window through which I'd seen the dark-haired girl just that morning—some twenty hours ago—when I hugged naked Astoria while Daryl was getting my Doctor of Veternary Dentistry degree out of his station wagon, where Astoria was soon to be fucked. Daryl had interrupted our love-making when he brought Storee the puppy. Muggs had then eaten the bonds. Was Daryl, then, because of his interference, the one responsible for Astoria losing her home and security.

Perhaps, yes. Perhaps.

But the Pook sisters had asked for the bonds back—after Harriet had told Astoria about them, and gotten her hopes up. Are, then, the Pook sisters partly responsible for Astoria's coming pain?

In a way, yes, one could say so.

But what about me?

When I had gone back to the condo with the dark-haired girl, and went into the bedroom to change my clothes, I could have done something with the bonds then. I could have suspected there was something fishy about them, and to protect these riches—knowing what Muggs was like—I could have put him under the bed with a couple of the cheaper bonds, and hidden the rest in a safe place so that later I would be sure to be able to buy Astoria a house and cashmere sweaters, and get expensive tennis shoes for our kids. I could have protected Astoria that way.

Or how about this: since I was so suspicious Astoria was going to fuck us over again, perhaps I did hide the bonds and have kept them for myself. I can understand that some people could believe I did that. After all it's hard to trust a man who'd make veal scallopini out of chicken legs.

Could I do that, though? Really? After all these years, could I really scheme to finally abandon Astoria? Could I do that?

Could I forget about our years together, forget the grin on her face when she had me feeling her up outside the restaurant as crowds walked by?

What would happen to her if I did? Would she continue to live in a dream world full of hopes? Would she still pretend there exists for her—if only she works and schemes hard enough—a place of comfort and safety? Perhaps. But more probably with me out of the way, her world would begin collapsing around her, and she would struggle ceaselessly to keep a hold on the remaining people and things in her life. But almost certainly, fatefully, everything was bound to collapse. Then she will feel pure pain. She will scream in agony.

"Wing?" Bertie said. "What is it?"

"Pardon."

Harriet said, "You were clenching your jaws, you looked like some kind of animal."

"I was thinking that we are going to give Astoria the gift of pain."

Bertie snorted, "With friends like us, who needs enemies?"

As if in answer to her question, we heard the front door open; someone had come into the condo. "Let's go," I said to the sisters, and we all got up and went into the living room.

It was Storee. She stared at me, fear and defiance mixed in her eyes.

Everyone stood still, silent for a few moments, until Harriet went to Astoria and put her arms around her, to console her.

Dear Harriet, bless you for that.

Astoria kept her eyes on me, like I was the enemy.

Bertie said, "We'd best be going now."

The clock on the kitchen wall said 4:17 am. The group of us wrapped things up like it was the end of a business meeting. I asked Harriet to do a favor for me: to call Bruno at his room at the Eight Ball Tavern, and have him assemble all the Holy Yessers that he could for a meeting on our beach at eight-thirty that morning.

Certainly, he would be able to convince some of them to come, I thought.

If Bruno was gone would she herself try to assemble as many of the Yessers as possible, I asked. She took the phone list I handed her, and promised to do her best. But Bertie looked agitated.

"I'm sorry, Wing," she said, "but we have an airplane to..."

"Of course," Harriet said to me. "Of course, we'll come."

"Bertie, too?" I asked.

"I have many things," Bertie said, "that must be done before we...."

"Of course," Harriet said. "If Bertie wants me to cooperate with her, she'll have to cooperate with me."

"Good. Thanks. And something else?"

"What?"

"Bring a camera?"

"If you like, I suppose."

"You have one of those handy, little instant cameras right? A Polaroid?" Saying she'd bring it, Harriet gave me a quick peck on the cheek, then did the same to Astoria who accepted it stiffly. Taking Bertie by the hand, Harriet said, "See you at 8:30 then," and they left, leaving Astoria and I staring silently at one another.

Storee stood there opposite me with her head held high. Proud. Her hands hung loosely at her sides. Then she rubbed the palms downward against her thighs. "Well..." she said, and stood there waiting, with her chin in the air, as though she were full of courage. Had she done anything wrong, she seemed to be saying. Anything at all wrong? Head high. Proud. Standing tall. "Well..." she began, wanting me to begin speaking, to get the talking started. Her hair was mussed. What was there to say? It seemed like all the words and surprises were in the past. She swallowed hard. "Say something," she demanded. "Are you just going to stand there staring?"

373

"We've been together a long time."

"Yes. But I may have lost my interest in continuing this relationship."

It was the sort of thing she used to say to bring me to my knees.

"Maybe that's a good idea."

She looked down at her hands, then stared up at me, and said in a softer tone, "But every marriage has it's rough spots."

"I guess you're right about that."

There was dead air between us. Irritation flickered across her face. Perhaps she was annoyed that I was doing little to move the conversation forward, maybe she wanted my words to come tumbling out full of pleading, full of ideas and reasons to keep us going. Now it was she who had to reach out across the Grand Canyon and reach me on the other side.

She swallowed hard. "I suppose for the children's sake, we just have to start over," she said. "We've both made our mistakes." She repeated it, softly, admitting it, sounding so sorry about the mess we'd made of our lives. She took a step toward me, and I started to take a step toward her. It was the first movements of coming together, of hugging, of reconciliation. As I started to step to her, she smiled a sad smile. I stopped. The world was so clear, at that moment. Little details stood out. The light from the lamps was extra bright, and the colors of the room stood out in sharp contrast from one another. The electric clock on the table was whirring like a turbine in my ears. The dog's scratching sounded like sandpaper. Instead of us coming together, I hammered another nail into the coffin of our marriage. "Tell me about some of your mistakes. What are they?"

She turned angry. "What about you? What kind of person would follow me like that? Sneaking...?"

She stopped. It was as though she realized she was speaking to stone and that it was useless.

...oh, we had been fighting, she and I, for so long. And now she had lost, and she refused to admit it, she refused to see it, refused to surrender and ask for peace...

"Well...?" she said. "I suppose we're even."

"Pardon?"

"You did what you did. And I..." She had a hard time getting it out, and so she blurted it, spilling the words out in a rush. "I did what I did and that's that. Now we just have to pick up the pieces and keep our marriage going."

It would have been smarter for her to ask me, "Wing, what do you think we should do?"

Instead, she said, "Harriet told me about the bonds she's given us. We can make a new start."

"The dog ate the bonds."

"What?"

"The dog *ate* the bonds. All of them."

I pointed toward the bedroom. Full of hesitation, she went into the room with me following. Standing next to the bed, she stared down at the pile of scraps that the Pook sisters and I had dragged from underneath. Slowly, she sat on the bed edge.

Then she started to cry. Something in her just gave up. She gave a small moan, and her eyes moistened. She lost control and all her sorrow poured out in huge, racking sobs that shook her body. She had fought so hard for so long, and now everything was finished. She let it all pour out of her. All that was left was the pain, everything else was done. It was then I realized that she had known all along that this was coming. Far before me, she had known our marriage was ending. She is so smart and sensitive, and that's why she'd been so desperate, so close to tears, when she was showing Marcie Tarwater our wedding pictures. That was why she was so angry the following night when I told Quentin *Yes*, he could borrow the car. She is so perfect in her understanding of me that she must have realized in those very first seconds of my rebirth that she had lost control over me.

I went around to the other side of the bed and laid down on my back. Reaching out, I touched her shoulder and pulled her down beside me. She laid her head on my shoulder. Gradually, her crying subsided and we fell asleep in each other's arms, Daryl's sperm still swimming inside her.

Live On

東 said, "A revolution travels a crooked road. It must wander where it can. It retreats before superior forces, advances where it has room to advance, and is possessed of enormous patience."

It is different from a dinner party.

Many friends and lovers may be lost.

We do what we have to do, regardless.

Live on, my friends.

The future belongs to you.

Example

Without an alarm, I awoke a few hours later, at 8:30 am. Leaning over, I kissed Astoria on the forehead. She awoke. Our faces were grim and our sentences short as we arose and only splashed water on our faces before descending the steps of the condo. Crossing the beach we advanced toward the small group of Yessers who had been willing to show up.

Bruno was there, of course. Alice, Toby and Darlene who sat drowsily in a beach chair. Even Daryl made it. (Was that because Bruno had strongly requested his presence, or because Daryl wanted to show his courage? Who knows? I was glad to see him.) Harriet and Bertie, of course. (With relief I noticed the camera dangling from a strap on Harriet's wrist.) Astoria and I were the last to arrive. Bruno took me aside as my wife and I arrived at the spot near the water's edge where the little group waited. He told me that when I had started my sermon the night before, and then begun crying he'd become concerned. He said that while his attention was on me, Joe Wagonewti and Frenando Clip had slipped out of the room. Suspecting they meant to harm me, he'd left to search for them, and had spent most of the night scouring Laguna, contacting various people who might know my enemies' whereabouts. Bruno cautioned me that his contacts during the night had convinced him that Joe, Fernando, and Shifty Eddie were surely involved in various sorts of criminal activities, and—in his alarmist manner—Bruno said we should plan some way to deal with the threat these men posed on me. They were convinced I'd been dealing with the police, and that made them nervous, particularly Joe who had recommended me to Shifty Eddie.

I told Bruno that his worrying was useless, and that *Yes* would protect me. He accepted that. Astoria, standing by my side, shook her head as though she was tired of hearing me resort to *Yes*. She looked at the little group of remaining Yessers that waited patiently a little way from us. Although it was only a quarter to nine in the morning, the sun was shining nicely, promising that the day would be pleasant.

Out in the parking lot adjacent to the beach a spiffy green Dodge with fright lights across the top rolled to a stop.

That was all right with me because I had very little to say to my friends anyway. Taking Bruno and Astoria over to the main group, I quickly assembled them into a semi-circle around Darlene, asleep in her beach chair. Already, Gilford and Kim were out of their vehicle and crossing the sand. Silently, I wished they could have been in the picture too. Alice, her strawberry blonde hair glinting in the sun, came to me and whispered in my ear. "Wing, every time I go into a market and see a zucchini, I start to giggle."

We laughed together, and I hugged her. Quickly, we were all

378

assembled for the photo, but then I realized that we needed a photographer or else one of us would be left out. It would be like a part of myself missing. Already, Norleen was gone. It would be awful to lose anymore. For a moment I thought of how nice it would have been to have had her there, and Winslow K. Smaggers, too.

The cops were getting closer.

Yes would have to come to my rescue soon or else I would have to leave without the picture, and I dearly wanted to take a visual reminder of my people with me. Of course, *Yes* did come through for me once again. As though impelled by an inner voice, I turned around and spotted a jogger coming to our rescue. Jogging in place, he listened as I told him of our dilemma. He said "Yes", and we quickly formed a group. Astoria and I were shoulder to shoulder in the center behind Darlene's chair. I took Storee's right hand in my left and raised our arms over our heads as though we had won a prizefight or some great victory. The jogger stopped moving, snapped the picture, tossed the camera to me, and resumed his healthful run.

Gilford and Kim were only a hundred yards away now, and closing in at a trot.

The instant camera whirred, and the photograph appeared at the bottom. Without inspecting it, I stripped the thing from the camera and slipped it beneath my toga into the back pocket of my cut-offs. Taking a few steps forward, I turned and addressed my family, all these persons whom I'd so recently gotten to know.

It was to be my last sermon.

It was short.

"Good-bye," I said.

They looked surprised and shuffled in place, uneasily.

To Bruno, I nodded in the direction of the oncoming cops, and said, "Get me out of this, Crunch."

He nodded although he looked sorrowful, having finally

realized what this morning meeting was all about. Astoria's jaw hung slack.

She looked so tired.

I turned and ran.

I passed the jogger.

Veering left, I sprinted across the beach toward the parking lot, shedding my toga as I reached the pavement. Looking back, it appeared that Bruno had momentarily delayed my law enforcement friends, and they were now running in my direction. How fitting it was to end my stay in Laguna the same way I'd begun it.

Crossing the parking lot, and the street beyond it, I ran the few blocks that separated me from the downtown area and the main highway that went through it. There, at the first traffic signal, I stuck out my thumb and was immediately given a ride by a teenage black fellow in a new Cadillac with 29 coats of Georgia peach lacquer.

"Hey," he said as we drove north out of Laguna, "that T-shirt's all right. I like that. Where'd you get it?"

"France," I said, and started laughing. Looking behind me, the road was completely free of spiffy green Dodges. That meant escape. My only possessions were my T-shirt, cut-offs, sneakers, the photograph of my family, and the six hundred dollars that I'd kept of the money Joe Wagonewti had fronted me. To carry so little baggage made me feel light and free. It felt as if I was fleeing on the breeze like...like a butterfly, I thought.

Oh, God!

I laughed.

All this time I had thought of myself as a rock.

Yet, it was *I* who had fled from L.A.

Astoria had chased after me.

And now I was fleeing from Laguna.

And she was staying behind.

Who then had the real endurance, and courage, and humility?

Who then was the rock, who was the butterfly?

Maybe all this time, *I* was the butterfly...a butterfly that thought he was a rock.

But I felt so perfectly sane and humble. So maybe even though I was riding away in this car, I was actually a rock that just thought he might be a butterfly.

It was all too complicated. Later there would be plenty of time to figure it out. I laughed again, feeling my freedom, and my new friend asked me what was so funny and where I was going.

I laughed again.

Who knew?

Some fine place probably. Some place where *Yes*—in some wonderful way—would make clear to me what had just happened in my life. Some enchanted place where my mind would heal.

"I'm going north, man. I'm going north to the magic kingdom. You want to come?"

He must have thought I was offering some recreational chemicals or something.

"Hey, man, it's still morning." he said. "Besides, I gotta drive."

Hitchhiking, walking, even riding a bicycle for a while, I continued north until I reached sheep country, and here I have made my home. It's taken me these past three years, while working on this fucking sheep ranch, to understand and evaluate the lessons of all that had happened to me during that summer. Right from the beginning, I knew I'd discovered something in *Yes*. But it has taken me all this time to make those lessons a part of my self.

In the meantime I worked, just as any man has to work to support himself. I was right at home, here on the sheep ranch. At first they gave me odd jobs that had little to do with real sheep ranching, but I worked my way up, so to speak. Last summer I had my own flock, which I shepherded alone in the hills a hundred miles from here. Almost all of the ewes, lambs and rams came back safely with me; under my care they escaped the stalking wolves, coyotes and wildcats that inhabit the hills of this region.

"Come on, you farts, it's getting late. Let's get the balls off these little suckers before it's too dark to see."

The foreman has called out to us. Now it's time to castrate and shear, time to harvest the sheep we have tended since birth. But I'm going to skip it. I've had enough of preying on lambs. That part of my life is over.

And also, I am through allowing the wolves, coyotes and wildcats of life to feast on me, myself, as though I were some weak, wooly thing. I am coming home now, but sending this book on first, ahead of me, as a warning. Watch out, fuckers.

It has occurred to us that some bookstores may refuse to carry this book because of its title. If you are finding it difficult or impossible to find *FUCK, YES!* at a bookseller's, you can order it directly from us. If you can buy it at a bookseller's, please do so, as we'd prefer to avoid interfering with their making a living. Thank you.

ORDER FORM

Please send me _____ copies of *FUCK, YES!* at $12.50 each.

Name _____

Address _____

_____Zip_____

_____If you want your order sent airmail, add $2.90 per book, otherwise it'll be sent to you at book rate.

Please allow 2-3 weeks for delivery.

Mail To:

Shepherd Books
Box 2290
Redmond, WA 98073
